Embroidery
Techniques & Patterns

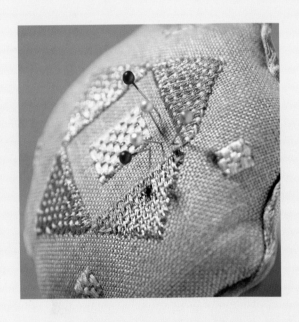

Marie-Noëlle Bayard

Photography by Charlie Abad

Translation by Kim M. Allen Gleed

Sterling Publishing Co., Inc.
New York

Translated from the French by Kim M. Allen Gleed

Library of Congress Cataloging-in-Publication Data

Bayard, Marie-Noëlle.
 [Broderie. English]
 Embroidery : techniques & patterns / Marie-Noëlle Bayard ;
photography by Charlie Abad ; translation by Kim M. Allen Gleed.
   p. cm.
 Includes index.
 ISBN 1-4027-1984-1
 1. Embroidery. 2. Embroidery--Patterns. I. Title.
 TT770.B3613 2005
 746.44--dc22

                    2005002758

10 9 8 7 6 5 4 3 2 1

Published in 2005 by Sterling Publishing Co., Inc.
387 Park Avenue South, New York, NY 10016
Published originally under the title *La broderie:
techniques et modèles*
© 2003 by Editions Solar, Paris
English translation copyright © 2005 by
Sterling Publishing Co. Inc.
Distributed in Canada by Sterling Publishing
c/o Canadian Manda Group, 165 Dufferin Street
Toronto, Ontario, Canada M6K 3H6
Distributed in Great Britain by Chrysalis Books Group PLC
The Chrysalis Building, Bramley Road, London W10 6SP, England
Distributed in Australia by Capricorn Link (Australia) Pty. Ltd.
P.O. Box 704, Windsor, NSW 2756, Australia

Sterling ISBN: 1-4027-1984-1

For information about custom editions, special sales, premium and
corporate purchases, please contact Sterling Special Sales
Department at 800-805-5489 or specialsales@sterlingpub.com.

CONTENTS

Introduction

Cross-stitch, stem stitch, chain stitch, knot stitch . . . even the absolute novices among us know these names and attribute them to the technique of embroidery. These famous stitches are the pretty trees that hide a vast luxurious forest, because embroidery is a technique of incomparable beauty.

Although the present work is far from being exhaustive, I have nonetheless done my best to gather in this volume more than one hundred stitches in families, allowing you to approach in a straightforward way the practice of embroidery. Chapter after chapter, you will discover that one family of stitches lends itself to derivatives which offer different appearances, textures, and design qualities as they adapt to the particular ornamental elements.

The selected stitches will allow you to become familiar with embroidery. Then, you can advance with more complex stitches. To guide you through your initiation, each stitch is described and illustrated with photos detailing the steps towards completion. Tips and helpful hints have been added to the explanations in order to give you all the keys to success.

One final word of advice before launching into the beautiful adventure of embroidery: make samplers. This is the key for all embroiderers, beginner and experienced! It is on these pieces of fabric that you will carry out your maneuvers. And why not, like our grandmothers, make a journal or picture out of these exercises in style? Once your spirit and your hand are accustomed to managing thread, needle and fabric, I suggest that you move into creating sophisticated works that will allow you to showcase your new artistic acquisition and to develop your creativity.

You will discover, page after page, the art of working with a simple thread and one of the most modest tools: the needle. Embroidery is, quite simply, a magnificent activity that generates hours of pleasure caressing fabrics and fibers, and blending stitches and colors. It's truly bliss . . .

Marie-Noëlle Bayard

1

Materials,
Preparation,
and Finishing Touches

Textile Foundations

Each embroidery technique requires the use of different textile foundations. This is an important basic concept, because the success of the final work depends upon it. Here is a summary of the fabrics available to the embroiderer.

THE CHOICE OF TEXTILE FOUNDATIONS

The foundation must be appropriate and the fabric must be chosen with the desired effect and the embroidery technique used in mind.

For border stitches and filling stitches

These stitches are usually worked on an already drawn tracing. Therefore, you can use fabrics with a fine, tight weave. The most frequently used fabrics are those made of natural fibers such as cotton, linen, silk, or wool.

Depending on the function of the work (clothing or decoration), cotton, linen-cotton blend, linen, or wool are excellent foundations for embroidery.

Satin silk and taffeta bring elegance to embroidery, even when it is done with cotton thread.

You will find these fabrics, sold by the yard, in certain fabric and craft stores, in the decorating section of large department stores, in specialized mail-order catalogs, but also in markets or second-hand shops that sell household linens.

For counted stitches

The fabrics used are single-weave or double-weave cottons and linens, called "even-threads." These simple cross-weaves allow you easily to count the threads in the weave over which you will embroider the counted stitches without first having to transfer the pattern.

Woven cotton is the most popular and the simplest to use, because it has a double weave. It is also sold under the name "Aida." It is available in different weave sizes (7 mesh, 11 mesh, 14 mesh, 16 mesh, and 18 mesh) and in many colors. Several sizes of pre-cut cloth are offered (from $\frac{1}{8}$ of a yard to several yards), according to the type of work envisioned.

The most popular Aida fabric is 14 mesh, and it is worked with two or three strands of DMC stranded embroidery floss.

Single-weave cotton or linen fabric, finer and lighter weight than muslin, allows you to work motifs with much finesse. These fabrics are available in different sizes, and have anywhere from six to twenty-eight threads per inch.

The higher the number of threads per inch, the finer the embroidered design will be. On single-thread muslin, one must work the stitches over two or three threads of the weave in height and length.

For drawn-thread stitches and cutwork embroidery

Linen, cotton, linen-cotton blends, and organdy are the fabrics used for these techniques. Choose fabrics with a tight weave and you will be able to make stitches with great finesse and precision.

For these embroideries, it is helpful to hot-press the fabric (see below) before beginning your work. This step stabilizes the dimensions of the fabric being used and also removes excess dye.

For couching stitches

Couching stitches are used to highlight exquisite embroidery made with fragile and rare thread, such as silk or metallics. Therefore, you should use exceptional fabrics such as cashmere, silk, velvet, organza, or silk taffeta. It is not advised to hot press or even wash these fabrics—dry cleaning is recommended.

As you are embroidering, be careful not to break the fibers of these delicate fabrics, when you tighten them in an embroidery hoop, for example.

Protect the inner circle of the hoop with a ribbon of cotton or other soft fabric wrapped around the frame (see box on page 13).

THE SAMPLER

Before working the final embroidery, make a test on a sample of the fabric you have chosen. It is important to know if the thickness and the type of thread are appropriate for the stitch, if the needle passes through the fabric without spoiling the weave, and if the eye of the needle does not wear out the embroidery thread too quickly. Finally, you must make sure that the fabric does not become misshapen in the course of your work.

CUTTING THE FABRICS

The dimensions of the embroidery pattern are given in the directions accompanying each project. Add four inches all around the work or follow the directions in the explanatory notes. It is important to leave enough fabric around the embroidery in order to position it easily in the embroidery hoop.

Cut the selvages

The borders of the fabric must always be trimmed along the straight of the goods. Using a graduated ruler and pins, transfer the dimensions indicated. Notch the edge of the fabric 3¾ inch with dressmaker's scissors, pull out a thread of the fabric, and cut along the path of this removed thread for the entire length of the cut. This thread path will guide you and will allow you to make a cut along the "straight of the goods."

HOT-PRESS THE FABRICS

A large number of fabrics can be embroidered. Cotton, poplin, organdy, and fine linen fabrics are most frequently used for household linens. For decorative embroidery, wool flannels, silk taffetas, large sheets of linen, and even raffia fabric bring a particular style to the work.

These fabrics must be hot pressed first, meaning the industrial finish on the new fabric must be removed. This step is critical for certain types of fabrics, such as linen or cotton, which may shrink by 20% in the first wash. Because of this reaction, make sure you allow enough fabric around the future embroidery pattern to be able to finish the final project without a problem.

Hot-press cotton fabrics

Pour hot water in a basin, add a few shavings of Marseille soap (available in specialty stores in the US), and allow the fabric to soak for at least an hour.

Rinse thoroughly, gently remove the water without wringing or twisting the fabric, and allow it to dry flat, away from all heat sources. Iron the fabric while it is still slightly damp.

If the dye in a colored fabric bleeds, you can fix this by adding a teaspoon of sea salt to the final rinse water and allow the fabric to soak overnight in this solution.

Hot-press linen fabrics

Fill the bottom of the bathtub with hot water and add a few shavings of Marseille soap. Place the fabric in the water so that it is entirely submerged, and make sure that the fabric is spread out evenly, avoiding folds (the fibers in linen can break, and the folds become permanent). Allow the fabric to soak overnight. Rinse and allow to it drip, then lay the fabric flat, without wringing, away from all heat sources. Iron the fabric while it is still slightly damp, and reestablish the selvages by starching them lightly (see p. 20).

Hot-press wool

Immerse the piece of fabric in cold water and allow it to soak for an hour. Drip dry, lay flat, then iron when dry.

Hot-press silk

In principle, silk, is not washed before working the embroidery. To hot-press it, take it in your hands and gently rub the surface with your palms. When you have finished this, iron the fabric with a slightly damp cloth.

Embroidery Equipment

Cotton, wool, silk, or even synthetic threads are not used indiscriminately or in the same way on all fabrics. The delicate alchemy of embroidery resides in the correct choice of the ensemble of fabric, thread, needle, and stitches. Understanding these elements well is a gauge of your success.

THE CHOICE OF THREADS

The most frequently used threads for creating the projects in this book are cotton ones, and synthetics for metallic thread.

DMC 100% cotton stranded embroidery floss

This is a 100% cotton floss composed of six easily separable threads and available in a wide variety of colors. The number of strands used differs according to the type of fabric used. Stranded embroidery floss is as effective for tradi-

tional embroidery as it is for counted cross-stitch. It is available in small 8.7 yard skeins in a range of over four hundred colors. The skein is immediately ready to use: all you need to do is pull on the thread to unwind it.

DMC metallic stranded embroidery floss

This is a synthetic thread which looks metallic. It is available like cotton floss, in small 8.7 yard skeins, is washable to 100 degrees Fahrenheit, and is made up of six easily separable strands. The number of strands used differs according to the type of fabric used. It is as effective for traditional embroidery work as it is for counted cross-stitch, and it is available in twelve colors. The skein is immediately ready to use: all you need to do is pull on the thread to unwind it. This thread is very fragile, and it must be worked in small lengths of thread (10 inches maximum), and you should replace the threads when you notice any amount of wear on the surface. You must use an embroidery needle with a large eye.

DMC pearl cotton

This very shiny thread is made of 100% cotton, has vibrant color and is tightly twisted. It is available in several thicknesses which are used based on the fabric and the effect desired. Size 5 (fine) is sold in 27 yard skeins, size 3 (thicker) is sold in 16 yard skeins. Sizes 5, 8, and 12 (very fine) are also available in balls with lengths of 87 to 131 yards. The spectrum of colors, depending on the thickness of the thread, offers over three hundred colors.

DMC matte embroidery cotton

A very thick, twisted, vibrantly colored, 100% cotton thread, DMC matte embroidery cotton is sold in 11 yard skeins in variety of over two hundred colors. It is used on loose-weave fabrics and large muslins.

DMC cutwork and embroidery thread

Satiny, twisted, 100% cotton, and vibrantly colored, DMC cutwork and embroidery thread is used mainly for drawn-thread work and cutwork embroidery and for monogram work. It is sold in 25 yard skeins in one hundred eighty-six colors for size 25, the most popular thickness for this kind of work. This type of thread is available in different thicknesses, ranging from size 12 (thick) to size 40 (very fine).

DMC Medicis embroidery wool

This is a fine thread made of slightly twisted 100% wool. It is mothproofed and its colors are fade-resistant. One or several strands of this thread may be used at a time. 27 yard skeins are sold in one hundred eighty colors.

DMC tapestry wool

This is a thicker thread than Medicis. It is twisted 100% virgin wool, is mothproofed and is fade-resistant. It is used for decorative embroidery, and is sold in 8.8 yard skeins in a spectrum of four hundred sixty colors. There is also a selection of fifty colors in 42.7 yard balls. This wool is used mostly for work on canvas.

THE SKEINS

There are several kinds of skeins. According to their method of manufacture, some must be prepared for easier use.

● **Cotton floss skeins** are immediately usable: all you need to do is pull on the thread to unwind it.

● **Twisted skeins** such as Pearl cotton, or folded skeins, such as cutwork and embroidery thread, must be worked before use. Remove the bands from the skein, unwind it to obtain a long skein, and cut the strands at one end. Braid the strands (this way, they will not tangle), and wrap the band from the skein with the color number around the braid. To obtain one length of thread, pull a strand at the end of the braid.

THE LENGTHS OF THREAD

In order to avoid wear on the thread as you work the embroidery, use short lengths of thread, about 12 inches long.

To slip the thread easily through the eye of the needle, proceed in the following manner: fold the thread in half, position it at the eye of the needle, and use the fold of the thread to push it through the eye.

You will prevent the abrasion of the thread in the eye of the needle by sticking the needle in the strand itself about 2 inches from its end. Pass the thread just through the eye, and the needle is then attached to the thread. This helpful hint allows you to use short lengths of thread without their coming unstrung, and the thread will not deteriorate except where it is attached. Moreover, you will save thread, because it will remain intact up to the point where it meets the eye.

TWIST THE THREAD

As you work the embroidery, the twist of the thread changes. You must, therefore, from time to time, allow the twist to return to the strands. Let go of the needle and let it hang. The thread will spiral until it finds its natural twist. Return to your work as usual when this is complete.

THE NEEDLES

Embroidery needles are short, with a long, large eye. Depending on the chosen embroidery technique, the needle has either a blunt or sharp tip.

The large eye of the needle allows you to thread strands of varying thickness, and to pass it through fabric by opening the threads of the weave in order to prevent the embroidery thread from becoming quickly worn out due to friction.

Blunt-tipped tapestry needles

These are specially made for work on loosely woven fabrics or canvas. They are numbered from 13-26, and the higher the number, the shorter and thinner the needle. On very fine linen fabric, a number 26 needle should be used.

Sharp-tipped embroidery needles

These are numbered 1 through 10. Similarly, the higher number corresponds with a thin needle. You must adapt the thickness of the needle to the nature of the fabric and the thickness of the thread used.

Beading needles

These are used to sew small loose pearls. They are very long so that several beads or pearls can be threaded at a time, if needed. Their eye, which is miniscule, allows you to use only those threads that are thin and somewhat stiff (nylon thread, for example).

Yarn needles

These are pointed, and are equipped with a very long, large eye that has been specially developed for threading thick strands of wool or cotton. The large eye opens the weave of the fabric and creates an opening that is larger than the thread used. Thus, the thread does not wear as you work.

Sewing needles

These remain useful for assembling and completing the finishing touches of the work. They are available in three types:
- long (for basting or tacking stitches);
- medium (for whipping stitches as well as for hems);
- short (for seams).

They are pointed, with a small round eye, and are numbered 1 through 12 (the standard numbers are 6, 7, 8, and 9).

CHANGING THE NEEDLE

A needle wears out or oxidizes upon touch. Change needles frequently so that the embroidery work remains uniform.

THE SCISSORS

You will need two types of scissors: sewing scissors and embroidery scissors. Both kinds are available for right-handed people as well as left-handed people.

Sewing scissors

These are used to cut fabrics. The large blades must be perfectly sharpened from end to tip. Don't forget to sharpen them regularly, and from time to time, pass a steel pin along the length of the blade, following the direction of the cutting blade. Proceed in back and forth

movements towards the tip of the blade. This method of sharpening is useful for all types of scissors.

Embroidery scissors

Small and with a tapered point, these are used for cutting embroidery thread as well as for piercing the fabric in certain stitches (such as Madeira embroidery, for example), or for trimming the threads of the weave of fabric (as in openwork embroidery). They measure about 5 inches long.

Choose embroidery scissors made of forged steel since they are the most solid and are more efficient than those made of molded metal.

THE FRAMES

The embroidery frame is an indispensable tool for obtaining beautiful embroidery. The fabric is permanently tightened during the work, so it does not become misshapen. The stitches are more uniform because they undergo a tension constant and equal to that of the fabric.

There are two types of embroidery frames:
- lath frame;
- embroidery frame or embroidery hoop.

Lath frame

This is a frame that professionals use, but you can find a form adapted for amateur use in craft shops.

This frame consists of two rods with mortises which form the top and bottom of the frame, and two vertical laths drilled with several holes which allow you to adjust the frame based on the height of the work.

There are two standard sizes of these frames: 24 and 36 inches. On certain models, an adjustable foot and stand are available. If not, this frame can rest on a pair of trestles.

Embroidery hoop

Very easy to use, the embroidery hoop is made up of two wooden circles. A vice mounted on the outer circle allows you to open the hoop and adjust the tension of the fabric. Embroidery frames are available in many sizes. You should use a smaller hoop (4 inches in diameter) for embroidering corners, and a larger hoop (6 inches in diameter) for the rest of the embroidery. Some embroidery hoops are equipped with a foot in order to place it on the edge of a table.

DO NOT BREAK THE FIBERS

So that the frame of the wooden hoop does not break the fibers of delicate fabrics, wrap the inner circle with a strip of white cotton.

As you are working your embroidery, make sure that your fabric is taut: the material should resonate like the skin of a drum if you give it a tap. Once you finish your work, loosen the vice and reduce the tension.

Preparing to Embroider

Based on her preferences, the embroiderer may choose her patterns in a heartbeat. Magazines, books, and old documents are infinite sources of creation. To reproduce themes on embroidery fabric, however, is an important step which requires great precision because it facilitates the embroidery work.

ENLARGE OR REDUCE THE PATTERN TO EMBROIDER

Certain embroidery patterns with large dimensions are reduced in order to be printed in the pages of a book or magazine. Therefore, you must enlarge the pattern to have the true size.

The amount of enlarging is generally indicated in the directions, and the easiest solution to enlarge a design is to use a photocopier. The same goes for the grid of a counted cross-stitch pattern, which is more readable once enlarged by a photocopier.

You can also adapt a pattern to the desired smaller dimensions by reducing it, and again, the use of a photocopier is the most practical solution.

TRANSFER THE PATTERN TO THE FABRIC

There are many ways to transcribe a pattern onto a piece of material. In general, the method chosen is based on the type of fabric.

By transparency

When the fabric is thin and the color is light, it is possible to transfer the design by transparency. In this case, place the pattern on the table and hold it in place with pieces of tape. Place the fabric, on which you have already marked the center with basting stitches, over the pattern. Be sure that the center of the pattern and the center of the fabric coincide. Maintain the shape of the fabric with adhesive ribbon if the format of the work permits. If it is a large format pattern, place heavy objects, large stones, or telephone books, for example, around the pattern to transfer.

With the help of a black, well-sharpened hard lead pencil, transfer the pattern onto the fabric. This tracing will disappear when you first wash the work. Embroider over the tracing in order to cover it as much as possible.

Carbon paper

When the fabric is thick or the color is dark, you will need to use carbon paper to transfer the pattern. You will find, in notions shops or in craft stores, dressmaker carbon paper for marking sewing patterns. These are sheets approximately 20 x 25 inches, prepackaged in three or four different colors. The dark-colored sheets are for use on light or medium colored fabrics, medium-colored sheets are for fabrics of all colors, and light-colored sheets are for dark fabrics.

Place the fabric, on which you have already marked the center with a basting stitch, flat on a table. Maintain the shape of the fabric with weights. Place the carbon paper colored-side down on the fabric. Then place the pattern on the carbon paper, making sure the center of the design coincides with the center of the fabric, and hold all three layers in place with pins.

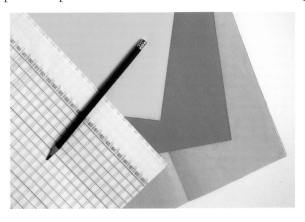

Transfer the pattern with the help of a ball-point pen. Press firmly enough so that the image transfers to the fabric, but be careful not to tear the pattern or the carbon paper. This tracing will disappear when you first wash the work. Embroider over the tracing to cover it as much as possible.

Transfer pencils

You will find in notions shops "transfer" pencils or felt-tip pens. Be careful to follow the instructions of the manufacturer. These pencils are easy, and as with other types of transfers, the tracing will disappear when you first wash the work. Embroider over the tracing to cover it as much as possible. Some felt-tip transfer pens disappear on their own after a few hours. If your work is more long-term, pens of this type are not recommended.

Tracing paper

This method is useful on thick woolens, flannel and velour, as well as on textured materials and in cases where carbon paper transfer is impossible.

With a black pencil, trace the embroidery design on a piece of tracing paper (in order to avoid any bleeding of the color). Place this tracing on the fabric and center it.

Pin the tracing to keep the paper and material from slipping. With a basting thread, sew all the lines of the pattern with small stitches. This is a bit tedious, but very effective. When the entire pattern is transferred with basting thread, tear off the tracing paper. Use tweezers to remove any small pieces of paper held prisoner by the stitches.

Embroider the pattern, and when the entire work is finished, pull out the basting thread. If some parts of the basting thread are sewn into the embroidery, do not pull them, but cut the thread level with the stitch.

READING COUNTED CROSS-STITCH GRIDS

Counted cross-stitch works are made using a design transferred onto a grid. Each square of the grid corresponds to an embroidered stitch.

The symbol diagram

Each color corresponds to a symbol inscribed in the squares of the grid. The squares that have been left white must remain untouched. The summary, or key of symbols used and corresponding colors is indicated at the corner of the grid.

The color diagram

This diagram, which is used more and more frequently, makes reading easier as you work. Each colored square corresponds to a color of embroidery thread to be used. A summary of colors is indicated at the corner of the diagram.

In general, you should begin the embroidery with the centermost point of the grid. A basting stitch should also be made in the center of the fabric. If the diagram does not indicate the center of the pattern, determine the center before you begin.

Sometimes, certain details of the pattern are surrounded by a larger line. This indicates that you must surround the embroidered part with a backstitch. Do this step only after the embroidery work in counted cross-stitch is completely finished.

RECYCLING

Using a black pencil, as you are working on your embroidery, cross out the rows you have completed or draw a line in the margin of the embroidered row. This method allows you to reuse the grid whenever you want, and all you need to do is erase the marks.

The ABC's of the Embroiderer

Like a musician, the embroiderer must practice her craft. Although hidden on the back of the work, the fastening stitches must be as discreet as possible. Some trials on samplers will allow you to practice and obtain a beautiful finish.

HOW TO BEGIN AND FASTEN AN EMBROIDERY STITCH

An embroidery stitch is never begun or fastened with a knot. The unattractive bumps of knots will appear when you iron the work. Moreover, knots are not very solid, and on works that will be used frequently, and washed often, they risk coming undone.

To begin a work of embroidery, allow ¾ to an inch of thread to hang from the back of the fabric and hold it with your index finger for three or four of your first stitches, which will catch and secure it.

Begin the next length of thread or stop the thread you are using by making two backstitches under the preceding stitches on the back of the work. Cut the end as close as possible to the backstitch.

UNDO A FEW STITCHES

It is possible to undo a few embroidered stitches or even several rows in the course of your work.

To remove a few stitches

Unthread the needle and, with the help of the eye, raise the stitches to pull them out. The round of the eye prevents ruining the surface of the fabric. Once the stitches are pulled out, fasten them with two backstitches into the preceding stitches on the back of the work. Cut off and throw away the used thread, re-thread the needle and start again.

To remove several rows

On the back of the work, raise the stitches and cut them with the help of embroidery scissors. Remove the cut threads. The holes left by the passage of the thread will appear (except in the case of Aida cloth), and these must be recovered by new embroidery work. If the fabric must remain empty in this area, gently rub it with your fingernail to close up the holes. If the marks remain, keep the fabric taut on a frame and spray a bit of water on the back. With the point of a needle, gently push the threads of the weave of the fabric to their original locations and then wait until the fabric is completely dry.

The Finishing Touches

Whether they will be functional or decorative, your works need a last step in their creation. Here is an overview of the many ways to finish and take care of your embroidery. Embroidered works will have a long life if you pay close attention to these finishing touches.

WHIPPING STITCH

So that fabrics do not fray during the course of your embroidery, it is advisable to whip stitch the edges of the fabric. You can make the whip stitch by hand or by machine using a zigzag stitch. Either way works equally well.

HEMS

Hems are needed on flat pieces such as table linens or bed linens, lap blankets, and stoles. The size of the hem is generally indicated in the directions. With an iron, form the first flap on the edge of the fabric towards the back of the work. In order to avoid over-thicknesses on the edges, trim each corner by cutting the fabric at an angle. Pin the first flap. With your iron, make a second flap, a bit larger than the first. Miter the corners. Pin or baste this hem, making sure to catch all three layers of fabric.

Sew the hem by hand with invisible stitches: make two backstitches to the right of the hem through all the layers. Moving to the left, make tiny stitches (less than $1/16$ inch in height), at regular intervals, alternately stitching in the thickness of the hem and in the fabric under the hem.

If you have a sewing machine, hems can be sewn using a thread that color coordinates with the color of the embroidered fabric.

OPEN THE SEAMS

When you are assembling the embroidered fabrics, it is generally recommended to open the seams with an iron.

Be careful, though, since in certain fabrics (such as wool or silk), the thickness of the seam can leave a mark.

Cut two long strips of brown wrapping paper and slide it on each side of the seam, making sure to place them between the wrong side of the fabric and the right side of the seam. Then open the seam with the tip of the iron. This method also allows you to form hems and to iron folds into delicate fabrics.

ASSEMBLING WORKS

Depending on the purpose of the work, you will find a few ideas for assembling below.

The Picture

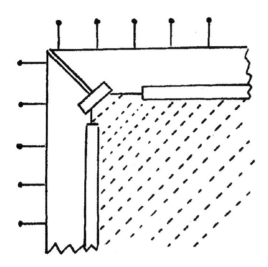

Cut a thick acid-free matboard to the exact dimensions of your embroidery. Cut the excess fabric around your embroidery, leaving 3 or 4 inches for the flap.

Cut two layers of quilt batting or table-felt to the exact dimensions of the cardboard.

Place the embroidery on the table, with the wrong side facing up. Place the two layers of batting on top, and then position the matboard on top of these three layers. Tighten the fabric around the matboard, and hold it in place by inserting pins into the rim of the matboard. Fold the edges of the fabric over the back of the matboard.

At the corners, fold the fabric at a right angle. Attach the edge of the fabric to the matboard with a thick framer's tape, and finish by attaching a fixture for hanging.

The Pillowcase

Because the cushion or pillow is easily removed from the pillowcase, this type of slipcover

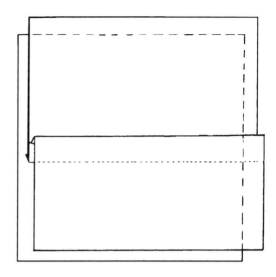

allows you to wash your embroidered work more easily.

The case is formed using three pieces of fabric: the front, which is embroidered, and two rectangles cut from the same fabric or a coordinating fabric for the back.

The dimensions of these rectangles corresponds in length to the size of the design on the case and in height to half of this size plus five inches. Whip stitch the edges of these pieces.

With an iron, form a half inch hem on the long end of each rectangle and stitch.

Place the front of the case on a table, embroidery facing up. Position the rectangles over it, with the right sides of the fabric facing each other. Overlap the center hemmed edges of the back.

Pin the fabric layers together and stitch the edges, making a $1/4$-inch seam.

Trim the edges and open the seams with an iron, then turn the case inside out, ironing the edges once more. Slip the pillow inside.

If you wish, you can use a strip of Velcro or snaps to close the case.

If you have a sewing machine, make three or four buttonholes on the back of the case on the edge of the top rectangle and then sew on some buttons.

CARING FOR EMBROIDERED WORK

Washing

Cotton or linen fabrics should be hand-washed or machine washed in hot water (up to 140°F) with detergent for delicate fabrics. In the washing machine, take care to place embroidered pieces in a special sack for delicate fabrics so that the embroidery threads do not get ruined by the friction. If you do not have one of these, place your embroidery in a pillowcase that can be buttoned or basted closed.

Use a gentle spin cycle and allow the embroidered piece to dry flat, away from all sources of heat, and in the shade if you dry your laundry outside. For embroidered wool or silk, dry cleaning is recommended.

Embroidered works composed of many kinds of fabrics and several types of embroidery threads must also undergo dry cleaning so that they do not shrink in certain places.

Starching

Table linen or bed linens require a light starching to keep their shape. Use spray starch—very easy to use—following the manufacturer's directions carefully. These products are useful for linen and cotton; however, they are to be avoided with satins, as well as silk and wool, because the starch can leave marks.

Ironing

Linen or cotton fabrics (and textiles containing a blend of these fibers) should be ironed while the material is still a bit damp. If necessary, dampen with a sprayer.

Place a thick layer of table felt or a bath towel on your ironing board. Place the embroidered work on top of the padding, with the right side facing down. Adjust the heat of the iron to the appropriate level for the fabric, and iron (use the "steam" function if the fabric will withstand it).

Use a piece of white cotton that you have already hot-pressed as a damp cloth for ironing. You do not need to moisten it, however, because the embroidered fabric is already damp. Place the cloth between the wrong side of the embroidery and the base of the iron. This helpful hint will prevent your fabric from becoming shiny.

Silk and wool are pressed when dry, with a dry iron (no steam) and a dry ironing cloth.

The family of outlining stitches is one of the most commonly used families of stitches in embroidery. It is made up of stitches allowing you to surround shapes of surfaces left empty or covered with filling stitches. The stitches described in this chapter are presented in order of increasing difficulty: the first stitches in each lesson are geared mainly towards beginners; the variations, often technically more complex and more ornamental, are used as single stitches or to highlight a detail of the embroidery.

Outlining stitches may take on more or less volume according to the manner in which they are made, the type of thread used, and the length of the stitch itself. Certain stitches are just slightly different from each other, and only the way of working the thread or pricking the needle sets them apart.

2

OUTLINING STITCHES

The Stem Stitch Family

The family of stem stitches includes basic stitches which are perfect for the beginning embroiderer. The lines of motifs, made with small, regular stitches, look like fine braided trimmings which outline the shape of the pattern. Depending on the effect sought, the stitches in this family can also be used to highlight surfaces that are entirely covered with embroidery.

THE STEM STITCH IN 2 STEPS

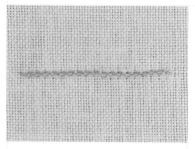

Level of Difficulty: Very easy, accessible to beginners.

Threads and Fabrics: This stitch can be made on any type of fabric, with embroidery cotton, linen, silk, or wool thread.

Direction: This stitch is worked horizontally, from left to right.

The stem stitch gets its name because it is frequently used to make stems and tendrils in floral embroidery patterns. It is most often used to highlight patterns. It can also be used as a filling stitch (for this, it takes the name "satin stitch"). In this case, you embroider line by line in tight, touching parallel rows.

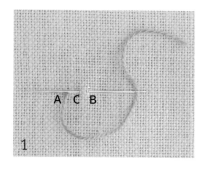

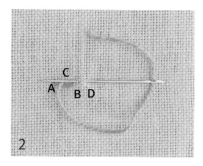

STEP 1

Bring your needle up on the left of the tracing, in A, and back down in B, directly to the right. Bring the needle back up in C, midway through the first stitch. Keep the working end of the thread looped below the stitch.

TIP:

On a curve, it is advised to keep the needle towards the outside. To obtain a uniform stitch, the needle must remain on the same side for the entire length of the tracing. If the curve reverses, continue with the needle on the inside and make small stitches to follow the circular design better.

STEP 2

Make a second stitch on the right, bringing the needle back up in B, in the hole made by the preceding stitch.

Proceed in this way for the remaining stitches.

THE CABLE STITCH IN 3 STEPS

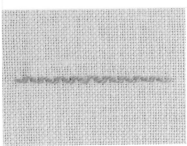

Level of Difficulty: Very easy, accessible to beginners.
Threads and Fabrics: This stitch can be made on any type of fabric, with embroidery cotton, linen, silk, or even wool thread.
Direction: This stitch is worked horizontally, from left to right.

TIP

It is not advised to use the cable stitch to carry out curves: the "broken" aspect of this stitch gives the impression that the arc is full of spikes. The cable stitch is better adapted to rectilinear designs.

A variation on the preceding stitch, the cable stitch offers a more broken appearance than the traditional stem stitch. It is used only to embroider shapes in a straight line.

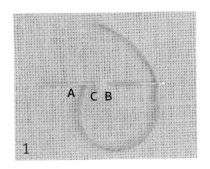
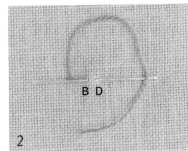

STEP 1

Bring your needle up in A, and down in B. Bring it up again in C, keeping the thread below the stitch.

STEP 2

With the working end of the thread now looped above the stitch, bring the needle down in D. Bring back up in B. Gently pull on the thread.

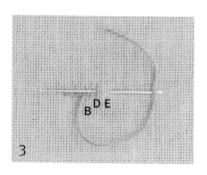

STEP 3

This time, keep the working end of the thread looped below the stitch, and bring the needle down through E. Bring it back up through D.

Return to step 2 to make the next stitch. Repeat the entire row with steps 2 and 3, alternating the direction of the thread from above to below the stitch.

THE SPLIT RUNNING STITCH IN 2 STEPS

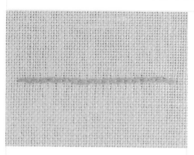

The split running stitch allows an even more precise tracing than the traditional stem stitch. Typical of Chinese embroidery, it is called "the Chinese stitch" when it is worked in tight lines to fill in an outline. The English call this "the Kensington stitch."

Level of Difficulty: Very easy, accessible to beginners.

Threads and Fabrics: This stitch must be made on delicate, thin fabric, with non-twisted embroidery cotton (such as cotton or silk floss).

Direction: This stitch is worked horizontally, from right to left.

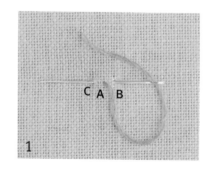 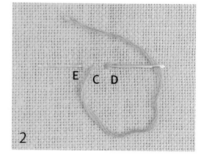

STEP 1

Bring your needle up at the right of the tracing, in point A. Bring it down directly to the right, in B, and bring it back up in C. Pull on the thread.

STEP 2

Bring your needle back down through the center of the first stitch, in D, splitting the center of the thread of this stitch. Bring your needle back up in E.

Repeat step 2 to continue your work.

TIP:
This very precise stitch is only made with embroidery thread whose strands can be easily separated, such as cotton or silk floss.

THE BACKSTITCH IN 2 STEPS

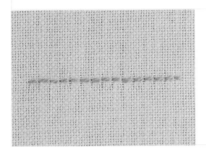

Level of Difficulty: Very easy, accessible to beginners.

Threads and Fabrics: This stitch can be made on any type of fabric, with embroidery cotton, linen, silk, or even wool thread.

Direction: This stitch is worked horizontally, from right to left.

TIP:

Make sure you always embroider stitches of the same length. The backstitch is also used to highlight patterns in counted cross-stitch. In this case, the length of the backstitch should be equivalent to the width or the height of the already-embroidered cross-stitch.

The backstitch is one of the most basic embroidery and sewing stitches. In embroidery, it allows you to make small, flat stitches, which are perfect for surrounding a motif. The solidity of the stitch makes it perfect for fabrics with a very loose weave. On the back of the work, the backstitch looks like a stem stitch.

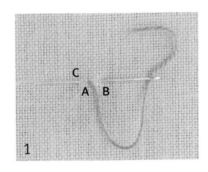

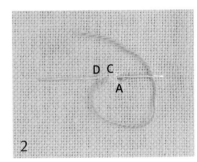

STEP 1

Bring your needle up on the right of the tracing, in A, and bring it back down in B, directly to the right on the tracing, as if you were making a horizontal stitch. Bring your needle back up in C, directly to the left of the first stitch. Gently pull on the thread.

STEP 2

Make a backstitch by bringing the needle down in A and back up in D, directly to the left on the tracing.

Repeat step 2 to embroider the remaining stitches.

THE PEKINESE STITCH IN 3 STEPS

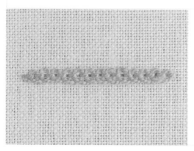

Level of Difficulty: Very easy, accessible to beginners.

Threads and Fabrics: This stitch can be made on any type of fabric, with embroidery cotton, linen, silk, or even wool thread.

Direction: This stitch is worked horizontally, from the right to the left for the first step, and then from the left to the right for the second.

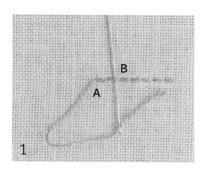

The Pekinese stitch is made on a basic backstitch. In the second step, the woven thread may be another color from that of the thread used to make the backstitch, which gives the Pekinese stitch a fancier look.

STEP 1

Make a row of regular backstitches, as explained on the previous page.

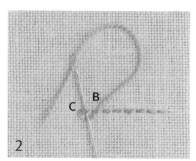

STEP 2

Thread a new needle. Bring your needle up in A, right below the backstitch, slip the needle up under the second stitch of the row, in B, and then slip the needle down under the first stitch, in C. Pull gently, leaving small loops above and below the back-stitch line.

STEP 3

Repeat step 2 as many times as needed, slipping the thread under the backstitches and forming small loops above and below the backstitches. Pull gently on the thread so that the loops remain a bit loose.

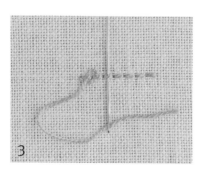

TIP:
During the second step, the embroidery thread has a tendency to quickly lose its twist. Don't forget to let it get its twist back frequently so that the loops do not become deformed.

THE SCROLL STITCH IN 2 STEPS

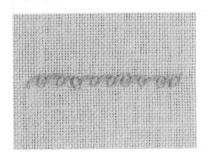

Level of Difficulty: Medium, for people who already have some experience.

Threads and Fabrics: This stitch can be made on any type of fabric, with embroidery cotton, linen, silk, or even wool thread (with a preference for Pearl or matte embroidery cotton).

Direction: This stitch is worked horizontally, from the left to the right.

TIP:

The scroll stitch looks best if you use a very round, twisted thread, such as Pearl cotton. The scrolls stand out nicely, which is perfect for a border on a pattern or to make a frame.

The scroll stitch happily combines a stem stitch with a knot stitch to form gentle spirals and arabesques. It allows you to make pretty borders.

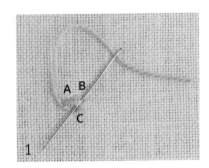
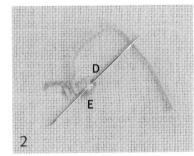

STEP 1

Bring your needle up in A, and back down at an angle in B and up against C, directly to the right of A. Slip the thread under the needle and pull gently to form a loose loop.

STEP 2

Directly to the right, bring your needle down in D and out in E at an angle, trying to keep the same slant as before. Slip the thread under the needle and pull gently on the thread.

Repeat step 2 for the remaining stitches

THE RE-EMBROIDERED BACKSTITCH IN 2 STEPS

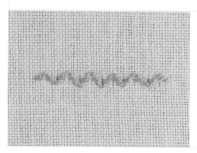

Level of Difficulty: Easy, accessible to beginners.

Threads and Fabrics: This stitch can be made on any type of fabric, with embroidery cotton, linen, silk, or even wool thread.

Direction: This stitch is worked horizontally, from the right to the left for the first step, and then from left to right for the second.

TIP:

Finish in the following way: slip the needle to the bottom of the following stitch; prick the needle right under this stitch and stop the thread by slipping it under the puncture points of the first row.

The re-embroidered backstitch is a new variation on the basic stitch, but this time it is embroidered to make it even fancier. This stitch takes on even more originality when it is made with two threads of different colors or materials.

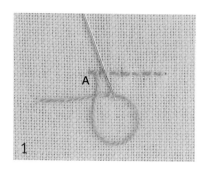
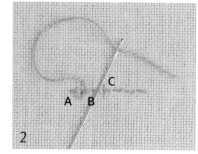

STEP 1

Embroider a row of backstitches (see p. 25). Change the needle and bring it up on the left at the end of the row of backstitches, in A, under the first stitch.

STEP 2

Slip the needle up under the second stitch, in B, then down through the third stitch, in C, leaving small even loops above and below the line of backstitches.

Repeat step 2 for the remaining stitches.

The Tea Tablecloth

A crown of Tokyo chrysanthemums decorates the center of this tea-colored linen tea tablecloth. The lightness of the petals of the flowers, simply highlighted with a stem stitch, gives subtlety to the whole. This work is designed for beginner embroiderers, who will find in it the finesse of the art of embroidery.

OVERVIEW

Level of Difficulty:
Easy; long-term project

Stitch Used:
Stem stitch (see p. 22)

Finished Dimensions:
The finished tablecloth measures 50 x 50 inches. The central embroidered pattern measures 12½ inches in diameter.

MATERIALS

60 x 60 inches tea-colored linen fabric, 32 threads/inch
3 skeins of DMC cotton embroidery floss, art. 177, pale pink (3770)
1 skein DMC cotton embroidery floss, art. 117, absinthe green (3819)
1 fine embroidery needle
Embroidery hoop
Red or blue carbon paper
Ball-point pen

PATTERN

Enlarge the pattern using a photocopier.

Whip-stitch the edges of the linen fabric with a sewing machine or by hand.

Fold the tablecloth in fours to determine the center. Place the pattern on the fabric and match the center of the pattern to that of the tablecloth. Pin two sides of the pattern. Slide the carbon paper between the fabric and the pattern, with the carbon side facing the fabric.

Trace the pattern with your ball point pen. Remove the carbon paper and pens once you have finished.

EMBROIDERY

Use two strands of cotton floss. Stretch the fabric in the embroidery hoop.

Begin working on the leaves, using the absinthe green (3819) thread, then make the flowers in pale pink (3770). This is a principle in embroidery: begin by working with the darker threads and finish with the lighter threads to avoid any staining.

Move the embroidery hoop as you complete each section of work.

FINISHING TOUCHES

Make a hem in the following manner: with an iron, make a first fold about ¾ inch high and baste, then make a second fold about 1¼ inches high; sew by hand or by machine.

Pattern reduced to 70%

ADVICE:

If you cannot find the appropriate color, you can dye your own linen fabric. Put the fabric through a first rinsing and hot-pressing (see p. 8). Prepare a very strong tea. Pour the tea in a large basin and dilute it with a bit of hot water. Dampen the linen fabric and place it in the basin and allow it to remain overnight, turning it one or two times so that it takes on the tint evenly.

Allow the fabric to dry flat (do not rinse). The color obtained is a result of the quality of the decoction of tea: it goes from deep ecru to pink-beige. This natural dye is not permanent, though, and the color of the fabric will lighten each time you wash it.

The Chain Stitch Family

The loop is the common denominator in this group of stitches. Made differently, the loops enchain themselves and form borders with remarkable depth. The chain stitch has many variations which can be used for the most complicated borders and friezes, as well as for the most simple filling stitches.

THE CHAIN STITCH IN 3 STEPS

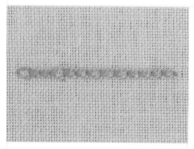

Level of Difficulty: Very easy, accessible to beginners.

Threads and Fabrics: This stitch can be made on any type of fabric, with embroidery cotton, linen, silk, or even wool thread.

Direction: This stitch is worked vertically, from top to bottom.

The chain stitch allows you to make very precise shapes and is also used for borders and for filling surfaces when it is worked in tight rows.

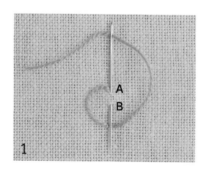
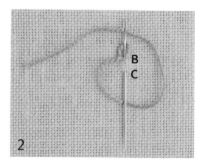

STEP 1

Bring your needle up in A, bring it down in the same hole, and then bring it out directly below A, in point B. Slip the thread under the needle and pull gently.

STEP 2

In the same way, make a second stitch, bringing your needle to B, then back down in the same hole at B, and back up below B, in point C. Slide the thread under the needle and gently pull the thread. Repeat step 2 to continue the row.

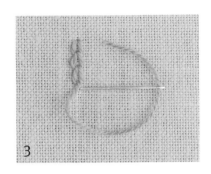

STEP 3

The row of chain stitches must be attached to the fabric at the final stitch or else it will unravel like a sweater. Make a small straight stitch over the thread of the final loop in order to keep it flat against the surface of the fabric.

THE TWISTED CHAIN STITCH IN 2 STEPS

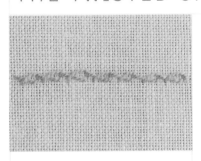

Level of Difficulty: Very easy, accessible to beginners.

Threads and Fabrics: This stitch can be made on any type of fabric, with embroidery cotton, linen, silk, or wool thread.

Direction: This stitch is worked vertically, from top to bottom.

Very easy to make, the twisted chain stitch is used to give depth to a border. Its twisted aspect is particularly fun. It is made with all types of threads, but Pearl cotton or matte embroidery cotton bring out its best qualities.

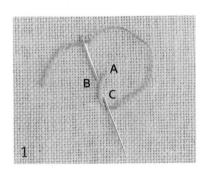

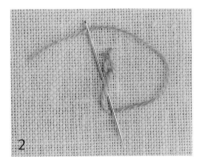

STEP 1

Bring the needle up in A. Bring the needle back down in B, to the left and slightly below point A. Bring the tip of the needle back up at point C, vertical with point A. Slide the thread under the needle and pull gently to form the loop.

STEP 2

Work the row repeating step 1. As with all chain stitches, end the row with a small straight stitch over the thread of the final loop.

THE CABLE CHAIN STITCH IN 3 STEPS

Level of Difficulty: Difficult, reserved for people with experience.

Threads and Fabrics: This stitch can be made on any type of fabric, with embroidery cotton, linen, silk, or even wool thread.

Direction: This stitch is worked vertically, from top to bottom.

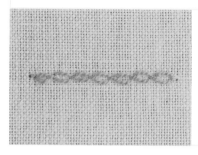

The cable chain stitch is a sophisticated variation of the classic chain stitch which gives the look of a metal chain with distinct links.

STEP 1

Bring the needle up in A and wrap the thread around it from left to right. Bring the needle back down in A.

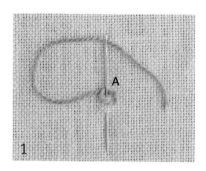

STEP 2

Bring the needle up in point B, below A. Slide the thread under the needle, then pull gently on the thread to form the loop.

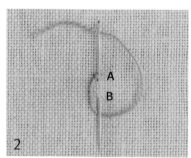

STEP 3

Wrap the thread around the needle from left to right and bring your needle down in C, below point B. Bring the needle back up directly below, in D. Slide the thread under the needle and pull the thread.

Work the row repeating step 3, and finish with a small straight stitch over the thread of the final loop.

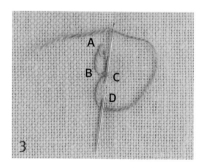

TIP:
The cable chain stitch is interesting because it gives dimension. Do not hesitate to work with a very twisted thread, such as matte embroidery cotton or size 3 or size 5 Pearl cotton. In this case, work with a larger embroidery needle so you don't wear out the surface of the fibers too quickly.

THE LADDER STITCH IN 3 STEPS

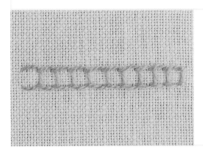

Level of Difficulty: Very easy, accessible to beginners.

Threads and Fabrics: This stitch can be made on any type of fabric, with embroidery cotton, linen, silk, or even wool thread.

Direction: This stitch is worked vertically, from top to bottom.

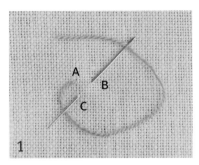

The ladder stitch, also known as "the open chain stitch" or "the square stitch," is a version of the classic chain stitch with open loops which evoke the rungs on a ladder.

STEP 1

Bring your needle up in A and bring the tip back down directly to the right in B. Points A and B are parallel. Bring the tip of your needle back up in C, directly below point A. Slide your thread under the tip of the needle and pull gently in order to form a large loop.

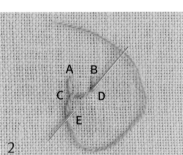

STEP 2

Finish the stitch by bringing the tip of your needle down in point D, below point B, and level with C. Bring the tip of your needle up in E, below points A and C, and then slide the thread under the tip of the needle.

STEP 3

Work the row following the above directions. To finish it, make a small straight stitch on the right and left over the thread of the final loop, in order to keep its large and open characteristic.

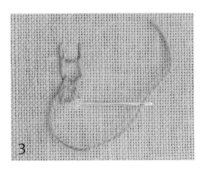

> **TIP:**
> For beginning embroiderers, working a ladder stitch is easier to master on fabric that has a visible weave because it allows you to follow the threads to work uniform heights and lengths for the stitches.

THE REVERSED CHAIN STITCH IN 4 STEPS

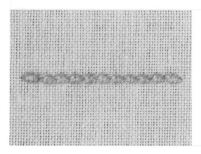

Level of Difficulty: Very easy, accessible to beginners.

Threads and Fabrics: This stitch can be made on any type of fabric, with embroidery cotton, linen, silk, or even wool thread.

Direction: This stitch is worked vertically, from top to bottom.

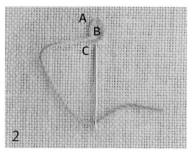

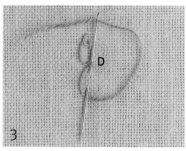

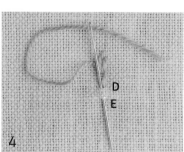

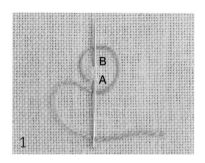

Here is an even easier way to make the chain stitch. The technique for the reversed chain stitch, also known as "heavy chain" or "braid stitch," is great for beginners or for children who wish to try embroidery.

STEP 1

The first stitch is made in the reverse direction from the rest. Bring your needle up in A, bring the tip back down in the same point, and bring it back up in point B, directly above A. Slide the thread under the tip of the needle.

STEP 2

Pull to make a loop. Turning work upside down, make a small straight stitch over the loop, bringing your needle down in C.

STEP 3

Bring your needle up in D, below point A. Slip the needle under the loop of preceding chain stitch from right to left, without pricking the fabric.

STEP 4

Bring your needle back down in point D, and bring the tip of the needle back up in point E.

Repeat steps 3 and 4 to form the entire row. Finish it by bringing the needle back up in the fabric after the final loop. To make loops without snagging the fibers of the thread, slip the needle eye-side-first under the loop.

THE LAZY DAISY STITCH IN 2 STEPS

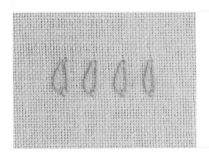

Level of Difficulty: Very easy, accessible to beginners.

Threads and Fabrics: This stitch can be made on any type of fabric, with embroidery cotton, linen, silk, or even wool thread.

Direction: This stitch is worked vertically, from top to bottom.

TIP:

Some thin fabrics, because of their transparency, allow you to see the working end of the thread between the daisy stitches on the back of the work. To prevent this unsightly appearance, fasten off your stitch at the back of each loop, cut the thread, and then move to where you need it on the fabric and begin your work again.

The lazy daisy stitch is a chain stitch for which each loop is isolated. It is used for light fillings or to form simple flowers when the loops are clustered around a center.

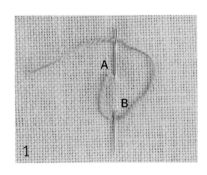 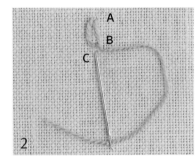

STEP 1

Bring your needle up in A. Bring it back down through the same point and bring the tip back up through B, directly below point A. Slide the thread under the tip of the needle and pull gently to make a loop.

STEP 2

To finish the stitch, make a small straight stitch over the thread of the loop, bringing the needle back down in point C.

Move to the next loop, at any distance from the first, and repeat steps 1 and 2.

THE DOUBLE LAZY DAISY STITCH IN 4 STEPS

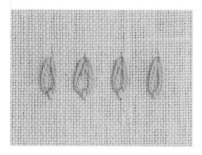

Level of Difficulty: Medium, for people who already have some experience.

Threads and Fabrics: This stitch can be made on any type of fabric, with embroidery cotton, linen, silk, or even wool thread.

Direction: This stitch is worked vertically, from top to bottom.

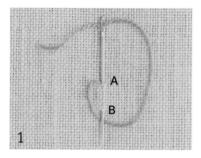

This is a more complex version of the previous stitch. The double lazy daisy stitch is best used in forming the petals of flowers. So that the petals remain balanced, orient them in the following way: the side on which you make the straight stitch to fasten the loop should be placed toward the outside of the flower.

STEP 1

Bring your needle up in A. Bring it back down in the same point and bring the tip back up in B, directly below A. Slide the thread under the tip of the needle and pull gently to form the loop.

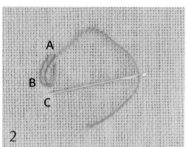

STEP 2

Make a small straight stitch over the thread of the loop, and bring the needle back down in C.

STEP 3

Return slightly above point A and bring your needle up through D. Slide the needle under the straight stitch to hold the loop.

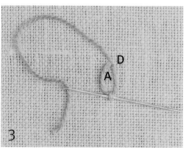

STEP 4

Bring your needle back down in point D. Pull gently so that the thread meets up with the thread of the inner loop. The stitch is complete.

Move to the next loop, a bit further away, and repeat steps 1 through 4.

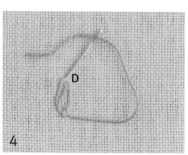

THE WHIPPED CHAIN STITCH IN 2 STEPS

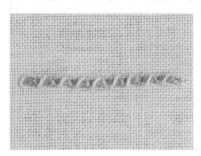

Level of Difficulty: Medium, for people who already have some experience.

Threads and Fabrics: This stitch can be made on any type of fabric, with embroidery cotton, linen, silk, or even wool thread.

Direction: This stitch is worked vertically, from top to bottom.

TIP:

Do not hesitate to use this stitch to make monograms on your household linens. The whipped chain stitch is very versatile, and it adapts to any curve. To make it stand out as much as possible, use Pearl, matte embroidery cotton, or cutwork and embroidery thread.

The whipped chain stitch is classified among composite border stitches. It is made on a base of chain stitches, and then a second row is worked over them. When it is done well, the stitch looks like a round braid, and the effect is best when two colors are used.

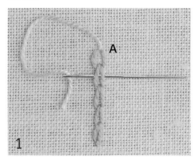
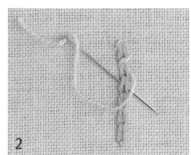

Begin by making a row of chain stitches (see p. 32).

STEP 1

Thread a new needle. Bring the needle up at the beginning of the row of chain stitches, in A, and slide the needle from left to right under the next stitch.

STEP 2

Gently pull to make a slightly slanted stitch. Under the next loop, slide the needle from left to right.

Embroider the entire row, and finish by bringing your needle down into the fabric just to the right of the last loop after having slid the needle from left to right.

The Shopping Bag

A mistletoe pattern inscribed within a circle decorates an elegant linen shopping bag. This pattern can have an even better effect on other materials, such as silk taffeta, cotton velour, or good quality wool. It is up to the embroiderer to experiment with combinations of colors and textiles.

OVERVIEW

Level of Difficulty:
Easy

Stitches Used:
Chain stitch (see p. 32)
Knot stitch (see p. 74)

Finished Dimensions:
The shopping bag measures 13 x 15 inches. The central embroidered pattern measures 6 inches in diameter.

MATERIALS

1 natural-colored linen shopping bag
1 skein DMC cotton embroidery floss, art. 117 in each of the following colors: off-white 3866, Verona green 3813, pale green 504, absinthe green 734, brown 3032
1 fine embroidery needle
Embroidery hoop
Tracing paper
Blue carbon paper
Ball-point pen
60 inches absinthe green velour ribbon, ½ inch wide

PATTERN

Trace the mistletoe pattern on tracing paper.

Measure the front of the shopping bag to determine the center.

Place the pattern on the fabric, match the centers, and pin two sides of the pattern.

Slide the sheet of carbon paper between the fabric and the pattern, with the carbon side down on the fabric. Trace the outline of the pattern with your pen, then remove the carbon paper and the pins.

EMBROIDERY

Use two strands of cotton floss.

Stretch the fabric in the embroidery hoop.

Begin the work with the absinthe green (734) and pale green (504) leaves, and then make the stems in Verona green (3813).

Continue the embroidery with the berries. Make a knot stitch (see p. 74) with Verona green at the center of each berry.

Finish the work with the brown (3032) line around the pattern.

Move the embroidery hoop as you complete each section of the work.

FINISHING TOUCHES

Remove the linen handles on the shopping bag and replace them with doubled velour ribbon.

Pattern reduced to 90 %

ADVICE:

To obtain a uniform fill, begin by outlining the pattern with chain stitches. Then, without fastening off your needle, place a second row against the first, then a third, etc. Fill the pattern in this fashion, little by little, from exterior to interior.

The Featherstitch Family

The featherstitch is derived from the chain stitch. Here, the loops which make up rows are wide open and projecting. Because of the feathery appearance of these stitches, this family is used for large, dense borders which are as fun to make on clothing as they are on household decorations.

THE FEATHERSTITCH IN 4 STEPS

Level of Difficulty: Very easy, accessible to beginners.

Threads and Fabrics: This stitch can be made on any type of fabric, with embroidery cotton, linen, silk, or even wool thread.

Direction: This stitch is worked vertically, from top to bottom.

The featherstitch is generally found in smocking. It is also used to decorate crazy quilt patchwork.

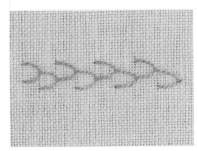

STEP 1

Bring your needle up in A. Bring it down to the right, in B, level with point A. Bring the tip of the needle up in C, below and between points A and B. Slide the thread under the needle and pull gently to make an open loop.

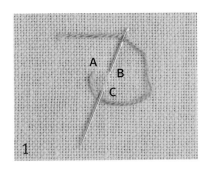

STEP 2

Directly to the left of point C, but at the same level, bring your needle down in D. Bring the point of your needle back up in E, below and between points C and D. Slide the thread under the needle and pull gently to form an open loop.

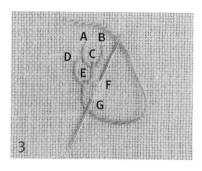

STEP 3

Bring your needle down in F, directly below point B. Bring the tip of the needle back up in G, below and between points E and F, in line with C. Slide the thread under the needle and pull gently to form an open loop.

STEP 4

Proceed, repeating steps 2 and 3. To finish the row, make a small straight stitch over the final open loop.

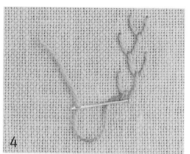

TIP:
Because it is made in a sweeping way, the featherstitch allows you to obtain wide open loops, alternating their directions between right and left.

THE DOUBLE FEATHERSTITCH IN 3 STEPS

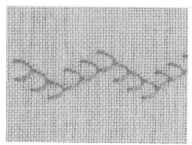

Level of Difficulty: Medium, for people who already have some experience.
Threads and Fabrics: This stitch can be made on any type of fabric, with embroidery cotton, linen, silk, or even wool thread.
Direction: This stitch is worked vertically, from top to bottom.

TIP:
The size of the chevron will depend on the number of open loops composing each branch. Here, we have worked three stitches: this is the minimum to obtain a pretty design. By adding one, two, or three more loops per branch, the chevron will become larger.

Like the preceding stitch, the double featherstitch is used for smocking and fancy borders. Its chevron design makes it one of the most decorative border stitches.

To make the chevron, this stitch is worked by making the same number of open loops for each of the branches. It is made by forming the diagonal stitches from top to bottom, alternating from left to right.

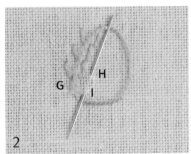

STEP 1

Bring your needle up in A. Bring it down in B, to the right, level with point A. Bring the tip back up in C, below and between points A and B. Slide the thread under the needle and pull gently to form an open loop. Continue working in points D, E, F, and G, shifting each stitch more towards the left.

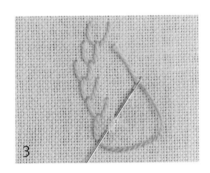

STEP 2

The fourth stitch shifts to the right and is situated directly below the second stitch. Bring your needle down in H, level with G and directly to the right. Bring the needle back up in I, then slide the thread under the needle and pull gently.

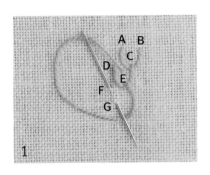

STEP 3

Continue the row of chevrons, alternating three stitches to the left with three stitches to the right.

To finish, make a straight stitch over the thread of the final open loop.

THE FISHBONE OUTLINE STITCH IN 3 STEPS

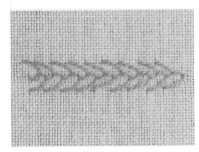

Level of Difficulty: Very easy, accessible to beginners.
Threads and Fabrics: This stitch can be made on any type of fabric, with embroidery cotton, linen, silk, or even wool thread.
Direction: This stitch is worked vertically, from top to bottom.

The fishbone outline stitch is a featherstitch whose branches, in chevrons, may be of different lengths. As its name indicates, it looks like the bones of a fish.

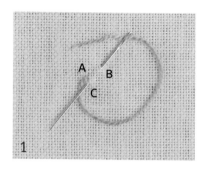

STEP 1

Bring your needle up through A. Shift to the right and up a bit and bring it down in B. Bring the tip of your needle back up in C, under point A. Slide the thread under the needle and pull gently to form an open loop.

STEP 2

Shift to the left, and bring your needle down in D. Bring the tip of the needle back out in E, under points A and C. Slide the thread under the needle and pull gently.

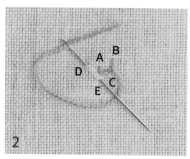

STEP 3

Continue the work, alternating a stitch on the right and a stitch on the left, then finish the row by making a small straight stitch over the thread of the final open loop.

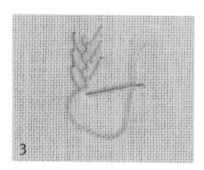

TIP:
The slant and length of the branches of the stitch must be uniform along the whole length of the row. To achieve this, it is best to work on fabric with an obvious weave (such as cotton muslin or linen, for example).

THE WHEAT STITCH IN 4 STEPS

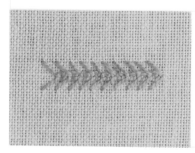

Level of Difficulty: Medium, for people who already have some experience.
Threads and Fabrics: This stitch can be made on any type of fabric, but it is preferable to use twisted embroidery cotton, such as Pearl or matte embroidery cotton, which will stand out more.
Direction: This stitch is worked vertically, from top to bottom.

Frequently used to make stalks of wheat in embroideries of landscape patterns, the wheat stitch is made up of a chevron stitch of which the center is highlighted with a closed-loop stitch.

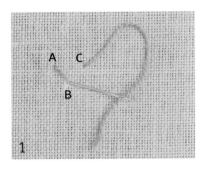

STEP 1

Bring your needle up in A. Bring it down again in B, shifting very slightly to the lower right. Point B will be the center of the row. Bring your needle back up in C, level with A, and bring it back down in B.

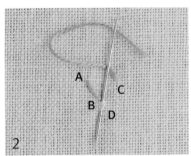

STEP 2

Bring your needle up in D, directly below point B. Pull gently on the thread.

STEP 3

To form the chain stitch, slide the needle from right to left under the two branches of the chevron.

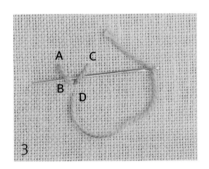

STEP 4

Bring your needle back down in D, gently pulling on the thread to form the loop and bring the needle back up in E, directly below point A.

Start again at step 1 to continue the row, which you will finish off with the final chevron stitch.

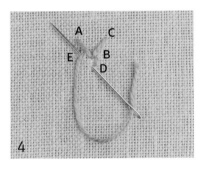

TIP:

If you use this ribbed stitch for work on feathery motifs, you will obtain a very beautiful effect. Tighten the stitches against each other to cover the entire surface of a pattern, and adapt the length of the branches of the chevrons to the size of the design of feathers.

THE CROSSED FEATHERSTITCH IN 3 STEPS

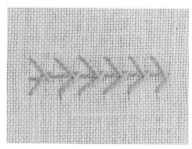

Level of Difficulty: Very easy, accessible to beginners.

Threads and Fabrics: This stitch can be made on any type of fabric, with embroidery cotton, linen, silk, or even wool thread.

Direction: This stitch is worked vertically, from top to bottom.

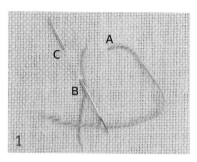

The crossed featherstitch, also known as the "feather couching stitch," is used for work on stems, branches, and leaves in landscape motifs when the stitches are closely embroidered. The first large stitch, called the couching stitch, may be embroidered in a contrasting color to the other stitches. Made with a metallic thread, your work will be even more spectacular.

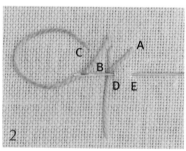

STEP 1

Make a large straight stitch (see p. 97). Bring your needle up in A, directly to the right of the couching stitch top. Bring your needle down in B, to the left of the couching stitch. Bring it back up in C, above and to the left, level with A.

STEP 2

Bring your needle down in D, to the right of the couching stitch, level with B. Bring it back up in E, directly below point A.

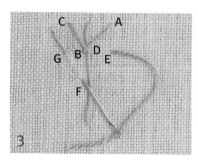

STEP 3

Bring your needle down in F, to the left of the couching stitch and directly below point B. Bring your needle back up to the left in G, level with E and in line below C.

Continue the row alternately forming the branches of the chevron to the right and left, keeping the couching stitch central on the fabric with the crossing of stitches.

TIP:
To adapt this stitch to curves, make the couching stitch with large backstitches (see p. 25), following the tracing of the pattern to embroider.

THE CLOSED FEATHERSTITCH IN 4 STEPS

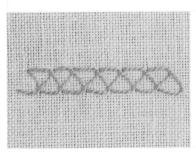

Level of Difficulty: Very easy, accessible to beginners.

Threads and Fabrics: This stitch can be made on any type of fabric, with embroidery cotton, linen, silk, or even wool thread.

Direction: This stitch is worked vertically, from top to bottom.

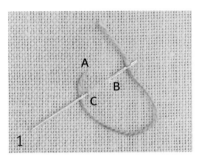

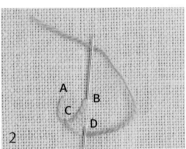

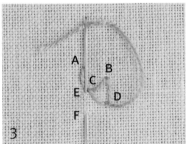

The closed featherstitch is an easy-to-make variation of the simple featherstitch. By orienting the branches of the points against each other, you close the design.

This stitch can also be embroidered on a thin colored ribbon.

STEP 1

Bring your needle up in A. Bring it down in B, diagonal to A. Bring the tip back up in C, directly below point A. Slide the thread under the needle and pull gently to make an open loop.

STEP 2

Bring your needle down in B, then bring the tip of the needle back up directly below, in D. Slide the thread under the needle and pull gently to form an open loop, which is actually now closed by the branch of the preceding stitch.

STEP 3

Bring the needle back down in E, below C, and bring the tip of the needle back up in F, directly below E. Slide the thread under the needle and pull gently to form the loop.

STEP 4

To make the row, repeat steps 2 and 3, alternating a stitch pointing to the right with a stitch pointing to the left. Finish with a small straight stitch over the thread of the final loop.

THE CRETAN STITCH IN 4 STEPS

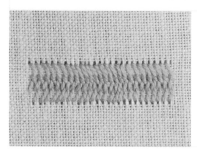

Level of Difficulty: Very easy, accessible to beginners.

Threads and Fabrics: This stitch can be made on any type of fabric, with embroidery cotton, linen, silk, or even wool thread.

Direction: This stitch is worked vertically, from top to bottom.

In this derivation of the featherstitch, the loops are embroidered very openly, almost horizontally. The Cretan stitch is often used on traditional garments embroidered by the inhabitants of Crete, where the stitch gets its name. It is also known as "the Cretan featherstitch."

STEP 1

Bring your needle up in A, then, shifting to the right, bring it down in B. Bring the tip back up in C. Slide the thread under the needle and pull gently. The slightly slanted stitches give the impression of being worked on the same horizontal plane.

STEP 2

Bring your needle down in D, to the left of point A. Bring the tip back up in E, just below point A, and then slide the thread under the needle and pull gently on the open loop.

STEP 3

Bring your needle down on the right, in F, below point B, and bring the tip back up in G, below point C. Slide the thread under the needle and pull gently on the open loop.

STEP 4

Continue the row by repeating steps 2 and 3. Alternate a stitch to the right with a stitch to the left. To finish, make a small straight stitch over the loop of the final stitch.

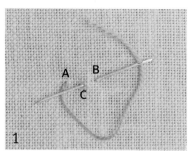

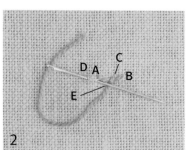

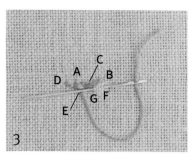

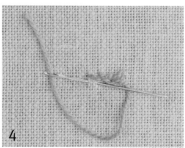

The Frame

The play of arabesques in this pattern evokes the foliage patterns of classical frames. One clearly sees here that the featherstitch is well-suited to supple and relatively complex designs. Enlarged, this pattern adapts for other uses: a border for a pillow, the frame for the center of a lap blanket, or as decorative corners on a tablecloth and napkins.

OVERVIEW

Level of Difficulty: Medium

Stitch Used:
Featherstitch (see p. 43)

Finished Dimensions:
The frame measures 10 inches square. The pattern of embroidered arabesques measures 3½ inches square.

MATERIALS

16 x 16 inches lavender blue cotton fabric
2 skeins of DMC cutwork and embroidery thread, art. 107, white
1 medium embroidery needle
Embroidery hoop
Tracing paper
Blue carbon paper
Ball-point pen
Thick, heavyweight acid-free matboard
Pins
Fabric glue

PATTERN

Trace the arabesque pattern on a piece of tracing paper.

With thread, baste an outline on the fabric to mark the edges of the frame. Place the pattern on the fabric, and center the pattern on the frame.

Pin two sides of the pattern to the fabric.

Slide the carbon paper between the fabric and the pattern, with the carbon face down on the fabric. Trace the pattern with your pen, then remove the carbon and the pins.

EMBROIDERY

Stretch the fabric in the embroidery hoop.

Begin working from the outer edges of the pattern of arabesques towards the inside. When the embroidery is finished, bring the thread to the back of the fabric, cut the end, and begin again at the next corner.

Move the embroidery hoop as you finish each section of your work.

FINISHING TOUCHES

Cut the shape of the frame out of the matboard.

Using scissors, cut the central square in the embroidered

To obtain the look of braided trimmings, it is important to record the dotted lines that surround the arabesque pattern on the tracing paper. The outer edges of the featherstitch should be positioned with this border to maintain the same stitch length throughout the entire embroidered work.

fabric, ¾ inch from the dotted line. Stretch the fabric over the matboard, holding the fabric with several pins in the matboard. Fold the excess fabric over the back of the matboard.

Resize the corners of the fabric and glue the fabric on the back of the matboard.

Cut another piece of matboard, 10 inches square, and attach it to the back of the frame. If desired, cover the inner edge of the opening with grosgrain ribbon.

Pattern reduced to 50 %

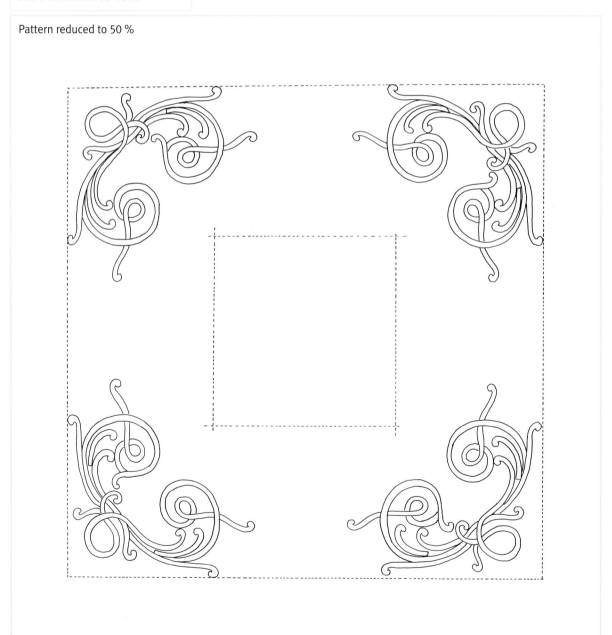

The Herringbone Stitch Family

The herringbone family of stitches brings together works made with long, crossed stitches. These stitches have been know since antiquity, and they are used in large decorative friezes which cover very expansive surfaces. They are sometimes made as counted stitches and are therefore associated with other types of embroidery, such as patterns made using counted cross-stitch.

THE HERRINGBONE STITCH IN 3 STEPS

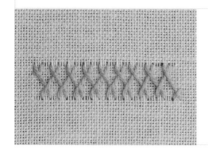

Level of Difficulty: Very easy, accessible to beginners.

Threads and Fabrics: This stitch can be made on any type of fabric, with embroidery cotton, linen, silk, or even wool thread.

Direction: This stitch is worked horizontally, from left to right.

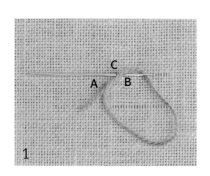

As a sewing technique, the herringbone stitch is sometimes used to make hems. In embroidery, it may be worked as counted stitches on fabric with an obvious weave, or on a tracing of a motif on finer materials. For a clearer understanding of how to work this stitch as it comes and goes between the top and bottom lines, two drawn threads mark the outer limits of the stitches.

STEP 1

Bring your needle up in A, to the left of the row and slightly below the upper line of drawn thread. Bring it down in B, to the right, in the upper drawn thread. Bring it back up in C, to the left and still on the upper drawn thread. You have a slanted half-stitch.

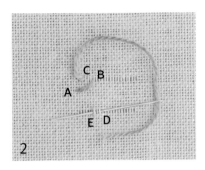

STEP 2

Bring your needle down in D, below and to the right, in the lower line of drawn thread. Bring it back up in E, to the left and still in the lower drawn thread. The first two stitches will cross.

STEP 3

Come back to the upper drawn thread. Bring your needle down in F, to the right of B, and bring it back up in G, to the left of F and close to B.

Repeat steps 2 and 3, and finish with a slanted half-stitch.

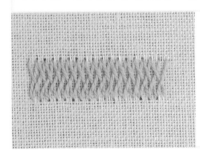

> **TIP**
>
> This stitch offers best results when it is made with a thick twisted thread. Use Pearl cotton or matte embroidery cotton.

THE CROSSED BACKSTITCH IN 3 STEPS

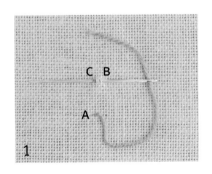

Level of Difficulty: Very easy, accessible to beginners.
Threads and Fabrics: This stitch can be made on any type of fabric, with embroidery cotton, linen, silk, or even wool thread.
Direction: This stitch is worked horizontally, from left to right.

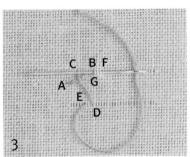

Also called the "tight herringbone stitch," the crossed backstitch is made like the previous stitch, but its stitches are tight against each other to form a grill of slanted stitches which cover the surface of the fabric. For a clearer understanding of how to work this stitch as it comes and goes between the top and bottom lines, two drawn threads mark the outer limits of the stitches.

STEP 1

Bring your needle up in A, on the lower line of drawn thread. Bring it down in B, above and to the right, in the upper drawn thread. Bring it back up in C, to the left on the same line.

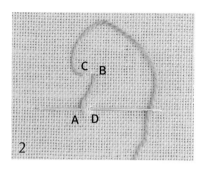

STEP 2

On the lower line of drawn thread, bring your needle back down in D, to the right of and close to point A. Bring the needle back up in A.

STEP 3

On the upper line, bring your needle down in E, to the right of and close to point B, and bring your needle back up in B.

Continue the row by repeating steps 2 and 3. The back of the work will reveal two parallel lines of backstitches.

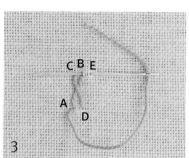

TIP

For best results with this stitch, it is important to stretch the fabric taut in the hoop, because if the long, crossed stitches are not taut, they run the risk of floating on the surface of the fabric.

THE CHEVRON STITCH IN 4 STEPS

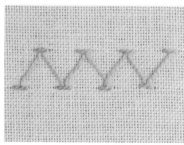

Level of Difficulty: Very easy, accessible to beginners.
Threads and Fabrics: This stitch can be made on any type of fabric, with embroidery cotton, linen, silk, or even wool thread.
Direction: This stitch is worked horizontally, from left to right.

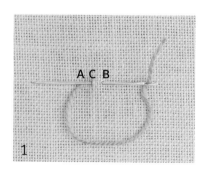

More airy than the classic herringbone stitch, the chevron stitch allows you to make light borders or to attach a flat braid or trimming. A variation of this stitch is used in sewing to baste or tack two pieces of material together.

STEP 1

Bring your needle up in A, bring it down to the right in B, and bring it back up in C, between the two preceding points. Position the thread below the needle and pull gently to form the stitch.

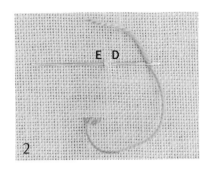

STEP 2

Above, shift the work to the right, bringing the needle down in D. Bring it back up on the same line and to the left, in E.

STEP 3

Shift to the right and bring your needle down in F and back up in D. Position the thread above the needle and pull gently to form the stitch.

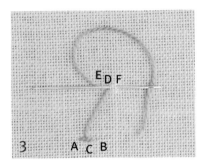

STEP 4

On the bottom line, bring your needle down in G and bring it back up in H, to the left. Bring your needle back down on the same line and to the right, in point I, and then back up in G.

Repeat steps 2, 3, and 4 to continue the row. Begin and finish the row with a small flat stitch situated at the top or bottom of the chevrons.

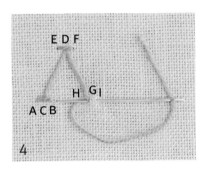

> **TIP**
>
> Be sure to make uniform stitches. The small horizontal stitches must be the same length, and the diagonal stitches must always keep the same angled slant.

THE ROMAN STITCH IN 3 STEPS

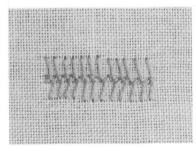

Level of Difficulty: Medium, for people who already have some experience.

Threads and Fabrics: This stitch can be made on any type of fabric, with embroidery cotton, linen, silk, or even wool thread.

Direction: This stitch is worked in all directions, but for better understanding of the stitch, the explanation here is given from top to bottom.

Unlike other stitches derived from the herringbone stitch, the roman stitch is only used to fill in forms. The length of its stitches adapt easily to the pattern being worked. The middle of the stitch is marked with a vein.

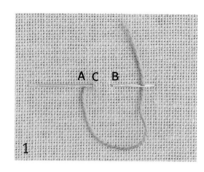

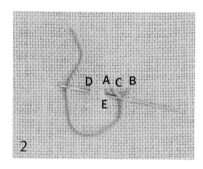

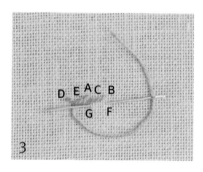

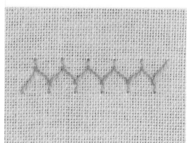

STEP 1

Bring your needle up in A, on the left. Bring it back down in B, to the right and level with A, and bring it back up in C, between A and B. Position the thread below the needle.

STEP 2

Bring your needle down in D, to the left and just slightly below the preceding stitch. Bring the needle back up in E, towards the center of the stitch, below point A. Position the thread below the needle.

STEP 3

Bring your needle down in F, to the right and below point B, and then bring the tip of the needle up in G, below point C, and slide the thread under the needle. To continue your work, repeat steps 2 and 3, alternating the stitches on each side of the central vein.

TIP

To fill a leafy pattern, for example, begin by tracing the shape of the leaf and the central vein on the fabric. The length of the stitches alternating to the left and the right varies based on the size of the pattern. Tighten your stitches close together to cover the surface of the fabric completely.

THE RUSSIAN STITCH IN 3 STEPS

Level of Difficulty: Very easy, accessible to beginners.
Threads and Fabrics: This stitch can be made on any type of fabric, with embroidery cotton, linen, silk, or even wool thread.
Direction: This stitch is worked horizontally, from left to right.

Easy to make, this chevron stitch, also called "open Cretan stitch," is also one that is quick to embroider. Unlike the chevron stitch, the tops of which are marked with small horizontal stitches, the tops of the Russian stitch are marked with small vertical stitches.

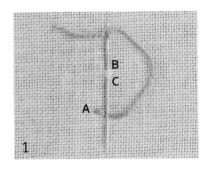

STEP 1

Bring your needle up in A, at the bottom of the leg of the first chevron. Bring it down in B, shifting up and to the right. Bring the tip of your needle back up directly below, in C, and slide the thread under the tip of the needle.

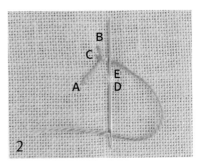

STEP 2

Bring your needle down in D, on the bottom line, level with and to the right of A. Bring the tip back up directly above, in E, to make a small vertical stitch. Slide the thread under the needle and pull gently to form the second branch of the chevron.

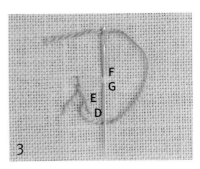

STEP 3

On the top line, bring your needle down in F, and back up in G, directly below, to form a small vertical stitch. Slide the thread under the tip of the needle. To continue the row, repeat steps 2 and 3.

TIP

Similar to the preceding stitches, the Russian stitch requires a great deal of uniformity. The length of the stitches must always be identical, and the same goes for their spacing. Also, you must not forget to slide the thread under the needle at each small vertical stitch, otherwise, the twisted angle effect is lost.

The Pillow

The herringbone stitch is not only assigned to filling friezes and borders. Discover its other uses with this finely embroidered tone-on-tone cover for a pillow. This pattern can also be adapted easily for the top of a footstool.

OVERVIEW

Level of Difficulty:
Easy

Stitch Used:
Herringbone stitch (see p. 54)

Finished Dimensions:
The pillow cover can be adapted to the dimensions of the pillow. The embroidered motif measures 12 x 8 inches.

MATERIALS

40 x 32 inches blue linen DMC cloth
2 skeins of DMC Pearl cotton, art. 115, blue (597)
1 medium embroidery needle
Embroidery hoop
Tracing paper
Blue carbon paper
Ball-point pen
16 x 12-inch pillow
Blue sewing thread

PATTERN

Fold the fabric in two and cut it in order to obtain two rectangles with the dimensions of 20 x 16 inches. Whip stitch the edges of the linen.

Trace the scallop motif onto tracing paper.

Place the pattern on the rectangle of fabric, with the center of the pattern matching the center of the fabric.

Pin two sides of the pattern.

Slide the carbon paper between the fabric and the pattern, with the carbon side facing the fabric. Trace the outline of the pattern with your pen, then remove the carbon paper and the pins.

EMBROIDERY

Stretch the fabric in the embroidery hoop. Begin the work with the stylized flower motifs, then bring the thread to the back of the work. Cut the thread and begin the work on the next motif, so that you avoid having threads floating on the back of the work.

Continue the work with the scalloped border.

Move the embroidery hoop as you complete each section of your work.

FINISHING TOUCHES

Press the embroidery on the opposite side.

With right sides of the fabric together, pin the edges of the rectangles.

ADVICE

Angle the stitches on the curves to follow the direction of the design. To do this, tighten the stitches toward the inside of the curve and then lightly loosen them on the outside of the motif. Keep the same space between stitches throughout the entire work.

Sew the edges making 2-inch seams and leaving a 10-inch opening on one side.

Cut the excess fabric to ¾ inch from the seam, and clip the corners.

Press the seams open. Turn the pillow cover inside out, slip the pillow inside, and slipstitch the opening closed by hand.

Pattern reduced to 50 %

The Palestrina Stitch Family

Made up of a line of knots, the Palestrina stitch is an outlining stitch with a very raised appearance. This family of stitches has the same characteristics as knot stitches. These stitches are a bit more difficult to make than previous ones, but their very original finish rewards embroiderers for their efforts in learning them.

THE PALESTRINA STITCH IN 3 STEPS

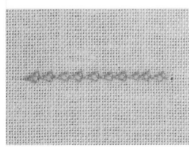

Level of Difficulty: Medium, for people who already have some experience.
Threads and Fabrics: This stitch can be made on any type of fabric, preferably with non-separable, twisted embroidery cotton, silk, or wool.
Direction: This stitch is worked vertically, from top to bottom.

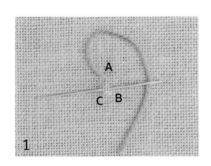

The Palestrina stitch is generally worked on a tracing, but it may also be adapted for counted stitches. When it is made horizontally from left to right on a tracing, it is called the "Italian scallop stitch." It keeps the same raised quality, and is also used as a border.

STEP 1
Bring the needle up in A, and down in B, directly below A. Bring it back up in C, just to the left of B, and pull the thread to make a small vertical stitch.

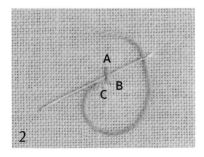

STEP 2
Slide the needle under the vertical stitch from right to left.

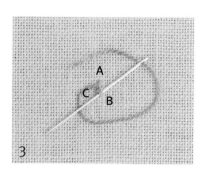

STEP 3

Without catching the fabric, slide the needle between the two branches of the stitch you just made. Slide the thread under the needle to form a knot, then pull gently on the thread.

Continue the work, beginning at step 1 and point B.

THE PEARL STITCH IN 2 STEPS

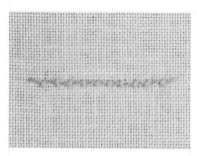

Level of Difficulty: Medium, for people who already have some experience.

Threads and Fabrics: This stitch can be made on any type of fabric, preferably with non-separable, twisted embroidery cotton, silk, or wool.

Direction: This stitch is worked horizontally, from left to right or from right to left.

Also called the "coral stitch," this outlining stitch perfectly adapts to making linear motifs, monograms, and decorative lines. The pearl stitch can be worked either from left to right or from right to left, always stitching over the tracing. The version shown below is being worked horizontally from right to left.

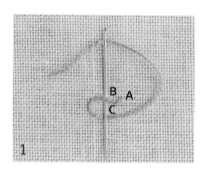 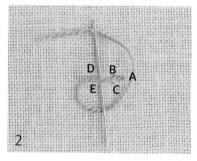

STEP 1

Bring your needle up in A and back down in B, directly to the left of A. Then bring the tip of the needle back up vertically in C, just below B. Place the thread over the needle from right to left, then slide it under the needle from left to right to form a knot. Pull gently on the thread.

STEP 2

Bring your needle down in D, directly to the left. Then bring the needle tip back up vertically in E, just below D. Place the thread over the needle from right to left, and then slide it under the needle from left to right to form a knot. Pull gently on the thread. To continue working, repeat step 2.

TIP

To obtain a straight line with regularly spaced knots, be sure to tie the knot on the tip of the needle after having formed the loop. Then gently pull the thread in order to maintain the size of the knot.

THE LINK STITCH IN 3 STEPS

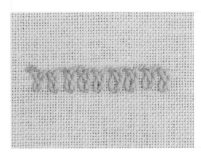

Level of Difficulty: Medium, for people who already have some experience.

Threads and Fabrics: This stitch can be made on any type of fabric, preferably with non-separable, twisted embroidery cotton, silk, or wool.

Direction: This stitch is worked horizontally, from right to left.

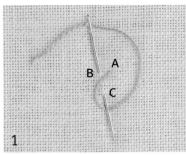

The link stitch resembles a twisted chain stitch and is sometimes called a rosette chain stitch. Nonetheless, its technique and formation, because of the large open knots, brings it closer to the family of knot stitches.

STEP 1

Bring your needle up in A. Bring it down to the left in B, and bring the tip of the needle back up at a slight angle below and to the right, in C. Slide the thread under the tip of the needle from left to right and pull gently to form a large loop.

STEP 2

Slide the needle from right to left under the right branch of the loop, next to point A. Pull gently on the thread.

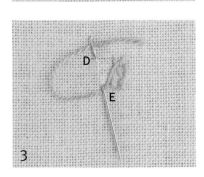

STEP 3

Bring your needle down directly to the left, in D, and bring the tip of your needle back out at a slight angle below and to the right, in E. Slide the thread over the needle and under the tip of the needle from left to right, then pull gently to form a large loop.

Repeat steps 2 and 3 to form the row.

> **TIP**
>
> This stitch is even more decorative when it is used as an isolated border. Worked evenly, it offers the appearance of a lace trimming. To obtain the perfect finish, the stitch must not exceed fi inch in height.

THE CORDED DOUBLE KNOT STITCH IN 4 STEPS

Level of Difficulty: Difficult, for people who are experienced.

Threads and Fabrics: This stitch can be made on any type of fabric, preferably with non-separable, twisted embroidery cotton, silk, or wool.

Direction: This stitch is worked horizontally, from right to left.

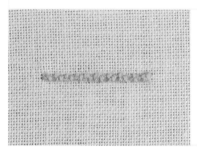

The corded double knot stitch made on a couching stitch offers a very raised appearance. It requires a work of great regularity, both at the level of rhythm of the stitch and tension of the thread.

STEP 1

Make a long horizontal stitch. Bring the thread up through A, on the right and below the couching stitch. Pass the needle vertically under the couching stitch and bring it back down in B. Bring your needle up in C. Pull gently on the thread.

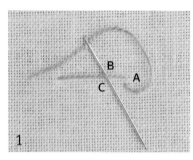

STEP 2

Without catching the fabric, pass the needle under the couching stitch once more, from top to bottom, and slide the thread under the point of the needle. Pull gently on the thread and tighten the loop on the couching stitch.

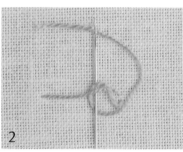

STEP 3

Bring your needle down vertically, directly to the left, in point D. Bring the tip of your needle back up in E, below the couching stitch, and pull gently without tightening to maintain the loop you just formed.

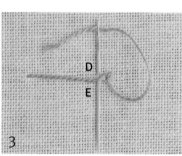

STEP 4

Slide the needle under the couching stitch from top to bottom without catching the fabric. Slide the point of the needle in the loop you just formed, pull gently and tighten the loop on the couching stitch. Repeat steps 2 and 3 to form the row.

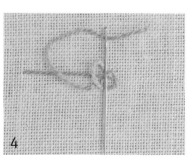

THE ZIGZAG CORDED PEARL STITCH IN 3 STEPS

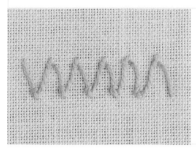

Level of Difficulty: Medium, for people who already have some experience.

Threads and Fabrics: This stitch can be made on any type of fabric, preferably with non-separable, twisted embroidery cotton, silk, or wool.

Direction: This stitch is worked horizontally, from right to left.

Fun to make, the zigzag corded pearl stitch combines a chevron stitch with a knot stitch. It is made in the same way as a pearl stitch, but in working on two parallel lines. The back and forth between the two lines forms the branches of the chevrons.

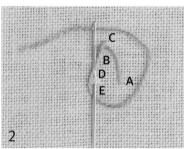

STEP 1

Bring the needle up in A. Shift up and to the left, bringing your needle back down in B and the tip back up vertically in C, directly above B. Place the thread over the needle from the right to the left, then slide it under the tip from left to right to form a knot. Pull gently on the thread.

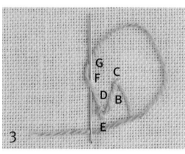

STEP 2

Shift to the lower left, level with point A. Bring your needle down in D and back up vertically in E, directly below D. Place the thread over the needle from right to left and then slide the thread under the needle from left to right to form a knot. Pull gently on the thread. The second branch of the first chevron is formed.

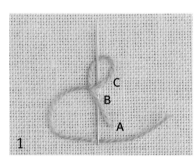

STEP 3

Shift to the top left, level with B. Bring your needle down in F and bring the tip of it back up vertically in G, directly above F. Place the thread over the needle from right to left, then slide the thread under the needle from left to right to form a knot. Pull gently on the thread.

Alternate the work from top to bottom. Repeat steps 2 and 3 to continue the row.

TIP

The zigzag corded pearl stitch is perfect for embroidering smocks. The knots, placed at the top and bottom of the chevron stitches, make this very pretty decorative stitch solid and uniform.

THE SIND STITCH IN 3 STEPS

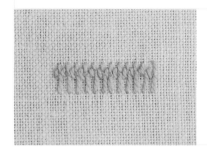

Level of Difficulty: Difficult, for people who are experienced.

Threads and Fabrics: This stitch can be made on any type of fabric, preferably with non-separable, twisted embroidery cotton, silk, or wool.

Direction: This stitch is worked vertically, from top to bottom.

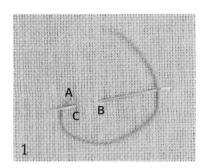

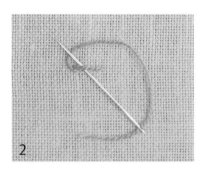

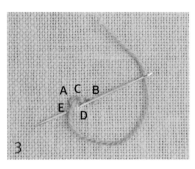

The Sind stitch gets its name from a region of Pakistan situated in the lower Indus River valley. Used to decorate clothing, this stitch is often made with cotton or silk thread worked on indigo-dyed cotton. It is made up of knots worked on a long support stitch.

STEP 1

Bring the thread up in A. At the same level and directly to the right, bring it down in B. Bring the tip of the needle back up to the left and slightly at an angle and below A, in point C. Reposition the thread above the work and pull on the thread—a large horizontal stitch will be formed.

STEP 2

Slide the needle from bottom to top under the large horizontal stitch. Place the thread under the tip of the needle to form a loop and pull gently on the thread to tighten it on the horizontal stitch.

STEP 3

To attach the knot, bring your needle down in D, next to C. Bring the needle up in E, below and to the left of A. Pull gently on the stitch to attach the knot to the surface of the fabric.

Repeat all three steps to make the next stitch.

THE CORAL STITCH IN 3 STEPS

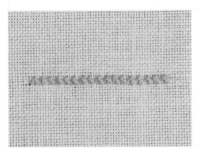

Level of Difficulty: Medium, for people who already have some experience.

Threads and Fabrics: This stitch can be made on any type of fabric, preferably with non-separable, twisted embroidery cotton, silk, or wool.

Direction: This stitch is worked horizontally, from right to left.

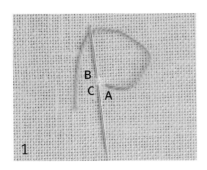

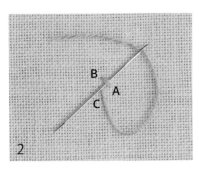
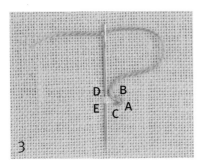

Issuing from the family of knotted line stitches, this French version of the coral stitch is very decorative, especially when its knots are made tightly against each other, as if to form a pearl necklace.

STEP 1

Bring your needle up in A. Shift slightly up and to the left and bring it down in B. Bring the tip of the needle up vertically in C, below B. Pull on the thread, and a slanted stitch is formed.

STEP 2

Slide the needle under the slanted stitch from right to left, and pull gently so the stitch stands out.

STEP 3

Bring your needle down directly to the left of B, in D, and bring the tip of the needle back out vertically in E, below D. Continue the row by repeating steps 2 and 3 as many times as necessary.

TIP

To obtain a truly vertical small stitch, make sure that the needle is brought down and back out directly under and perpendicular to the tracing of the motif.

The Tray Cloth

Restrained and elegant, this pattern of knots perfectly decorates a tray cloth or table-cloth. You can place four patterns in a crown on the center of the fabric, or even work the motif on each corner of a tablecloth. This version is reserved for the most patient of embroiderers.

OVERVIEW

Level of Difficulty:
Difficult

Stitch Used:
Palestrina stitch (see p. 63)

Finished Dimensions:
The size of the tray cloth depends on the dimensions of your tray. The embroidered motif measures 16 x 7 inches.

MATERIALS

20 x 14 inches ice blue linen fabric (dimensions based on the size of your tray)
2 skeins of DMC No. 5 Pearl cotton, art. 107, white
1 fine embroidery needle
Embroidery hoop
Tracing paper
Black hard lead pencil

ADVICE

It is important to embroider the Palestrina stitch regularly. The knot stitches must be placed every $1/4$ inch (or less) for a well-spaced work.

PATTERN

Enlarge the pattern using a photocopier.

Place the pattern under the fabric and match the center of the pattern with the center of your fabric. Pin the pattern and the fabric together.

Trace the outline of the pattern, which will show through your fabric, with the pencil, and then remove the pattern and the pins.

EMBROIDERY

Stretch the fabric in the embroidery hoop.

Begin the work at the center with the knot motif. At the end of each line, bring the thread to the back of the work, cut the thread, and begin your work again on the next line. In doing so, you will avoid having threads floating on the back of the work.

Move the embroidery hoop as you complete each section of your work.

FINISHING TOUCHES

Trim the linen fabric to fit the dimensions of your tray, allowing 2 inches all around for the hem.

With an iron, make a first fold of $3/4$ inch to form the hem of the edge of the doily. Baste, and form a second fold of $1 1/4$ inches and baste again. At the corners, trim the excess fabric to avoid over-thickness.

Sew the hem by machine, or by hand with slip stitches if you do not have a machine.

Pattern reduced to 50 %

Filling stitches are used to cover the surface of an embroidered motif partially or completely. Some are also used in traditional embroidery. The thirty-six stitches explained in this chapter are grouped according to their appearance and the way in which they are worked.

Depending upon the technique used, filling stitches are embroidered in patterns with isolated stitches, or row by row in stitches close against each other to cover the fabric completely.

Stitches based on knots, large taut stitches, or long crossed threads exert a great deal of tension on the supporting fabric. Here again, it is important to stretch the fabric on a frame so that the embroidery keeps its neat shape and uniform stitches.

3

FILLING STITCHES

The Knot Stitch Family

The knot stitch is one of the most basic stitches in traditional embroidery. One finds it in different embroidery techniques, such as cutwork embroidery or counted cross stitch, where it is used sparingly to highlight a detail. Like its derivatives, it gives interesting depth to the work of floral motifs, details of people, or geometric patterns.

THE KNOT STITCH IN 2 STEPS

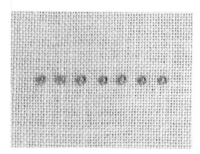

Level of Difficulty: Medium, for people who already have some experience.

Threads and Fabrics: This stitch can be made on any type of fabric, with embroidery cotton, linen, silk, or even wool thread.

Direction: This stitch is worked in patterns; the direction does not matter.

TIP

The success of this stitch depends upon four elements:
• the loop must be formed in the right direction (step 1);
• point B must be a very short distance from point A in order to give volume to the stitch. If you bring the stitch back down in A, the knot risks disappearing into the back of the fabric;
• the knot must be tightened against the surface of the fabric before the needle is finally pushed through to the back of the fabric (step 2);
• the thread must be pulled gently when you form the knot in order to maintain good volume.

The knot stitch, called the French knot in America, can be embroidered in patterns to form a light filling. Be careful of floating threads found between two stitches on the back of a work, because on lightweight fabrics, these threads can show through the material. In this case, fasten the thread of each stitch on the back and begin again with the next stitch.

STEP 1

Bring up the needle in A. Wrap the thread over, then under the needle. Holding the thread to keep it wrapped in place around the needle, bring your needle down in B, inside the loop you just formed, a few threads of the weave away from A.

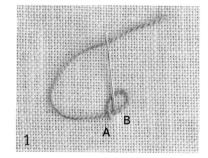

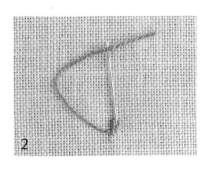

STEP 2

Tighten the thread of the loop around the needle, against the fabric. Push the needle through to the back of the fabric.

Make another knot stitch a bit further away, repeating steps 1 and 2.

THE BULLION STITCH IN 3 STEPS

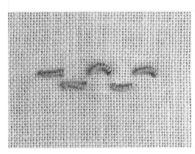

Level of Difficulty: Difficult, for people who are experienced.

Threads and Fabrics: This stitch can be made on any type of fabric, with embroidery cotton, linen, or silk thread (if possible, a twisted thread like Pearl or Cutwork and Embroidery thread).

Direction: This stitch is worked in patterns; the direction does not matter.

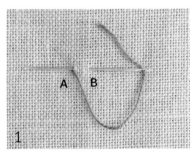

The bullion stitch, also known as the "minute stitch" or "chenille stitch," looks like a cord of trimming. It can be worked in isolation or in patterns for filling. In sewing, it is used to form button loops for small buttons, such as the ones found on lingerie.

STEP 1

Bring up the needle in A. Bring it down in B, horizontally and to the right. Bring the tip of the needle back up in A.

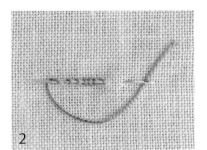

STEP 2

Wind the thread several times (five to seven, depending on the desired length of the stitch) around the tip of the needle. Keep the loops flexible.

STEP 3

Hold the loops in place against the surface of the fabric with your thumb and pull the needle. Continue to hold the stitch in place and bring the needle down in C, just behind point B. Repeat these three steps to form additional bullion stitches.

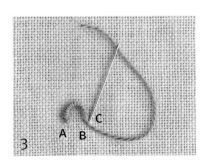

THE SEED STITCH IN 2 STEPS

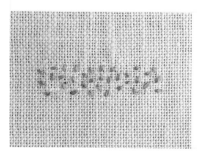

Level of Difficulty: Easy, accessible to beginners.

Threads and Fabrics: This stitch can be made on any type of fabric, with embroidery cotton, or linen or silk thread.

Direction: This stitch is worked in patterns; the direction does not matter.

TIP

The small backstitches must be of equal length. Make each of them in a different direction, right next to the preceding stitch. In this way, you will obtain a pattern as light or as dense as you wish. For an attractive, uniform pattern, make sure to stretch the fabric taut over the frame.

Also called the "sand stitch," the seed stitch allows you to fill patterns with great subtlety. It is used to decorate initials and monograms, on lingerie and household linens.

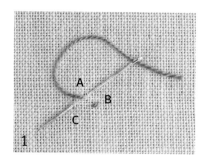 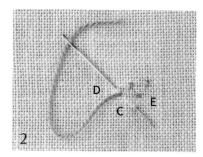

STEP 1

Bring the needle up in A and down in B, in such a way as to make a small, slightly slanted backstitch. Bring the tip of the needle back out in C, a bit further away on the surface of the fabric.

STEP 2

Bring your needle down in D to make a small, slightly slanted backstitch. Bring the tip of the needle up in E, a bit further away on the surface of the fabric.

Repeat step 2, and cover the entire surface of the motif in this fashion.

THE GERMAN KNOT STITCH IN 4 STEPS

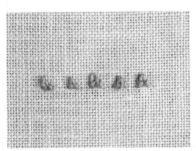

Level of Difficulty: Medium, for people who already have some experience.

Threads and Fabrics: This stitch can be made on any type of fabric, with embroidery cotton, linen, silk, or even wool thread.

Direction: This stitch is worked in patterns; the direction does not matter.

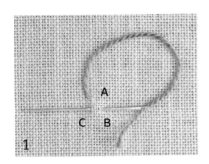

Shaped like a triangle, the German knot stitch has a great deal of character. It may be used in two ways: on its own to mark the stamens of flowers, or in a line to surround a motif embroidered with another stitch.

STEP 1

Bring the thread up in A and down in B to make a diagonal stitch. Bring the needle up in C, level with and slightly to the left of B.

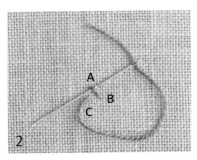

STEP 2

Slide the needle under the diagonal stitch, from the top right to the bottom left, with the working end of the thread below the stitch. Pull gently to form a loop.

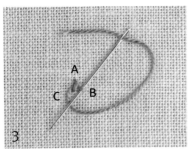

STEP 3

Slide the needle under the diagonal stitch again, from top right to bottom left. The point of the needle passes between the loop and point B. Slide the thread under the needle, and pull gently on the thread to form the knot against the fabric.

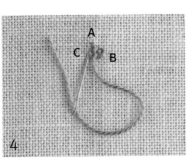

STEP 4

Attach the double knot by bringing the needle down in C.

Form another German knot stitch about ¼ inch away from the first, beginning the work again at step 1.

THE SORBELLO STITCH IN 4 STEPS

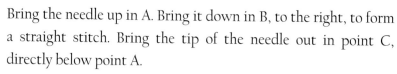

Level of Difficulty: Medium, for people who already have some experience.

Threads and Fabrics: This stitch can be made on all types of fine fabric or fabric with obvious weave, with twisted embroidery cotton such as Pearl, Cotton Matte, or Cutwork and Embroidery thread.

Direction: This stitch is worked in vertical or horizontal rows.

Of Italian origin, the sorbello stitch forms a square. Made on fabrics intended for counted cross-stitch work, it may be embroidered like a cross-stitch. Its exceptional depth brings true originality to the work.

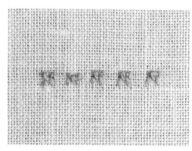

STEP 1

Bring the needle up in A. Bring it down in B, to the right, to form a straight stitch. Bring the tip of the needle out in point C, directly below point A.

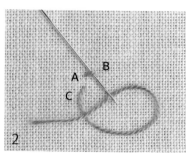

STEP 2

Slide the needle upwards under the straight stitch from bottom to top.

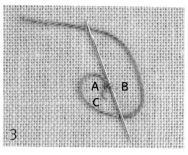

STEP 3

Slide the needle under the straight stitch again, downwards this time. Pass the needle from top to bottom between the preceding loop and point B. Slide the thread under the tip of the needle and pull gently.

STEP 4

Attach the work of knot stitches by bringing the needle down in D, directly below point B.

To make another sorbello stitch, begin again at step 1. In the case of counted cross-stitch embroidery, close the stitches against each other.

At the end of the row, fasten off the stitch and begin the next row at the left.

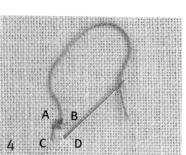

THE KNOTTED STEM STITCH IN 2 STEPS

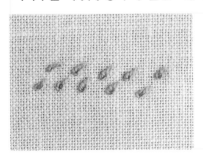

Level of Difficulty: Medium, for people who already have some experience.

Threads and Fabrics: This stitch can be made on any type of fabric, with embroidery cotton, linen, silk, or even wool thread.

Direction: This stitch is worked in patterns; the direction does not matter.

TIP

When the fill is very compact and the knotted stem stitches overlap to give more depth to the work, make sure that all the tails are made in the same direction.

The knotted stem stitch has many different uses. In patterns, it serves as a light filling stitch. In corollas, with the knots facing out, it is used to embroider fine flower designs. In a dense filling, the stems of the stitches are superimposed for a very richly textured effect.

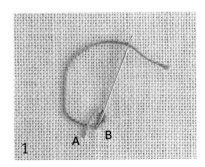 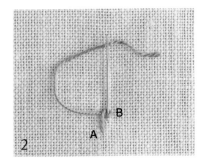

STEP 1
Bring your needle up in A. Form a loop by winding the thread over then under the needle. Holding the thread to keep it wrapped in place around the needle, bring the needle down in B, inside the loop, directly to the right of A.

STEP 2
Pull the thread to tighten the loop on the needle, against the fabric. Push the needle through to the back of the fabric. The knot is situated above point B.

Make another knotted stem stitch a bit further away, repeating steps 1 and 2.

THE CABLE STITCH IN 2 STEPS

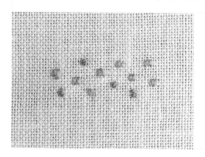

Level of Difficulty: Easy, accessible to beginners.

Threads and Fabrics: This stitch can be made on all types of fine fabric or fabric with obvious weave, with twisted embroidery cotton such as Pearl, Cotton Matte, or Cutwork and Embroidery thread.

Direction: This stitch is worked horizontally, from the left to the right.

TIP

The cable stitch is especially intended for working dots that are too small to be embroidered using the satin stitch (see p. 176). It also advantageously replaces the knot stitch when it is made on fabric that is not stretched in a frame.

To give the most depth to the motif, the two backstitches may overlap, the needle stitching points A and B twice consecutively.

The cable stitch is also called the "seeding stitch" or "double backstitch." It is made up of two small backstitches and is generally used to highlight and give a bit of depth to a motif or to fill a surface that is already surrounded by another stitch.

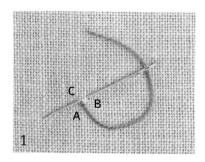 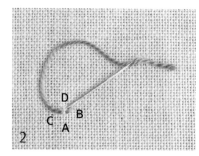

STEP 1

Bring your needle up in A and back down in B, forming a small backstitch, either at an angle or straight, depending on the desired effect. Bring the tip of the needle up in C, right next to A. Pull gently to form a small backstitch.

STEP 2

Bring your needle down in D, right next to point B, forming a second backstitch parallel to the preceding one.

Repeat steps 1 and 2, and cover the surface of the motif to embroider.

THE KNOTTED CABLE STITCH IN 2 STEPS

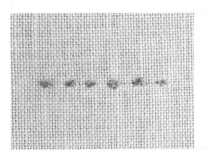

Level of Difficulty: Very easy, accessible for beginners.

Threads and Fabrics: This stitch can be made on any type of fabric, with embroidery cotton, linen, silk, or even wool thread.

Direction: This stitch is worked in horizontally, from right to left.

TIP

The knotted cable stitch is intended for people without experience. It is even more easily made from top to bottom, like the lazy daisy stitch (see p. 37).

At first glance, the knotted cable stitch closely resembles the simple knot stitch, but it is much easier to make. Composed of a small chain stitch held in place by a backstitch, it is perfect for beginning embroiderers.

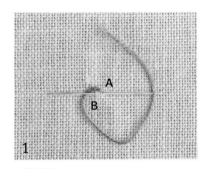
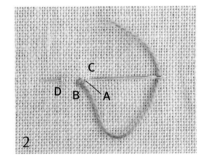

STEP 1

Bring the needle up in A and back down in the same point, A. Bring the tip of the needle up laterally in B, directly to the left of point A. Slide the thread under the needle and pull gently to form a small loop.

STEP 2

Hold the loop in place with your thumb. Bring your needle down in C, right behind A. Bring the tip of the needle up in D, a bit further away, to make a new knotted cable stitch.

Repeat steps 1 and 2 to form additional stitches.

THE BASQUE KNOT STITCH IN 4 STEPS

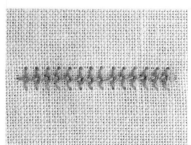

Level of Difficulty: Medium, for people who already have some experience.
Threads and Fabrics: This stitch can be made on any type of fabric, with embroidery cotton, linen, silk, or even wool thread (it is best to use twisted thread, such as Pearl, Cotton Matte, or Cutwork and Embroidery thread).
Direction: This stitch is worked horizontally, from right to left.

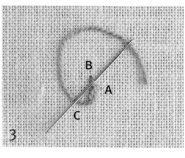

This raised cross in the center is embroidered in lines on men's shirts, aprons of traditional Basque costumes, and on the table linen of that region. One finds traces of the Basque knot stitch in the entire southwest of France and in the northern Iberian peninsula.

STEP 1

Bring your needle up in A, then bring it down in B, above and to the left of A, and back up in C, vertical to B, to form a stitch slanting up. Point A is halfway between B and C.

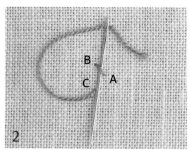

STEP 2

Slide the needle under the slanted stitch from right to left and from top to bottom, making sure to keep the working end of the thread to the left. Slide the loop formed to the lower right of the slanted stitch.

STEP 3

Slide the needle under the slanted stitch again, from right to left and from top to bottom. Place the thread under the needle, and then pull gently to form a complete knot.

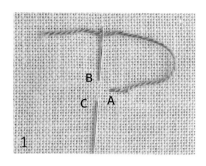

STEP 4

Move to the next stitch, bringing your needle down in D and back up in E, vertical with D, shifting a bit to the left.

Repeat steps 2, 3, and 4 to form additional stitches.

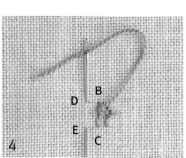

The Ring-Bearer's Pillow

Precious and silky, this pillow serves as a delicate holder for rings on a wedding day. The pattern, which is repeated at each corner, is entirely composed of small knot stitches, worked side by side to obtain the look of damask fabric with beautiful depth.

OVERVIEW

Level of Difficulty:
Medium

Stitch Used:
Knot stitch (see p. 74)

Finished Dimensions:
The ring-bearer's pillow measures 8 x 8 inches. The corner motif measures 2½ x 2½ inches.

MATERIALS

10 x 24 inches antique rose colored silk taffeta
2 skeins of DMC cotton embroidery floss, art. 177 in each of the following colors: fresh butter (746), yellow orange (3855), tangerine (3854)
1 coverable button, 1 inch in diameter
12 inches antique rose colored satin ribbon, ½-inch wide
1 fine embroidery needle
Embroidery hoop
Black hard lead pencil
Synthetic stuffing
Pins

PATTERN

Cut two 10-inch squares from the taffeta, then fold one in four to determine the center of the fabric.

Place the pattern under the fabric, matching the center of the pattern (indicated with dotted lines on the design) with that of the squares of taffeta. Pin the pattern to the fabric. With the black pencil, trace the outline of the pattern onto the fabric. Remove the pattern and the pins once you have completed the tracing.

On a small piece of fabric, trace the button motif.

EMBROIDERY

Stretch the material in the embroidery hoop.

Use three strands of cotton floss. Work section after section.

Begin the work with the darkest color, tangerine. Tighten the stitches against each other to cover the surface of the motif entirely. Continue embroidering and finish with the lightest color, fresh butter.

Make the four corner designs and the button decoration in this manner.

FINISHING TOUCHES

Press the work. Place the squares of fabric with right sides together and pin the edges of the pillow. With a sewing machine or by hand, seam 1 inch in from the edges, leaving a 4-inch opening along one side. Trim off the excess fabric, leaving ½-inch seams, then open the seams with an iron. Turn the pillow inside out, stuff it with the stuffing, and neatly slipstitch the opening closed.

Mount the embroidered motif onto the button following the manufacturer's directions. Sew the button on the center of the pillow, pulling on the needle to give the pillow a padded look. Wind the satin ribbon around the back of the button and tie the wedding rings onto the ribbon.

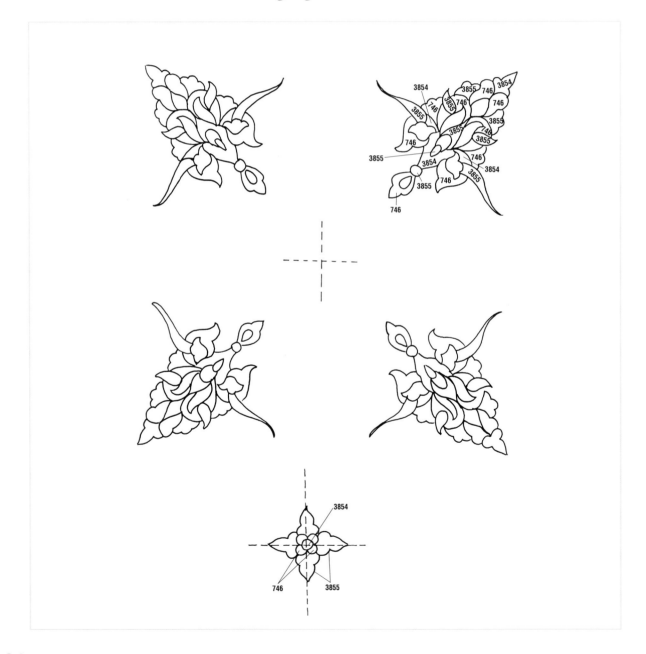

The Leaf Stitch Family

As its name implies, the family of leaf stitches includes stitches used mainly for filling leaf shapes; these stitches can also serve, of course, for making petals, as well as for making the curved designs found in traditional embroidery. In general, they are made on a tracing which shows the shapes of the embroidered motif. The work consists of passing the needle from one side to the other of the traced shape.

THE LEAF STITCH IN 3 STEPS

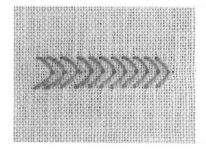

Level of Difficulty: Easy, accessible to beginners.

Threads and Fabrics: This stitch can be made on any type of fabric, with embroidery cotton, linen, silk, or even wool thread. Floss-type threads cover surfaces well.

Direction: This stitch is worked vertically, from top to bottom.

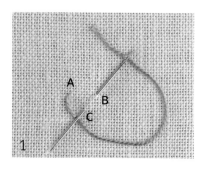

The leaf stitch, also known as the "fly stitch," when worked in single units, is perfectly suited for fillings. The embroidered motif, in the shape of a "Y," looks like a fern with a well-marked central vein. You can make the stitches as close together as you wish, depending on the desired effect.

STEP 1

Bring your needle up in A. Bring it down in B, to the right and level with A. Bring the tip of the needle up in C, directly below, halfway between A and B. Slide the thread under the needle.

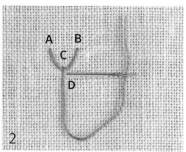

STEP 2

Bring your needle down in D, right below C and over the "V" of the stitch you just made.

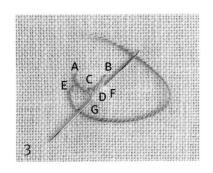

STEP 3

Bring your needle up in E, on the left, under point A. Bring it down in F, to the right and below point B. Bring the tip of your needle up in G, directly below points C and D. Slide the thread under the needle and finish the stitch with a small straight stitch at the center, in the "V" of the stitch.

Repeat step 3 to continue the filling.

THE DOUBLE LEAF STITCH IN 2 STEPS

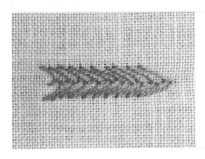

Level of Difficulty: Easy, accessible to beginners.

Threads and Fabrics: This stitch can be made on any type of fabric, with embroidery cotton, linen, silk, or even wool thread. Floss type threads cover surfaces well.

Direction: This stitch is worked vertically, from top to bottom.

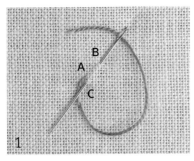

The double leaf stitch is a variation of the preceding stitch. It is called "double" because each side worked is made up of an open loop. This type of stitch can only be worked on fabric that is stretched on a frame.

STEP 1

Begin the work with the right side of the stitch. Bring the needle up in A, then back down in B, on the upper right, as if to make a slanted stitch. Bring the needle back up in C, below point A. Slide the thread under the needle. Pull the thread through.

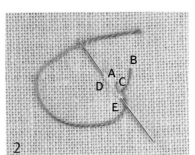

STEP 2

Bring your needle back down in D, horizontal with B, as if to make a stitch slanted to the left. Bring the tip of the needle up in E, directly below point C, and slide the thread under the needle. Pull thread through. To continue the work, repeat steps 1 and 2, alternating stitches to the left and right. Always come back to the center to keep each loop open.

THE BASKET STITCH IN 3 STEPS

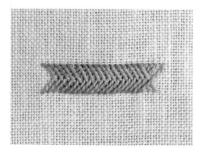

Level of Difficulty: Medium, for people who already have some experience.

Threads and Fabrics: This stitch can be made on any type of fabric, with embroidery cotton, linen, silk, or even wool thread. Floss type threads cover surfaces well.

Direction: This stitch is worked vertically, from top to bottom.

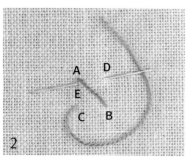

The overlapping crossing of threads offers this very pretty stitch the look of basket weave. Also known as the "raised cross stitch," the basket stitch uses a great deal of thread because of its couched work of crossed and overlapped threads.

This stitch is made as a series of squares.

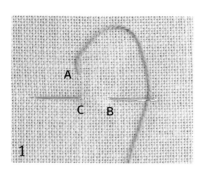

STEP 1

Bring your needle up in A. Bring it down in B, diagonally, on the lower right. Bring the tip of your needle back up in C, horizontal with B and below point A.

STEP 2

Bring your needle down in D, horizontal and to the right of A, above point B. The square is thus formed, and the stitches cross each other to form equidistant branches. Bring the tip of your needle up in E, below point A.

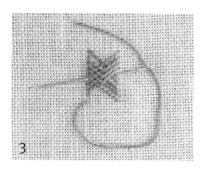

STEP 3

Alternate the stitches from left to right to cross them regularly. Bring your needle up and back down in line with the points you already used (and in the same points as you work farther down). The crossed threads will overlap.

Repeat steps 1 and 2 to form the remaining stitches.

TIP

Using a floss thread, you will obtain a very smooth basket stitch. The effect of light on the slanted stitches is sumptuous, and will highlight vivid or dark colors.

THE PLUME STITCH IN 3 STEPS

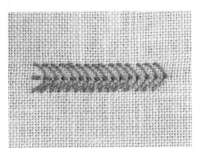

Level of Difficulty: Easy, accessible to beginners.

Threads and Fabrics: This stitch can be made on any type of fabric, with embroidery cotton, linen, silk, or even wool thread.

Direction: This stitch is worked vertically, from top to bottom.

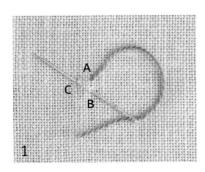

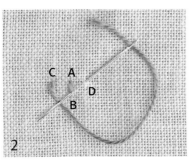

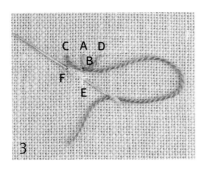

Ideal when you need to make a light filling, the plume stitch, called "fishbone stitch" in America, adapts to all surfaces to be covered. The way in which it is made—a succession of "Y" shaped stitches—is close to that of the leaf stitch or the French fishbone filling stitch.

STEP 1

To form the point of the stitch, bring the needle up in A. Bring it down in B, directly below point A. Bring the tip of the needle up in C, diagonal and to the left of point A. Pull on the thread to form the first vertical stitch, situated at the center of the plume stitch.

STEP 2

Bring your needle down in D, to the right of A and the same distance from A as C is on the opposite side. Bring the tip of the needle up in B. Pull gently on the thread to form the stitch in the shape of a chevron.

STEP 3

Bring your needle down in E, directly below point B. Bring the tip of the needle up in F, to the left and directly below point C. Pull gently on the thread to form the small central vertical stitch.

Repeat steps 2 and 3 to continue the filling.

TIP

To maintain a pretty look, the small vertical stitch must not be too small. Because of this, the plume stitch cannot be used to cover a surface entirely. Consider checking the back of the work. If the stitch is done properly, a line of chevrons will appear there.

THE FERN STITCH IN 3 STEPS

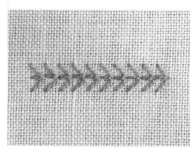

Level of Difficulty: Very easy, accessible to beginners.

Threads and Fabrics: This stitch can be made on any type of fabric, with embroidery cotton, linen, silk, or even wool thread.

Direction: This stitch is worked vertically, from top to bottom.

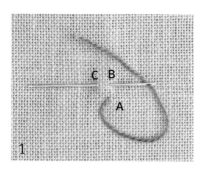

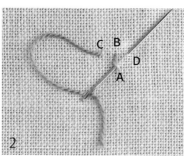

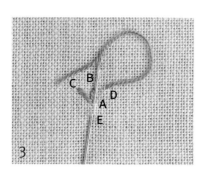

Similar in appearance to the plume stitch, the fern stitch is embroidered stitch by stitch. It adapts to thicker fabrics with obvious weaves, such as cotton muslin. Because it is so easy to make, it is ideal for those who are just becoming familiar with the techniques of embroidery.

STEP 1

To form the point of the stitch, bring the needle up in A. Bring it down in B, directly above A, and bring the tip of the needle back out in C, to the left of point B. Pull on the thread to form the first vertical stitch situated in the center of the fern stitch.

STEP 2

Bring your needle down in A and up in D, directly to the right of point B. Pull on the thread to form the first branch of the chevron stitch.

STEP 3

Bring your needle back down in A to complete the chevron. Bring the needle up in point E, directly below point A.

Repeat steps 1, 2, and 3 to continue the row.

TIP

You must use a fine, pointed needle to make this stitch since the central stitch requires three passages through the same hole. The embroidery will be easier if made on a thick fabric with an obvious weave.

THE OVERLAPPING CROSS-STITCH IN 4 STEPS

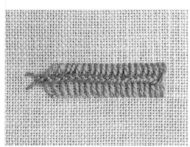

Level of Difficulty: Medium, for people who already have some experience.

Threads and Fabrics: This stitch can be made on any type of fabric, with embroidery cotton, linen, silk, or even wool thread.

Direction: This stitch is worked vertically, from top to bottom.

The overlapping cross-stitch highlights the very large central vein, which is made by the crossing of stitches. The stitch is perfectly suited for filling leafy motifs.

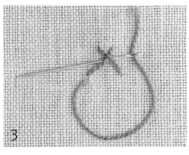

STEP 1

Bring your needle up in A, on the left. Bring it down in B, diagonally, about ¼ inch to the right, above A. Bring the tip of the needle back up in C, to the left of and level with B. Pull on the thread to form the first branch of the cross.

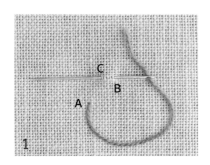

STEP 2

Bring your needle down in D, horizontal with and to the right of A. Bring the tip of the needle back up directly below point A. Pull the thread to form the second branch of the cross. You will make an elongated cross-stitch, the intersection of which is situated at the top.

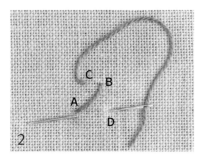

STEP 3

Slide the needle under the cross from right to left. Pull gently to bring the thread against the branch of the preceding cross-stitch.

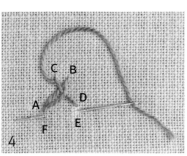

STEP 4

Bring your needle down in E, directly below point D. Bring the tip of the needle up in F, directly below point A, and pull gently. The new cross is in fact a twisted loop maintained by the crossing of the first cross.

Repeat steps 3 and 4 to continue working.

THE CROSSED STITCH IN 2 STEPS

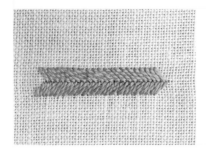

Level of Difficulty: Easy, accessible to beginners.

Threads and Fabrics: This stitch can be made on any type of fabric, with embroidery cotton, linen, silk, or even wool thread.

Direction: This stitch is worked vertically, from top to bottom.

TIP

You will know if the crossed stitch is made well if the back side of the fabric is identical to the front, in other words, if you obtain rows of chevrons that close up against each other.

This is the ideal stitch for filling small-format leaf patterns. Despite that fact that it is called "crossed stitch," it is only composed of slanted straight stitches placed on one side and the other of the shape to fill, and these stitches never actually cross.

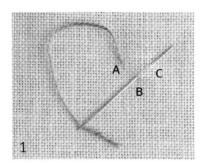
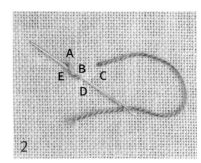

STEP 1

Bring the needle up in A and back down in B, diagonally down and to the right. Point B is the center of the row. Bring the tip of your needle back up in C, level with A and to the right. Pull on the thread to form the first branch of the chevron.

STEP 2

Bring your needle down in D, below point B, and back up in E, below point A. Pull the thread to form the second branch of the chevron. Space the stitches only one or two threads of the weave apart so that they remain close to each other.

Repeat steps 1 and 2 to continue the work.

THE FISHBONE FILLING STITCH IN 2 STEPS

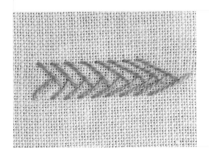

Level of Difficulty: Very easy, accessible to beginners.

Threads and Fabrics: This stitch can be made on any type of fabric, with embroidery cotton, linen, silk, or even wool thread.

Direction: This stitch is worked vertically, from top to bottom.

TIP

In the course of your work, do not forget to allow the embroidery thread to get its twist back, especially if you are using a tightly twisted thread, such as Pearl Cotton or DMC cotton matte.

The fishbone filling stitch is a variation of the other filling stitches in the form of chevrons. Here, the center of the stitch is slightly shifted to the left. Composed only of slanted stitches, it is very easy to make.

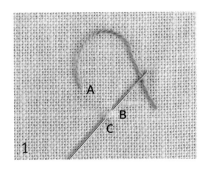
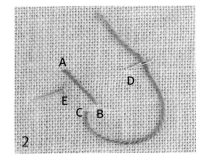

STEP 1

Bring your needle up in A. Bring it down in B, slanted towards the right. Bring the tip of your needle back up in C, below and a bit to the left of point B. Pull the thread to form the first branch of the chevron.

STEP 2

Bring your needle down in D, horizontal with and to the right of A. Pull the thread to form the second branch of the chevron. This branch, which is situated to the right of the stitch, is longer than the branch on the left.

Repeat steps 1 and 2 to continue the row.

The Bolster

When the leaf stitch decorates several different types of leaves, one sees that is does so with mastery. This is the case for this bolster cover made of beautiful vivid colors, which will bring energy and refinement to the décor of your home.

OVERVIEW

Level of Difficulty:
Easy

Stitches Used:
Leaf stitch (see p. 86)
Stem stitch (see p. 22)

Finished Dimensions:
The bolster measures 6 inches in diameter and 20 inches in length. The motif of leaves, inscribed in a square, measures 6½ x 6½ inches.

MATERIALS

For a bolster measuring 6 inches in diameter and 20 inches in length:
16 x 36 inches anise colored cotton
2 skeins of DMC cotton embroidery floss, art. 117 in each of the following colors: absinthe (3819), turquoise (564), mauve (340)
1 fine embroidery needle
Embroidery hoop
Black hard lead pencil
Pins
Compass

PATTERN

From the cotton fabric, cut a 16 x 24-inch rectangle. On the leftover fabric, trace two circles with a 6-inch diameter with a compass. Cut the rounds, adding a 1-inch seam allowance all around. Whip stitch the edges of the fabric with a sewing machine or by hand.

Fold the rectangle of fabric in four to determine the center, and then mark the center with pins.

Place the pattern under the fabric. The four leaf design inscribed in a square is repeated on the left and on the right half of the fabric.

Match the center of your fabric with the middle of the side edge of your pattern.

Pin the pattern and the fabric together. Trace the outline of the pattern, which will show through your fabric, with the black pencil, then remove the pattern and the pins. Place the pattern on the other side of the center of your fabric and trace the pattern a second time.

EMBROIDERY

Stretch the fabric in the embroidery hoop.

Use three strands of cotton floss to work the leaves and two strands to embroider the stems.

Work one motif at a time.

Begin the work with the leafy shapes using the leaf stitch (see p. 86). Follow the color directions indicated on the pattern.

Begin the motif of leaves at the top with a vertical stitch, then embroider by filling the motif from the top to the bottom.

When the embroidery of the leaves is complete, make the stems with the stem stitch using two strands of mauve cotton floss. Press the work.

FINISHING TOUCHES

Fold the fabric in half lengthwise, with right sides together. Pin and sew the long edges together, leaving an opening of 10 inches in the middle.

Notch the edges of the circles, forming ½-inch notches every 1½ inches. With right sides together, baste a circle to the body of the bolster at each edge and sew them, following the circular tracing. Turn right side out and insert the bolster before closing the opening.

Pattern reduced to 60%

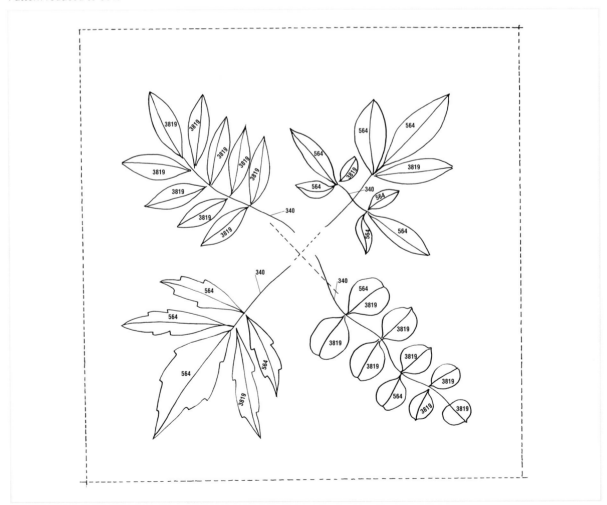

The Straight Stitch Family

The straight stitch family is one of the most well known and most frequently used for filling small or large surfaces. Master embroiderers of centuries past especially used stitches of this type on precious materials such as velour or silk. The threads used were also silk, and served to make the sumptuous decorations called "needle paintings." In our times, we use these embroidery techniques on cotton, linen, or wool fabrics mainly with cotton or wool thread, which offer the advantage of easier maintenance.

THE STRAIGHT STITCH IN 1 STEP

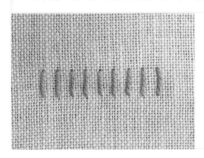

Level of Difficulty: Very easy, accessible to beginners.

Threads and Fabrics: This stitch can be made on any type of fabric, with embroidery cotton, linen, silk, or even wool thread.

Direction: This stitch is worked in any direction.

TIP

On light or transparent fabrics, be sure to hide threads floating between the straight stitches on the back of the work. Slide these threads under existing stitches. The fastenings of threads must be clean, and cut as close as possible to the embroidered surface.

This is the basic embroidery stitch, and it is one of the easiest to make. This stitch is called the straight stitch when it is made in light patterns or when it is placed in a circle to make the center of a flower.

When it is worked tightly, with stitches side by side, it takes the name "satin stitch" (see p. 98).

The straight stitch explained here is worked horizontally, following a right to left progression.

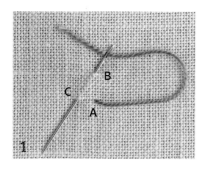

STEP 1

Bring your needle up in A and down in B, about ¼ inch above point A. Bring the tip of your needle up in C, level with A and about 1¼ inch away.

Repeat this step to form additional straight stitches.

THE SATIN STITCH IN 1 STEP

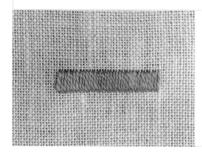

Level of Difficulty: Easy, accessible to beginners.

Threads and Fabrics: This stitch can be made on any type of fabric, with embroidery cotton, linen or silk thread, or even floss type wool.

Direction: This stitch is worked vertically or horizontally, according to the shape of the motif to be embroidered.

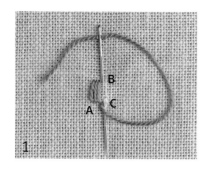

The satin stitch is made in the same way as the straight stitch, but stitches are made tightly against each other. Like other stitches in this family, the satin stitch uses a large amount of thread because the opposite side of the work is just as covered as the front.

The satin stitch explained here is worked horizontally and from left to right.

STEP 1

Bring your needle up in A and back down in B, about ¼ inch above A. Bring the needle back out in C, level with and right next to point A.

Repeat this step to form additional stitches.

> **TIP**
>
> If you work this stitch "economically," in other words, by bringing your needle back up right next to the preceding stitch and not on the lower line, you will use much less thread. You will also save your embroidery cotton with this technique, but the satin stitch will appear much less dense on the front of the work, and the stitches will appear much less uniform.

THE LONG AND SHORT STITCH IN 4 STEPS

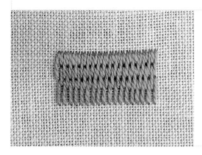

Level of Difficulty: Medium, for people who already have some experience.

Threads and Fabrics: This stitch can be made on any type of fabric, with embroidery cotton, linen, silk, or even wool thread, but preferably floss threads.

Direction: This stitch is worked horizontally, from left to right for the first row and from right to left for the second row. The work moves from top to bottom.

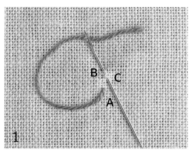

Generally used to cover foundations, the long and short stitch is made up of vertical straight stitches all embroidered in the same direction. This technique allows the effect, row by row, of covering a large surface while blending the colors.

STEP 1

Bring the needle up in A and down in B, vertical with point A. Bring the needle back up in C, slightly below and to the left. Pull the thread to form the first stitch.

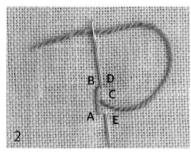

STEP 2

Bring the needle down in D, right next to point B. This line of stitches forms the upper limit of the surface to be embroidered. Bring the tip of the needle up in E, at the bottom and level with A, and pull the thread to form the second stitch, which is shorter than the first.

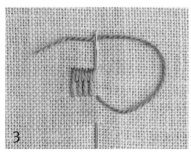

STEP 3

Continue the work, moving to the right and alternating large and small stitches.

STEP 4

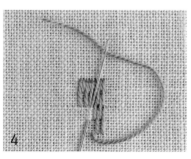

Work the next row, below the first, from right to left. For this row and all following rows, work all stitches as equally long stitches with the top of each new stitch just below the bottom of the stitch above. The new row of stitches will automatically alternate at the bottom. On the last row of the area, fill in the half-spaces with short stitches to even the bottom edge.

THE RE-STITCHED SATIN STITCH IN 3 STEPS

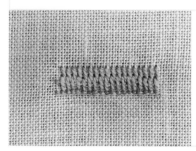

Level of Difficulty: Medium, for people who already have some experience.

Threads and Fabrics: This stitch can be made on any type of fabric, with embroidery cotton, linen, silk, or even wool thread.

Direction: This stitch is worked horizontally, from left to right. The work moves from top to bottom.

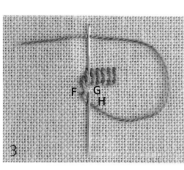

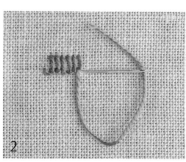

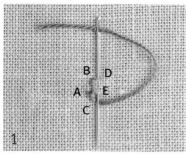

The re-stitched satin stitch is formed on a base of blanket stitches made row by row and slightly overlapped. It is especially used in borders, bringing depth and imagination to the embroidery. It is even more impressive when it is worked in a gradation of colors.

STEP 1

Bring your needle up in A and back down in B, situated above and very slightly to the right. Bring the tip of the needle back up in C, below B, slide the thread under the needle, and pull gently to form the first stitch. Bring your needle back down in D, to the right of point B. Bring the tip of the needle up in E, to the right of point C and below D, then slide the thread under the needle and pull gently.

STEP 2

Continue the row by forming blanket stitches, and finish with a small horizontal straight stitch made over the final blanket stitch in order to maintain it. Fasten off the thread.

STEP 3

The second row and all following rows begin again at the left. Bring the needle up in F, below point A. Bring it down in G, between the stitches of the preceding row. Bring the tip back out in H, below G, slide the thread under the needle and pull gently.

Continue the blanket stitches and embroider them side by side over the preceding row.

TIP

For gradation, begin with the light color, situated at the top of the motif to fill, and continue down through to the darkest color.

THE ENCROACHING SATIN STITCH IN 2 STEPS

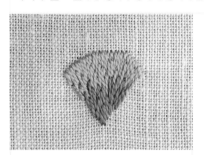

Level of Difficulty: Difficult, reserved for people who are experienced.

Threads and Fabrics: This stitch can be made on any type of fabric, with embroidery cotton, linen, silk, or even wool thread. For the best results, use floss threads, such as cotton floss.

Direction: This stitch is worked horizontally, from left to right for the first row of each new color and from right to left for the second, following the contours of the shape to embroider. The work moves from top to bottom.

Made up of different length stitches and similar to the long and short stitch, the encroaching satin stitch adapts itself to all types of shapes and allows a sophisticated shading of colors.

This very subtle stitch, one of the most beautiful in the art of embroidery, brings about effects of surprising realism, especially when worked on landscape motifs.

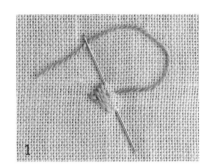
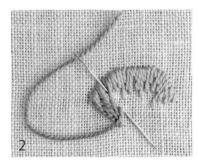

STEP 1

Proceed as you would with the long and short stitch, on page 99, alternating long and short stitches. Follow the contour of the shape along the upper edge. Work by loosening the stitches towards the exterior of the motif, and tightening them towards the interior. Proceed row by row, from the exterior to the interior of the shape.

STEP 2

For the next row, change the shade of the thread. Overlap the stitches by alternating long and short stitches.

TIP

To be successful at this stitch, it is important to practice your scales, just as a musician does. Practice the encroaching satin stitch on various shapes. It is important that the fabric be stretched tightly and that the thread keep a uniform tension. Work the stitches by bringing the needle down through the front of the work and then up though the back. This method allows the thread to stretch in a uniform way.

THE NEW ENGLAND LAID STITCH IN 3 STEPS

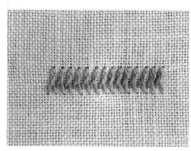

Level of Difficulty: Medium, for people who already have some experience.

Threads and Fabrics: This stitch can be made on any type of fabric, with embroidery cotton, linen, silk, or even wool thread.

Direction: This stitch is worked horizontally, from right to left.

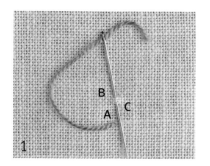

The New England laid stitch alternates long vertical stitches with slanted stitches. Very short stitches are formed on the back as a result, and this stitch saves a great deal of thread. It offers the look of damask rows, and is therefore mostly used to cover plain backgrounds.

STEP 1

Bring the tip of your needle up in A and back down in B, about ¼ inch above A. Bring the tip back up in C, vertical with B. Pull the needle to form the first vertical stitch.

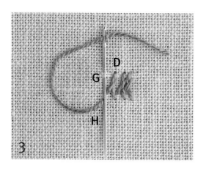

STEP 2

Bring your needle down in D, slightly above and to the left of A, and bring the tip of the needle up in E, next to point A and below point D. Pull gently on the needle to form the slanted stitch.

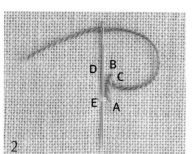

STEP 3

Bring the needle down in G, to the left of point D, and bring the tip back out in H, below G and level with point C. Pull the needle to form the next vertical stitch.

Repeat steps 2 and 3 to make the rest of the row.

TIP

For the second row (as well as the remaining ones), begin the work again at the right in order to work all the slanted stitches in the same direction. Be careful to make stitches of regular length, and preferably embroider on fabric with obvious weave or on muslin designed for counted cross stitch.

THE CROSSED SATIN STITCH IN 3 STEPS

Level of Difficulty: Medium, for people who already have some experience.

Threads and Fabrics: This stitch can be made on any type of fabric, with embroidery cotton, linen, silk, or even wool thread.

Direction: This stitch is worked in all directions around a template.

Fun to work, the crossed satin stitch is a quick solution for making small raised buttons. Cut a small disk of water soluble fabric stabilizer as a template to maintain a uniform shape.

STEP 1

Work large horizontal satin stitches over the template. Bring the needle up in A and down in B, situated on the opposite side of the edge of the template. Bring your needle back up in C, above point A, and make five or six horizontal stitches.

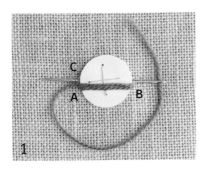

STEP 2

Work a group of vertical satin stitches over the horizontal ones. Make the same number of vertical stitches as you made horizontal ones.

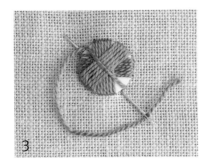

STEP 3

Make two more groups of stitches, diagonally this time, with one group pointing to the right and the other pointing to the left. On the back, fasten off the thread and begin again on the next template.

> **TIP**
>
> Keep the template flat against the fabric with two large basting stitches that cross at the center of the circle. Prepare as many templates as you will need out of white paper (other colors risk bleeding in the wash, and the templates will remain trapped under the embroidery stitches but will dissolve in washing).

The Advent Calendar

Placed near the chimney on the first day of December, the Advent calendar embroidered with the colors of Santa Claus will help kids stay patient until Christmas morning by allowing them to discover a gift each day.

OVERVIEW

Level of Difficulty: Medium

Stitches Used: Satin stitch
(see p. 98)
Encroaching satin stitch
(see p. 101)
Knot stitch (see p. 74)

Finished Dimensions: The hanging measures 13 x 13 inches. The embroidered motif measures 12 x 12 inches.

MATERIALS

16 x 16 inches beige and white large-checked (1¼ x 1¼ inches) cotton fabric
1 skein of DMC cotton floss, art. 117 in each of the following colors: white, Turkish red (321), dark red (815), soft green (966), fir tree green (3847), dark brown (779), pale pink (353), creamy beige (738), yellow ochre (3821), golden yellow (743), mandarin (3854)
2 skeins of DMC cotton floss, art. 117 in the following colors: suede beige (841) and brown (420)
24 small golden rings
2¼ yards white satin ribbon, ¼ inch thick
1 fine embroidery needle
Embroidery hoop
Ball-point pen
Blue carbon paper
13 x 13 inches heavyweight cardboard or adhesive mounting boards (sold in craft stores)
13 x 13 inches synthetic tablecloth backing
Textile glue and adhesive tape
Pins

PATTERN

Enlarge the pattern with a photocopier.

Whip stitch the edges of the cotton fabric with a sewing machine or by hand.

Fold the square of fabric in four to determine the center. Place the pattern on the fabric and match the center of the pattern with the center of your fabric. Pin two sides of the pattern and then slide the carbon paper between the fabric and the pattern with the carbon side facing the fabric. With a ball-point pen, trace the shapes of the pattern and then remove the carbon paper and the pins.

EMBROIDERY

Stretch the fabric in the embroidery hoop. Use two strands of cotton floss. Refer to the model for the correct direction of the stitches, which is indicated by dashes on the section to embroider.

Begin the work with the small details in the satin stitch, such as the Christmas tree balls, the ribbons on the gifts, or the reindeer's jingle bells. Continue the embroidery by filling the larger surfaces using the encroaching satin stitch. Finally, embroider the numbers and the holly leaves on the border. Don't forget to make a knot stitch in the center of the holly berries.

FINISHING TOUCHES

Sew a gold ring on the outer edges of the fabric next to each number. Cut the satin ribbon into twenty-four equal-sized pieces and tie them to the rings to attach small gifts.

ADVICE

This pattern presents a spectrum of different colors and numerous details. Save time by working with several needles and you will not need to unthread the needle every time you need to change colors.

When the work is finished, press it on the opposite side. Mount the embroidery on a purchased mounting board or glue the piece of tablecloth backing onto a piece of cardboard and center the embroidered work over the tablecloth backing. Fold the edges of the fabric over to the back of the cardboard, keeping everything taut with straight pins. Attach the embroidery permanently with adhesive tape.

(Within pattern, on Santa Claus and the gifts, the code "Blc" stands for "white."

The Spider Web Stitch Family

All the stitches in this family present the appearance of weaving or damask. These very spectacular effects make them unique; they are therefore used alone to form original motifs. Nonetheless, they can be highlighted with a stem stitch or a knot stitch. They take quite a while to make, and require a great deal of precision.

THE SPIDER WEB STITCH IN 4 STEPS

Level of Difficulty: Medium, for people who already have some experience.

Threads and Fabrics: This stitch can be made on any type of fabric, with embroidery cotton, linen, silk, or even wool thread.

Direction: This stitch is worked in all directions.

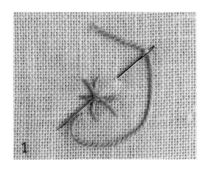

On the branches formed by long straight stitches, the weave is rolled in a spiral from the center to the outside edge of the shape. The spider web stitch generally illustrates simple flower motifs. It will have even more character if you use a variegated embroidery thread. This stitch is worked in two steps: the structural branches of the stitch and then the woven web.

STEP 1

Cross large straight stitches of identical length in the shape of a star inscribed within a circle. Make a star with six or eight branches.

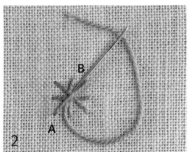

STEP 2

Bring the thread up in A, next to the center of the star, between two of the branches. Bring it back down in B, on the other side of the center. This little stitch fixes the center of the star.

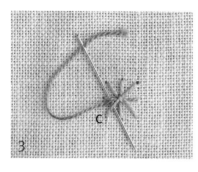

STEP 3

Change to a blunt-tipped needle to begin the weaving. Bring the needle up in C, as close to the center as possible, between two branches of the star. Slide the needle under the preceding branch and then under the next, and pull gently on the needle: the thread will surround the first branch. Proceed in this way, sliding the needle from behind to the front (under the preceding branch and under the next), turning counter-clockwise. A ribbed weave will appear. Tighten the rows against each other. The needle makes contact with the fabric only at the beginning and end of weaving the star.

STEP 4

The weave is finished once the star is entirely covered. At the final stitch, bring the thread through to the back of the fabric by making a small stitch over the final branch worked.

Fasten the thread on the back of the work. Cut it and begin another spider web stitch a bit further away on the fabric.

TIP

Change the needle before the weave work so that you do not catch the fabric in the branches of the star with the tip of your needle. In step 3, use a blunt-tipped tapestry needle.

THE WOVEN PORTUGUESE STITCH IN 4 STEPS

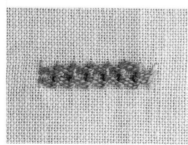

Level of Difficulty: Medium, for people who already have some experience.
Threads and Fabrics: This stitch can be made on any type of fabric, with twisted embroidery cotton such as Pearl, Cotton Matte, or Cutwork and Embroidery thread.
Direction: This stitch is worked vertically, from bottom to top and from top to bottom.

The woven Portuguese stitch is perfect as a border to highlight the edge of a collar or to decorate the button placket of a shirt. It is worked in two steps: the first consists of spacing stitches at regular intervals, around which the threads are woven on the second step.

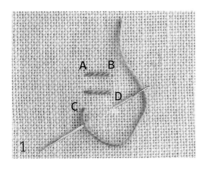

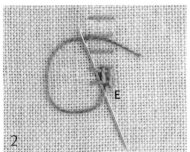

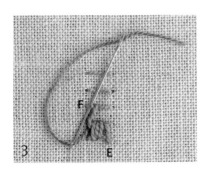

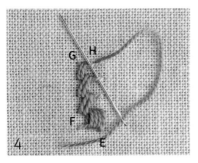

STEP 1

Bring your needle up in A and back down in B, on the right, to form a horizontal straight stitch (see p. 97). Bring the needle back up in C, about ¼ inch below A. Bring it down in D to form a second straight stitch, horizontal and parallel to the first. At regular intervals, make a line of horizontal stitches.

STEP 2

Thread another needle. Bring it up in E, on the lower right of the final horizontal stitch, and without entering the fabric make three vertical straight stitches sliding the needle under the two final horizontal stitches to cover the length of the stitches.

STEP 3

Moving upwards, slide the needle from top to bottom, under the third and then the second thread to embroider two vertical straight stitches and bring it back out in F. Make two vertical stitches under each base stitch. They will only cover the left side of the work.

STEP 4

At the top of the row, come back down the right side of the row, working toward the bottom. Bring your needle down in G and back up right next to it, in H, then slide your needle twice under the first two horizontal stitches. The needle direction should be from bottom to top, keeping the thread to the right.

Finish the weave in this manner. Make the final two stitches into the fabric to attach the embroidery to the surface of the fabric.

TIP

The woven Portuguese stitch is often made using two colors. The first color is used to make the base stitches which form the structural stitches, and the second color is used for weaving. In the second step, use long lengths of embroidery cotton (the thread wears out less quickly when it does not have to enter the fabric), and regularly allow the thread to regain its twist.

THE DARNING STITCH IN 2 STEPS

Level of Difficulty: Easy, accessible to beginners.

Threads and Fabrics: This stitch can be made on fabric for counted cross-stitch or on fabrics with an obvious weave, with embroidery cotton, linen, silk, or even wool thread. For best results, use floss threads such as cotton floss.

Direction: This stitch is worked horizontally, from left to right and from right to left.

First used to mend clothing or household linens, the darning stitch succeeded in seducing our grandmothers, who beat it at its own game: they invented all sorts of geometric designs made up of straight stitches woven into the weave of the fabric. These stitches because veritable decorations. Here is one example.

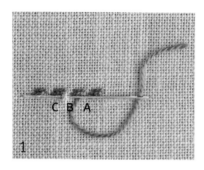
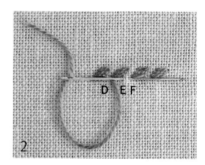

STEP 1

For the first row, work from right to left, Bring the needle up in A, skip six threads of the weave and bring it down in B, then bring the tip up in C, two threads of the weave away. Continue in this manner for the entire row.

STEP 2

For the second row, work from left to right. Bring your needle up in D, shifting one thread of the weave to the left with a running stitch (see p. 130). Skip six threads of the weave, bring your needle down in E, and bring the tip of your needle back up two threads of the weave away, in F.

Row after row, the stitches will shift first to the left and then to the right, making a woven chevron motif.

> **TIP**
>
> For the best results, this stitch must be made on an even number of threads of the weave. Here, we chose to make the stitch over six threads of the weave and skip two threads. However, we could have embroidered the stitch over eight threads and skipped four, etc.

THE WOVEN LADDER STITCH IN 5 STEPS

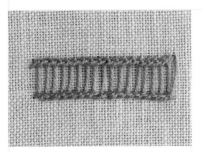

Level of Difficulty: Difficult, reserved for people who are experienced.

Threads and Fabrics: This stitch can be made on any type of fabric, with embroidery cotton, linen, silk, or even wool thread (for best results, choose a twisted thread, such as Pearl or cotton matte.

Direction: This stitch is worked vertically, from top to bottom.

Specifically developed to form borders, the woven ladder stitch offers the look of braided trimmings when it is worked with a fairly thick, twisted thread, such as Pearl cotton matte.

The woven ladder stitch is embroidered in horizontal stitches between two parallel lines.

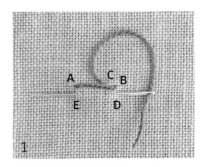

STEP 1

Bring your needle up in A, on the left, and back down in B, to make a large horizontal stitch. Bring the needle up in C, above and to the left of point B. Bring it back down in D, below point B, and bring the tip of the needle up in E, below point A.

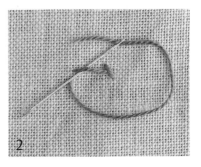

STEP 2

Pull the needle through and then slide it downward under the horizontal stitch. Slide the thread under the tip of the needle. Pull gently to form a loop.

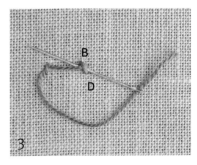

STEP 3

Slide the needle again under the large horizontal stitch, this time upward between points B and D. Pull gently on the thread to form a second horizontal stitch.

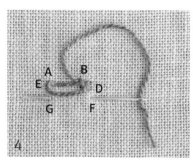

STEP 4

Bring your needle down in F, below point D, and back up in G, below point E. Pull gently on the thread.

STEP 5

Slide the needle upwards from right to left under the knot on the left of the ladder stitch.

Continue the work by repeating steps 3, 4, and 5.

> **TIP**
>
> The woven ladder stitch is only worked on fabric stretched on a frame. Moreover, to obtain a pretty effect, the horizontal stitches must measure at least $^1/_2$ inch. However, do not exceed $^3/_4$ inch, otherwise the stitches risk floating on the surface and giving the embroidery the impression of irregularity.

THE CHECKERBOARD STITCH IN 1 STEP

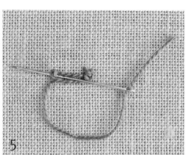

Level of Difficulty: Easy, accessible to beginners.
Threads and Fabrics: This stitch can be made on counted cross-stitch fabric or fabrics with a regular and obvious weave, with embroidery cotton, linen, silk, or even wool thread.
Direction: This stitch is worked vertically and horizontally.

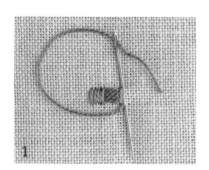

The checkerboard stitch truly deserves its name. The satin stitches, worked in horizontal and vertical groups, fit into each other to make a checkerboard. The result offers the appearance of a pretty, compact filling, similar to a weave.

STEP 1

Make the first square of five vertical satin stitches (see p. 98) over six threads of the weave of the fabric. To the right of this first square, embroider a second square also made of five satin stitches, except this time horizontal over six threads of the weave of fabric. Repeat these two squares, row by row, moving from top to bottom, alternating vertical and horizontal squares throughout.

THE CLOUD STITCH IN 3 STEPS

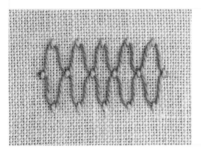

Level of Difficulty: Easy, accessible to beginners.

Threads and Fabrics: This stitch can be made on counted cross-stitch fabric or fabrics with a regular and obvious weave, with embroidery cotton, linen, silk, or even wool thread.

Direction: This stitch is worked horizontally, back and forth.

TIP

This stitch can be adapted to embroidering with ribbon. First, with a sewing machine, create the basic structure by making stitches ¹/₄ inch apart. Next, slide the embroidery ribbon through the small vertical stitches in loops. Take care to very regularly untwist the ribbon so that it remains flat.

The cloud stitch, also known as the "arch stitch," is made in two steps: first, you make the small vertical straight stitches of the structure, and then you create the weave made up of loops.

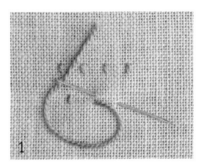 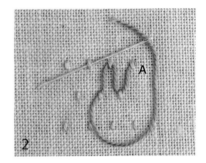

STEP 1

Embroider the horizontal rows of small vertical straight stitches (see p. 97). Here, the stitches are made over three threads of the weave and every eight threads of the same row. In the next row, place the stitches below and directly between the ones above. Alternate the stitch placement on following rows, evenly spacing the rows.

STEP 2

Change the thread on the needle. Bring your needle up in A, next to the last stitch on the right of the first row. Slide the needle under this stitch, then slide the needle under the last stitch on the right of the second row. Proceed in this manner for the whole row. Slide the needle under the stitch on the first row and then under the stitch on the second row. Work the needle horizontally, from right to left.

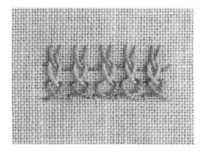

STEP 3

For the third row of arches, proceed from left to right. Bring the thread up next to the first stitch in the third row. Slide the needle under this stitch, then under the first stitch in the second row, and so forth. Work the needle horizontally, from left to right.

THE CEYLON STITCH IN 4 STEPS

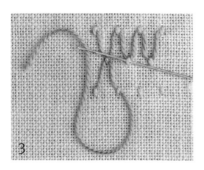

Level of Difficulty: Difficult, reserved for people with experience.

Threads and Fabrics: This stitch can be made on any type of fabric, with embroidery cotton, linen, silk, or even wool thread.

Direction: This stitch is worked horizontally, from left to right.

The Ceylon stitch covers fabric with a light weave of loops which are woven into each other. Worked in different shades of the same color, it offers a very pretty surface effect. The difficult mastery of the tension of the loops, however, means that this stitch is reserved for people who have a great deal of experience.

STEP 1

Bring your needle up in A and down in B, on the upper right. Bring the needle back up in C, about ¼ inch to the left of and level with B. Pull gently on the thread so that the stitch keeps a curved look.

STEP 2

Continue working the top line. Bring your needle down in D, to the right, and back up in E, between B and D. Pull the thread as before. Finish the row by bringing the final stitch down on the lower line.

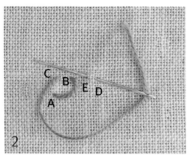

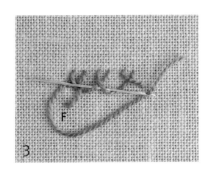

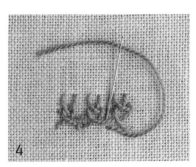

STEP 3

Begin the work on the left again. Bring your needle up in F. Slide the needle horizontally and from right to left under the first loop of the preceding row. Pull gently on the thread and form a loop of the same dimension as the one in the first row. Do not catch the fabric with your needle. Slide the needle horizontally from right to left under the second loop of the first row. Work the entire row in this way. The line of loops resembles a loose knit. Finish the row by bringing the final stitch down on the lower line.

STEP 4

On the final row, so that all the work does not come apart on the surface of the fabric, it is necessary to attach the bottom of each loop to the fabric with a row of small straight stitches embroidered over the thread between the two loops.

Napkin Rings

Typical of the 1920's and 1930's, the spider web stitch was very frequently used to decorate doilies, handkerchiefs, and pillows, just to name a few. Somewhat forgotten since then, it is still very much fun to embroider, as we have with this example, on napkin rings in joyful colors.

OVERVIEW

Level of Difficulty:
Easy

Stitches Used:
Spider web stitch (see p. 107)
Backstitch (see p. 25)
Lazy daisy stitch (see p. 37)

Finished Dimensions:
The finished napkin rings measure 6 x 2½ inches.

MATERIALS

14 x 18 inches rose (225) precut DMC embroidery linen (ref. DC 47)
1 skein of DMC cotton floss, art. 117 in each of the following colors: yellow (744), melon (3854), coral (3706) and pale green (369)
4 small mother-of-pearl buttons, ¼ inch diameter
1 medium embroidery needle
Embroidery hoop
Ball-point pen
Blue carbon paper
Pink sewing thread
Pins

PATTERN

From the piece of linen fabric, cut two 6 x 7 inch rectangles. With an iron, mark a fold in the middle of each rectangle to obtain two doubled bands of 3 x 7 inches each.

With a sewing machine, or by hand, whip stitch the edges of the linen bands.

Fold the bands in two to determine the center. Place the pattern on the front half of the first band, and match the center of the pattern with the center of this half. Pin two sides of the pattern. Slide the carbon paper between the fabric and the pattern, with the carbon side facing the fabric. Trace the outline of the pattern with your pen, then remove the pattern and the pins. Repeat this process for the second linen band.

EMBROIDERY

Stretch the band in a small embroidery hoop. Only the front of each band is embroidered.

Make the branches of the spider web stitch with the yellow thread, using six strands of cotton floss.

Then embroider the weave of the stitch, alternating the melon and coral threads. Use two strands of cotton floss.

Still using two strands of cotton floss, embroider the stems in pale green using the backstitch on the first napkin ring and the leaves with the lazy daisy stitch on both.

ADVICE

The pattern offered here offers the advantage of folding the napkin rings in half after they have been embroidered. When made in this way, the back side of the work stays tidy and does not run the risk of being pulled through use or in the wash. Make more napkin rings in other colors to match the shades of your tablecloths and napkins. They are easy and quick to embroider, and they also make delightful little gifts.

FINISHING TOUCHES

Press the work on the opposite side.

Refold the bands with right sides together. Pin and sew ¼ inch from the edge, leaving one side open. Open the seams with an iron.

Turn the napkin rings inside out. Turn in the raw edges and slipstitch the opening closed. Topstitch the edges of the band.

On one end, make two small loops for buttonholes. On the other end of the band, sew two small mother-of-pearl buttons on the front. Close the napkin ring.

Pattern reduced to 80%

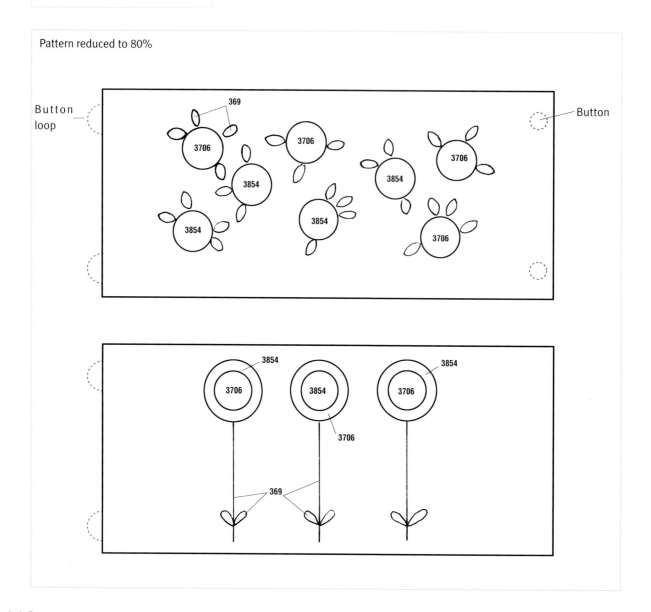

The Shadow Embroidery Stitch Family

The shadow stitch and the stitches which follow in this chapter have been selected for their appliqué effect. Discover the surprising results offered by the Shisha stitch, which borders a mirror or piece of mica added to embroidery, or by the Brocatello stitch, which imitates the weave of a textile so well that it gives the impression that a piece of fabric has been added. The use of these stitches brings much finesse and subtlety to embroidered works.

THE SHADOW STITCH IN 3 STEPS

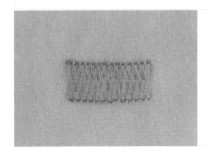

Level of Difficulty: Medium, for people who already have some experience.
Threads and Fabrics: This stitch can only be made on transparent cotton, silk or linen fabrics, with silk or cotton floss thread.
Direction: This stitch is worked horizontally, from right to left.

The shadow stitch is worked as a herringbone stitch on thin, transparent fabrics such as cotton or linen voile, organdy, or silk organza, in such a way as to create the effects of shadow on the opposite side of the work. Flowers with small petals work particularly well when made in this stitch.

The shadow stitch technique, probably of Indian origin, has been used in Europe for centuries, and is often associated with other stitches in cutwork embroidery as well as Dresden embroidery.

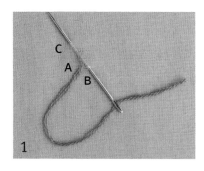

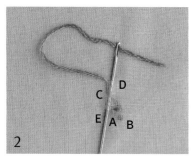

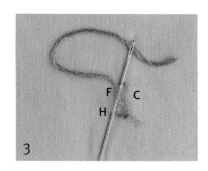

STEP 1

Bring your needle up in A, on the bottom line of the tracing and to the right, and bring it down in B, to the right to form the first stitch. Bring it back up in C, to the left, on the top line and a bit diagonal to the first stitch.

STEP 2

Bring your needle back down in D to finish the first stitch situated at the top of the tracing. Bring the tip of the needle up in E, just to the left of point A on the bottom line. Bring your needle back down in point A to finish the stitch situated on the lower edge of the tracing.

STEP 3

On the top edge, bring your needle up in F, just to the left of point C and bring it back down in C. Bring the tip of your needle back up in H on the bottom line. Complete as for step 2.

Continue the row by repeating steps 2 and 3, going back and forth between the upper edge and the lower one. The back of the work presents a row of herringbone stitches which appear through the transparent fabric between the two rows of back-stitches on the front of the work.

TIP

Whatever the shape of the motif you are working, it must be surrounded with backstitches. This detail gives the effect of appliqué on the background fabric. Begin the first stitch at the corner of the pattern, then work the back and forth between the two edges of the motif. On some complicated shapes, it may be the case that the first or the last of the herringbone stitches on the back of the work are very small. This is not a problem so long as the impression of filling is perfect on the front side of the work.

THE PARIS STITCH IN 2 STEPS

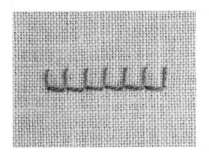

Level of Difficulty: Very easy, accessible to beginners.

Threads and Fabrics: This stitch can be made fabrics with obvious weave, with embroidery cotton, linen, silk, or even wool thread.

Direction: This stitch is worked horizontally, from right to left.

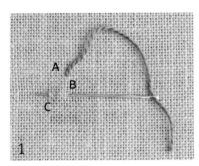

Extremely easy to make, the Paris stitch is placed on the edges of appliqué work, or even alone, as a finishing touch on a hem. There is another Paris stitch, used in drawn thread work, which is made in a different way.

STEP 1

Bring the needle up in A and down in B, on the bottom, to form a vertical straight stitch. Bring it back up in C, about ¼ inch to the left of and level with point B.

STEP 2

Bring your needle back down in B to form the horizontal stitch. Direct the tip of the needle diagonally up and to the left and bring it back out in D, about ¼ inch to the left of A and directly above C. Work the rest of the row in this manner, repeating steps 1 and 2.

TIP

In order for the Paris stitch to present a pretty finish, make sure to work the stitches vertically and horizontally over the same number of threads of the weave of fabric. Also be sure to allow some ease in the thread so as not to tighten the weave of the fabric, which can ruin the uniformity of the stitch.

THE BROCATELLO STITCH IN 3 STEPS

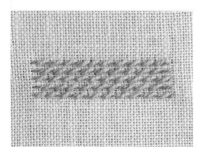

Level of Difficulty: Medium, for people who already have some experience.

Threads and Fabrics: This stitch can be made on fabrics with obvious weave, such as muslin and thin-ribbed cotton pique, with all types of thread.

Direction: This stitch is worked vertically, from bottom to top and top to bottom.

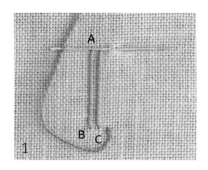

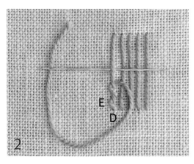

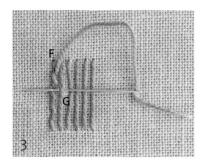

Of Italian origin, the Brocatello stitch was once reserved for filling backgrounds. This stitch, which follows the straight of the fabric, is made in two steps. The first consists of making, at regular intervals, large straight stitches which cover the surface of the fabric. The second step fastens the large stitches to the fabric with smaller ones.

STEP 1

Proceed from the left to the right. Bring your needle up in A and down in B to make a large vertical straight stitch. Bring your needle back up in C, next to B. In this manner cover the surface with large vertical stitches.

STEP 2

Thread a new needle. Bring the needle up in D, at the base and to the right of the first large stitch. Bring the needle down in E, diagonally to the upper left to form a small slanted stitch which will fasten the large stitch. Work the small slanted stitches upwards along the entire length of the large vertical stitch.

STEP 3

For the second stitch, work downwards. Bring the needle up in F, to the left of the stitch, and back down in D, diagonally down and to the lower right. Proceed in this manner along the length of the second large stitch.

Continue working the large stitches, repeating steps 2 and 3. Be sure to work so the small stitches always slant in the same direction.

THE MOSUL STITCH IN 2 STEPS

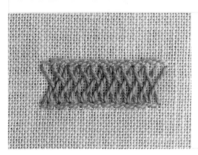

Level of Difficulty: Medium, for people who already have some experience.
Threads and Fabrics: This stitch can be made on any type of fabric, with embroidery cotton, linen, silk, or even wool thread.
Direction: This stitch is worked horizontally, from left to right.

The Mosul stitch, of Persian origin, is made up of two stitches we have already seen: the filling is made with the herringbone stitch, then it is surrounded with a stem stitch. The appliqué look of this stitch is thus made all the more spectacular.

STEP 1

Make a row of herringbone stitches (see p. 54): Bring the needle up in A, then down in B, on the upper right. Bring it back up in C, to the left, a short distance away from B. Bring it down in D, to the right of A, and below B. Bring your needle back out in E, midway between A and D. Proceed in this way to fill the row.

STEP 2

Work with a new needle and embroider a stem stitch (see p. 22) on the top and bottom of the herringbone stitch in order to completely border it. Bring your needle up in F and down in G, directly to the right. Bring it back up in H, halfway between points F and G.

TIP

With its stem stitch frame, the Mosul stitch has the advantage of offering a perfect finish to the borders of the embroidery. The stem stitch hides any imperfections in the herringbone stitch made in the first step.

You can also make this stitch by surrounding it with a thin braided trimming held in place by small slip stitches instead of the stem stitch. In this case, begin the work by placing the braid, then embroider the filling with the herringbone stitch as the second step.

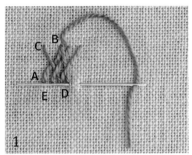

THE SHISHA STITCH IN 6 STEPS

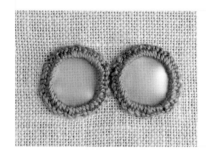

Level of Difficulty: Difficult, reserved for people who are experienced.

Threads and Fabrics: This stitch can be made on any type of fabric, with embroidery cotton, linen, or metallic thread.

Direction: This stitch is worked around the appliqué piece.

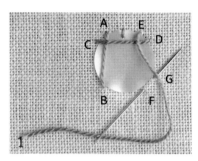

The Shisha stitch is reserved for appliqué work. It borders a piece of fabric or metal and holds it in place on the surface of the fabric. Of Baloutchistan Pakistani origin, where it decorates saris and blankets, it is also known as "mirror embroidery."

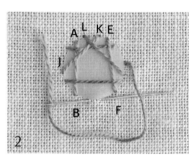

STEP 1

Place the element to be appliquéd on the fabric. Bring your needle up in A, at the top, and down in B to make a large vertical stitch. Bring your needle up in C and down in D to form a large horizontal stitch. In this manner, make a large stitch on top, bottom, and each side of the round piece to hold it to the fabric.

STEP 2

The second step consists of surrounding the round piece by making four more stitches, this time diagonally to the first four. Bring your needle up in J and down in K to form a large stitch. Continue in this way to surround the piece.

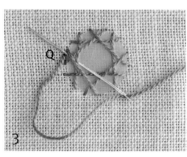

STEP 3

Bring the needle up in Q, right next to the side of the shape on the lower left. Slide the needle upwards under the border stitches, with the working end of the thread to the left.

STEP 4

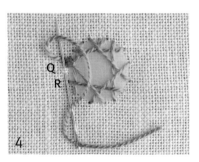

Working counterclockwise, bring your needle down in R, below Q, and bring it up two threads above R. Make a loop with the thread against the fabric and gently pull the needle through. You are forming the buttonhole stitch (see p. 182).

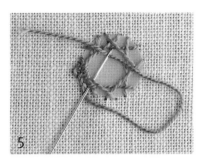

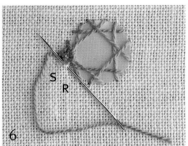

STEP 5

Slide the needle under the border stitches as you did in step 3. Move the needle from top to bottom, with the working end of the thread to the left and under the needle.

STEP 6

Bring your needle down in R and bring the tip back out in S, slightly to the left. Slide the thread under the needle and pull the thread gently to form the second chain stitch.

Repeat steps 5 and 6 all around the round piece. Once the frame is entirely embroidered, form a small stitch over the final loop of the chain stitch to hold it in place, and fasten off the thread on the back of the work. Begin again with step 1 for the next appliquéd element.

> **TIP**
>
> Originally, this stitch held bits of mirror or mica on fabrics. Today, it can be used to hold all sorts of materials such as large plastic or metal sequins. To keep these elements on the surface of the fabric you are working, apply a small dab of fabric glue on the back before placing it in the desired location.

The Stole

A wonder of subtlety, the shadow stitch plays on the transparency of the lightweight fabric. Choose harmonious shades of blue, embroider the bouquet of hydrangeas on an organdy stole, and you'll have very elegant accessory.

OVERVIEW

Level of Difficulty:
Medium

Stitches Used:
Shadow stitch (see p. 119)
Knot stitch (see p. 74)

Finished Dimensions:
The finished stole measures 20 x 69 inches. The hydrangea motif measures 6 x 13 inches.

MATERIALS

22 x 73 inches blue cotton organdy
2 skeins of DMC cotton floss, art. 117 in the following colors: lavender (792), mauve (340), porcelain blue (3839), sky blue (3840), leaf green (913), bud green (564), golden yellow (3822)
1 fine embroidery needle
Embroidery hoop
Black hard lead pencil
Blue sewing thread
Pins

PATTERN

The hydrangea motif is placed at each end of the stole, in the center of the width and 12 inches from each edge. Place the pins as markers. Place the pattern under one end of the fabric and match the edges of the pattern with the marker pins.

Pin the pattern and the fabric together. Trace the outline of the pattern, which will show through your fabric, with the black pencil, then remove the pattern and the pins. Begin again at the other end of the stole.

The tracing of the pattern is done on the right side of the fabric.

EMBROIDERY

Use two strands of cotton floss for the shadow stitches, and four strands for the knot stitches. Gently stretch the organdy in the embroidery hoop.

Begin the work by embroidering the petals, referring to the pattern for the color changes. Then embroider the leaves.

Finish the work by making the knot stitches, with golden yellow, where indicated by unmarked small circles on pattern. Move the embroidery hoop as you complete each section of your work.

Press the work on the back.

FINISHING TOUCHES

With your iron, make a ¼-inch fold along the side edges of the stole, then a second fold of ½ inch. Sew the hems by hand or with a sewing machine. On the ends, make a 1-inch fold, then a 3-inch fold. Sew the two hems.

ADVICE

The difficulty of the shadow stitch rests in the fastening of the stitches. This technique does not tolerate floating threads between motifs because of the transparency of the fabric. On the back of the work, fasten the thread with two backstitches slipped under the last two herringbone stitches situated on the back side of the work. Cut the thread at the level of the embroidery.

Make individual knot stitches, fastening off the thread on the back of the work, for the same reasons as above.

The most famous of the counted stitches is without question the cross-stitch. This very old stitch and its derivatives help to develop the qualities of precision and patience in beginning embroiderers. The stitches presented in this chapter are all embroidered on a simple fabric with an obvious weave so that you can count the number of threads in the weave of the material.

As for motifs, they are often presented on a graphed chart, also called a diagram. The symbol or the spot of color filling each square corresponds to one embroidery stitch. This detail generally allows you to make only geometric designs. Nonetheless, when the stitch is adapted to fine fabrics, more complex patterns may be created.

Counted stitches, furthermore, require using a needle with a blunt tip (a tapestry needle) which will not catch the fabric but will pass through it between the threads of the weave.

These details make counted stitches a homogenous and harmonious family.

4

COUNTED STITCHES

The Running Stitch Family

Very easy to make, the stitches in this family and their derivatives are accessible to beginning embroiderers and well as children who wish to try embroidery. The motif appears after a few stitches. It's as simple as drawing with a crayon.

THE RUNNING STITCH IN 1 STEP

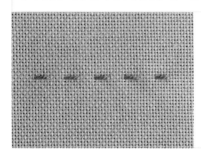

Level of Difficulty: Very easy, accessible to beginners.
Threads and Fabrics: This stitch can be made on fabrics with a simple weave or on muslins, with cotton, linen, silk or wool thread of the Pearl, Cutwork and Embroidery, or stranded cotton floss varieties.
Direction: This stitch is worked from right to left.

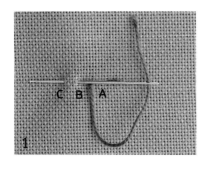

The running stitch is the simplest of all stitches. Its name alone already tells us how it's made. This stitch is best suited to straight lines rather than curves. The weave of the fabric guides the thread, and so the stitches are always regular and of identical length.

STEP 1

Bring the needle up in A and down in B, a few threads of the weave to the left.

Bring the tip of the needle back up a bit further to the left, in C, making sure that the distance between B and C is the same as the distance between A and B.

Continue the row in this manner, making sure to maintain the uniformity of the stitches and the intervals between them.

TIP

You will frequently find the running stitch as a step in making another stitch, where it serves as a base row before being covered entirely or partially by a fancier stitch.

THE LINE STITCH IN 2 STEPS

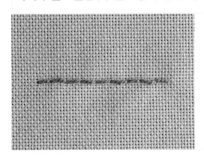

Level of Difficulty: Very easy, accessible to beginners.

Threads and Fabrics: This stitch can be made on fabrics with a simple weave or on muslins, with cotton, linen, silk or wool thread of the Pearl, Cutwork and Embroidery, or stranded cotton floss varieties.

Direction: This stitch is worked from right to left.

Also known as the "Holbein stitch" or the "double running stitch," the line stitch is a running stitch worked twice to obtain a continuous line. It offers many uses, especially for making geometric borders of simple lines, or even to frame motifs that are already filled with cross stitches.

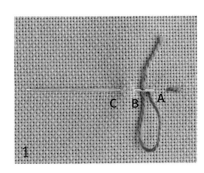 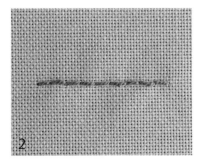

STEP 1

Bring the needle up in A, on the right, and down in B, a few threads of the weave to the left. Bring the tip of the needle back up in C, making sure that the distance between B and C is the same as the distance between A and B.

STEP 2

The second step consists of filling in the gaps left by the first row, by stitching in the same holes. Begin again at the right and make a second row of running stitches.

Continue the row in this manner, making sure to maintain the uniformity of the stitches and the intervals between them.

TIP

The only difficulty in this stitch comes at the second step, where you must take care not to catch your needle in the thread of the stitches from the first step. The thread used for the second step risks, under tension, being caught on the back of the fabric and, when tightened, can crimp.

To avoid this, use a needle with a blunt tip for the first step so that you spread open the threads of the weave, and a needle with a pointed tip for the second step. This way, if the needle catches the thread of the first step, it will not get caught on the back of the fabric.

THE JAPANESE LINE STITCH IN 2 STEPS

Level of Difficulty: Medium, for people who already have some experience.

Threads and Fabrics: This stitch can be made on fabrics with a simple weave or on muslins, with cotton, linen, silk or wool thread of the Pearl, Cutwork and Embroidery, or stranded cotton floss varieties.

Direction: This stitch is worked horizontally, from right to left and from left to right.

The Japanese line stitch is already a motif all on its own. Made on a base of running stitches, it allows you to work a filling on large surfaces. Its geometric honeycomb look evokes some woven materials originating in the land of the Rising Sun.

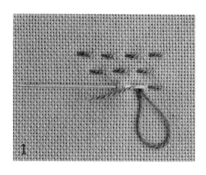

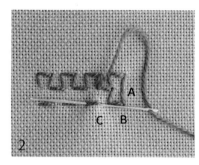

STEP 1

Make rows of horizontal, parallel running stitches (see p. 130). For the second row, embroider the stitches in a staggered fashion between the ones in the first row. Continue to alternate the position of surface stitches on the following rows.

STEP 2

Work the vertical stitches connecting two horizontal rows by stitching in the same holes you used for the running stitches in the first row. Bring your needle up in A, down in B, and back up in C, and continue this for the entire row.

> **TIP**
>
> The rows of running stitches in the first step should be placed parallel to each other. To be successful with the Japanese line stitch, the running stitches must be a bit longer than the intervals between them.

THE SIMPLE WOVEN STITCH IN 2 STEPS

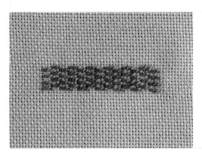

Level of Difficulty: Easy, accessible to beginners.

Threads and Fabrics: This stitch can be made on fabrics with a simple weave, with cotton, linen, silk or wool thread of the Pearl, Cutwork and Embroidery, or stranded cotton floss varieties.

Direction: This stitch is worked horizontally from right to left and from left to right.

TIP

The simple woven stitch can only be made on fabrics with a simple weave by following the straight of the goods, either vertically or horizontally. As with the preceding stitches, the woven appearance is not satisfying unless the uniform length of each stitch and the regular interval between stitches is maintained.

The simple woven stitch perfectly imitates the weave of fabric. In sewing, it is also called the "darning stitch." This stitch is found particularly in Moroccan and Rhodesian embroidery, where it is used to fill geometric motifs.

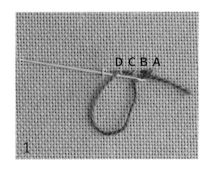
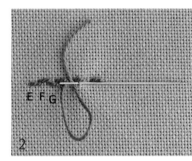

STEP 1

Bring the needle up in A and down in B, a few threads of the weave to the left. Bring the tip of the needle back up in C, skipping one or two threads (maximum) of the weave. Bring your needle back down in D. Continue in this way for the entire row.

STEP 2

Begin work on the left. Bring the needle up in E and down in F, a few threads of the weave to the right. The center of the first stitch of the second row is the end point of the final stitch of the first row. Bring the needle back up in G after having skipped one or two threads (maximum) of the weave.

Continue the horizontal rows in this manner, back and forth.

THE SYRNIE STITCH IN 3 STEPS

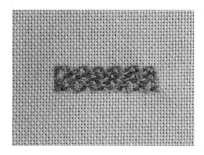

Level of Difficulty: Medium, for people who already have some experience.

Threads and Fabrics: This stitch can be made on fabrics with a simple weave, with cotton, linen, silk or wool thread of the Pearl, Cutwork and Embroidery, or stranded cotton floss varieties.

Direction: This stitch is worked horizontally, from right to left and then from left to right.

Because of its crinkled appearance, this stitch is also known as the "wave stitch." Originating in a region of Slovakia, the Syrnie stitch is found on embroidered ornaments of the folk costumes of the inhabitants of that country.

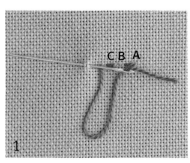

STEP 1

Bring the needle up in A, on the right, and down in B, a few threads of the weave to the left. Bring the tip of the needle back up in C, making sure that the distance between B and C is the same as the distance between A and B. Continue the row in this manner, maintaining the uniformity of the stitches and the intervals between them.

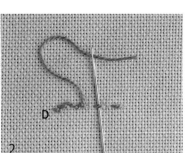

STEP 2

Work the second row from left to right. Bring your needle up in D, just below the first row. Then do not bring it down into the fabric but slide the needle upwards under the first running stitch. Then, slide the needle downwards and under the second stitch.

Continue in this manner for the entire row.

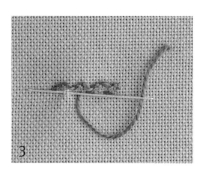

STEP 3

Make another row of running stitches below the row you made in step 1. Place the running stitches staggered between the ones you made in the first row.

Work another row of wave stitches into the running stitches as you did in step 2.

TIP

To give even more depth to this stitch, work the running stitches in a darker color than the one you will use in the second step.

The Place Mat

Easy to make, this place mat with geometric motifs is perfect for bringing color to your everyday table. It also nicely accompanies your party napkins for a more elegant effect. Play with the border by placing it at an angle, at the top and bottom of the place mat, or even around the entire edge, depending on the time you have and the results you want.

OVERVIEW

Level of Difficulty:
Easy

Stitch Used:
Running stitch (see p. 130)

Finished Dimensions:
The finished place mat measures 18 x 14 inches. The embroidered motif measures 5 x 5 inches.

MATERIALS

20 x 16 inches green DMC Aida fabric, size 16 mesh
1 skein of DMC cotton floss, art. 177, in each of the following colors: golden yellow (3854), yellow-green (734), coral (351)
1 blunt-tipped tapestry needle
Embroidery hoop

PREPARATION

Make a ¾-inch hem around the edges of the place mat. Baste, then machine sew the hem.

With pins, mark the edges of the motif. The marks indicated on the diagram are situated 22 threads from the edge of the place mat.

EMBROIDERY

Use two strands of cotton floss. Stretch the material in the embroidery hoop.

Begin the work with the diamond motifs made in coral (351). Each running stitch is made vertically, horizontally, or on a slant, over a single thread of the weave of the fabric.

Continue embroidering with the details in yellow-green (734), and then finish with the details in golden yellow (3854). The running stitches, situated at the center of the motif, in diamonds and embroidered in golden yellow, are made over two threads of the weave of the fabric.

Move the embroidery hoop as you finish each section and begin the next.

ADVICE

When the motif is fully embroidered, double check to make sure you have not forgotten any stitches.

Turn the work over and make sure all the ends of the threads are perfectly fastened off under the embroidered stitches.

Once your place mat is finished, cut the ends of the embroidery thread as close as possible to the fabric with sharp embroidery scissors to prevent the floating ends from being seen through the material.

The Cross-Stitch Family

Because it is so very simple to make, the cross-stitch is accessible to everyone who wishes to learn the basics of embroidery techniques. This is a universally known stitch, which today still retains its nobility in the spectrum of embroidery stitches. Discover in this lesson some elaborate versions of the basic stitch. Some, like the Assisi stitch are famous, while others, like the Hungarian cross-stitch, are less known, but all present remarkable decorative qualities.

THE CROSS-STITCH IN 2 STEPS

Level of Difficulty: Very easy, accessible to beginners.

Threads and Fabrics: This stitch can be made on fabrics with a simple weave, with cotton, linen, silk, or wool thread (preferably floss type so that it is possible to choose the number of strands to use based on the thickness of the fabric).

Direction: This stitch is worked horizontally or vertically.

The cross-stitch is the perfect example of embroidery made using counted stitches. The cross, formed by two equal-length stitches, is not composed of straight branches but rather, slanted ones, in order to cover the supporting fabric fully.

> **TIP**
>
> Check the back of the work. It must show small, uniform vertical stitches for the horizontal cross stitch, and small, uniform horizontal stitches for the vertical cross stitch.

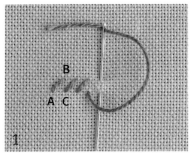

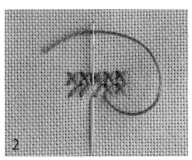

HORIZONTAL CROSS-STITCH

STEP 1

Work a row of half-stitches slanted to the right, moving from left to right. Each stitch is inscribed within a square formed by the same number of threads of the weave across and down. Bring the needle up in A and down in B, on the upper right, then bring the tip of the needle back up in C, vertical with point B.

STEP 2

At the end of the row, work from right to left, embroidering half-stitches slanted in the opposite direction over the stitches embroidered in the preceding step. Stitch in the same holes used in step 1.

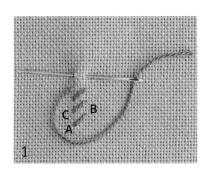

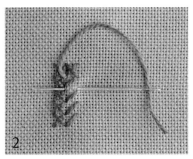

VERTICAL CROSS-STITCH

STEP 1

Work a row of half-stitches slanted to the right, moving from bottom to top. Each stitch is inscribed within a square formed by the same number of threads of the weave across and down. Bring the needle up in A and down in B, on the upper right, then bring the tip of the needle back up in C, horizontal with point B.

STEP 2

At the top of the row, work from top to bottom, embroidering half-stitches slanted in the opposite direction over the stitches embroidered in the preceding step. Stitch in the same holes used in step 1.

THE ASSISI STITCH IN 2 STEPS

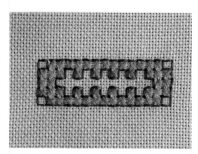

Level of Difficulty: Medium, for people who already have some experience.

Threads and Fabrics: This stitch can be made on fabrics with a simple weave, with cotton, linen, silk, or wool thread (preferably floss type so that it is possible to choose the number of strands to use based on the thickness of the fabric).

Direction: This stitch is worked in every direction for the shape of the line stitch motif, and horizontally for the background filling work in cross stitches.

Originating in the birthplace of Saint Francis of Assisi, this stitch brings character to embroidered geometric shapes or animal motifs that are left empty on the fabric; the motifs are outlined in darker colors with a line stitch, which stand out very well from the embroidered cross-stitches which are always done in a lighter color.

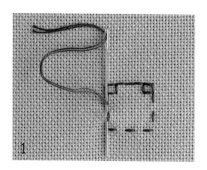
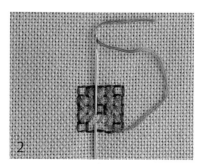

STEP 1

Begin the work with the shape of the motif, embroidering it with the line stitch (see p. 131). Make the first part of the stitch, and then fill it in during the second step to complete the entire outline.

STEP 2

Fill the background of the motif, leaving the motif itself empty. Embroider the cross-stitch (see p. 138) in horizontal rows, from top to bottom.

TIP

Make sure to choose a design adapted to this stitch, such as borders or motifs inscribed in geometric shapes, for example.

To follow the traditional and authentic style of the Assisi stitch, choose colors such as black, dark brown, navy blue or evergreen for the outline of the shape.

THE STAR STITCH IN 3 STEPS

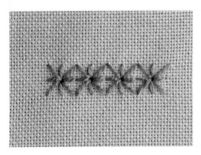

Level of Difficulty: Easy, accessible to beginners.

Threads and Fabrics: This stitch can be made on fabrics with a simple weave, with cotton, linen, silk or wool thread of the Pearl, Cutwork and Embroidery, or stranded cotton floss varieties.

Direction: This stitch is worked in every direction.

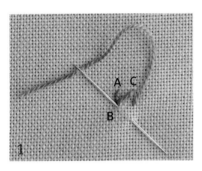

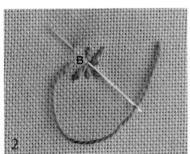

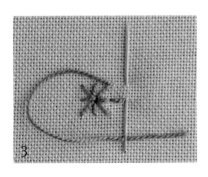

Very decorative, the star stitch is found in regions of the globe as diverse as the Ukraine, Algeria, and Denmark. It is always made in the same way, but it is embroidered with a variety of threads on different supporting fabrics. It is used in cutwork embroidery in Nordic countries, in golden embroidery in countries of the Maghreb, and in cotton and wool embroidery in the Ukraine.

STEP 1

The stitch is inscribed in a square, made up of the same number of threads of the weave in height and width. Bring the needle up in A and down in B, the center of the star stitch. Bring the needle back up in C and down in the center, point B.

STEP 2

Work clockwise in this manner, around point B, until a star with eight branches is formed.

STEP 3

Embroider the second star stitch right next to the first, being careful to stitch in the farthest hole on the right of the preceding stitch.

Continue the work in the same manner, until the stitches entirely cover the supporting material.

TIP

This stitch can be used in needle-work tapestry on canvas. For this, use embroidery wool and a large tapestry needle.

THE RICE STITCH IN 3 STEPS

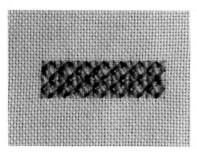

Level of Difficulty: Easy, accessible to beginners.

Threads and Fabrics: This stitch can be made on fabrics with a simple weave or on muslins, with cotton, linen, silk, or wool thread of the Pearl, Cutwork and Embroidery, or stranded cotton floss varieties.

Direction: This stitch is worked in every direction.

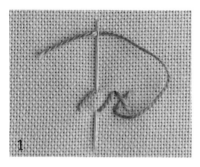

The rice stitch is also known in embroidery as the "overcast cross-stitch," a name which indicates precisely how this stitch is made. It is embroidered in two steps with two contrasting colors, giving it a pretty decorative effect.

STEP 1

The first step consists of covering the surface of the fabric with rows of large horizontal cross-stitches (see p. 139). Each cross-stitch is made over 6 threads of the weave of fabric.

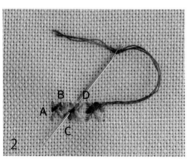

STEP 2

Change the color of the thread, and work in a shade that contrasts the color used for the cross-stitches. Bring the needle up in A and down in B, making a stitch slanting to the right, covering one branch of the first cross-stitch. Bring the needle up in C, between two cross-stitches, and back down in D. Embroider these stitches slanting to the right all the way to the end of the row. Come back from right to left with stitches slanting to the left to complete the chevron stitches which are formed on the upper half of the first row of cross-stitches.

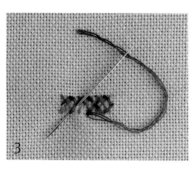

STEP 3

For the second row of chevrons, proceed in the same way as you did in step 2, making sure to form diamonds whose branches fit in between those of the cross-stitches in step 1.

TIP

Use a thick thread to make the large cross-stitches and a thinner thread for covering them with the rows of chevrons.

THE HUNGARIAN CROSS-STITCH IN 3 STEPS

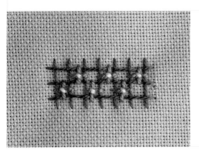

Level of Difficulty: Medium, for people who already have some experience.

Threads and Fabrics: This stitch can be made on fabrics with a simple weave or on muslins, with cotton, linen, silk, or wool thread of the Pearl, Cutwork and Embroidery, or stranded cotton floss varieties.

Direction: This stitch is worked in all directions.

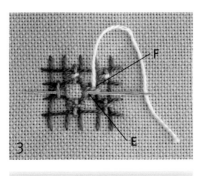

An original variation of the cross-stitch, the Hungarian cross-stitch is still used today in Magyar embroidery. It is made up of cross-stitches worked on a grid and held in place in the center with a small slanted stitch.

STEP 1

Make a grid of large straight stitches (see p. 97) on the surface to be covered. Work the vertical stitches first, then, maintaining the regular spacing, make the horizontal stitches of the grid.

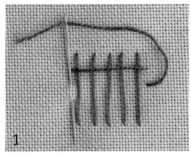

STEP 2

With a lighter-colored thread than the first, make a straight cross-stitch over a square of the grid. Leave every other square empty. Bring the needle up in A, at the bottom of the square, and bring it down in B, vertical to A. Bring it back up in C, on the left, and bring the needle back down in D, to the right and horizontal with C. On the second row, stagger the filling of squares to make a checkerboard effect.

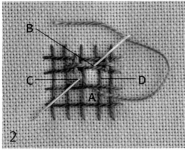

STEP 3

Take a light-colored thread and proceed row by row. Make a small stitch slanting to the right covering the center of each cross-stitch. Bring the needle up in E, to the left of the cross-stitch, and bring it down in F, diagonally.

TIP

To ensure that the straight cross-stitches on the squares of the grid are perfectly centered, make the straight stitches over an even number of threads of the weave.

THE TWO-SIDED CROSS-STITCH IN 4 STEPS

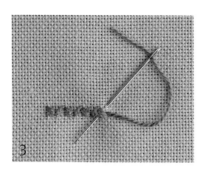

Level of Difficulty: Difficult, reserved for people who are experienced.

Threads and Fabrics: This stitch can be made on fabrics with a simple weave or on muslins, with cotton, linen, silk, or wool thread of the Pearl, Cutwork and Embroidery, or stranded cotton floss varieties.

Direction: This stitch is worked horizontally.

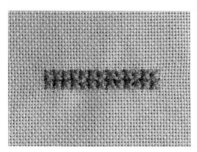

The two-sided cross-stitch is a complex stitch, used for works that need a front and a back that look the same, such as screen fabrics or blinds.

STEP 1

Each of the rows is made in four steps, counting an even number of threads of the weave for each cross-stitch. Proceed from left to right. Make a stitch slanting to the right. Bring the needle up in A and down in B, diagonally to the right. Bring it back up in C, after skipping the number of threads identical to that of the height of the cross, and bring it back down in D. At the final stitch of the row, make a slanted half-stitch, then bring your needle up in E and down in F to begin the return to the left.

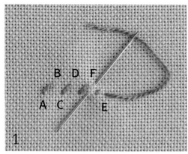

STEP 2

Work the next row of half cross-stitches to complete the crosses. To turn, finish the entire first cross of the row and bring your needle up at the right-hand base of the cross-stitch. Make half cross-stitches slanting to the right in the intervals left open.

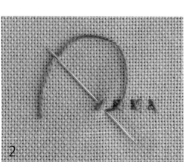

STEP 3

At the final stitch of the row, begin again with stitches slanted to the left. To start, bring the needle up at the left hand base of the final stitch in the row.

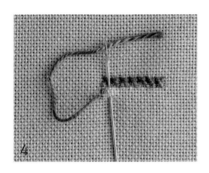

STEP 4

Complete the crosses of the second passage of the first row. To move to the next row, situated below the first, bring the needle up on the left hand base of the first stitch and make two small vertical stitches to bring the needle to the starting point for the second row.

Begin again at step 1.

> **TIP**
>
> Turn the work over regularly to verify that the stitch is identical on both sides of the fabric. It is very difficult to make the thread fastenings invisible. Leave the thread of each standing end dangling and finish them off once the entire work is completed. Slide the threads with small backstitches under the cross stitches and cut the ends as close as possible to the fabric.

The Commemorative Hanging

The commemorative hanging is a gift that is highly appreciated by young mothers, who are always happy to remember the birth of their child. This is also a way for beginners to practice. The dimensions of this motif are perfectly suited for novices because it only takes a few hours of work, and success is guaranteed.

OVERVIEW

Level of Difficulty:
Easy

Stitches Used:
Cross-stitch (see p. 138)
Line stitch (see p. 131)

Finished Dimensions:
The finished hanging measures 12 x 8 inches. The embroidered motif measures 10 x 4 inches.

MATERIALS

20 x 16 inches pink DMC Aida fabric, size 16 mesh
1 skein of DMC cotton floss, art. 177, in each of the following colors: white, coral (3705), orange (721), candy pink (3806), anise green (3819), golden yellow (744), dark gray (413), turquoise (959)
1 blunt-tipped tapestry needle
Embroidery hoop
12 x 8 inch heavyweight acid-free matboard
Pins
Framer's tape

PREPARATION

By hand or with a sewing machine, whip stitch the edges of the fabric so that it does not unravel as you work.

With pins, mark the center of the Aida rectangle.

Begin with the stitch situated at the center of the motif on this marking pin.

EMBROIDERY

Use two strands of cotton floss for the cross stitches and one strand for the line stitch which surrounds the motifs.

Stretch the material in the embroidery hoop.

Begin the work in the center of the composition, then embroider the motifs of toys one after the other. Finish the work with the baby's first name, drawing letters on graph paper before embroidering name.

Thread one strand of dark gray (413) and outline with a line stitch the toy motifs. Also embroider the outline of the baby's name in coral (3705).

Move the embroidery hoop as you finish each section and begin the next.

DMC cotton floss, art. 117

white ⁙

3705 ■ __

3806 ■

744 ▧

721 ■

413 ■ __

959 ■

3819 ■

ADVICE

Color your embroidery based on the colors indicated on the diagram. To make your work easier, use a different embroidery needle for each color. This method prevents your needing to unthread the needle and interrupt your work.

When you work with several needles at once, slip the ones you are not currently using through to the back of the work. Fasten the thread of the needle so that it does not get caught up in the stitches you are in the process of making.

The Damask Stitch Family

Derived from the Dresden weaving technique, these geometric stitches serve to cover the foundation of motifs. They were embroidered on fine cotton or linen fabrics. Made today on more solid fabrics with thicker threads, they have come to know a rebirth.

The geometric working of these stitches offers a refined look to this embroidery, especially when one uses a spectrum of complementary colors.

THE STRIPED DAMASK STITCH IN 2 STEPS

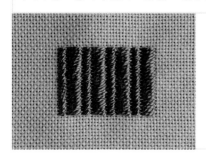

Level of Difficulty: Easy, accessible to beginners.

Threads and Fabrics: This stitch can be made on fabrics with a simple weave or on muslins, with cotton, linen, silk, or wool thread of Pearl, Cutwork and Embroidery, or stranded cotton floss varieties.

Direction: This stitch is worked vertically, from top to bottom.

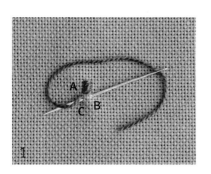

TIP

This stitch may be adapted in many ways. Work in different-sized stripes and take advantage of an assortment of colors.

The striped damask stitch is the simplest of the damask stitches. It is made up only of horizontal straight stitches which are parallel and of different lengths, to make a surface of raised stripes, with the final result looking like ribbed fabric.

STEP 1

The thin stripe is made over three threads of the weave. The stitches are situated on the straight of the goods with respect to the weave of the fabric. Bring the needle up in A, at the top of the motif to be made. Shift your needle three threads of the weave to the right and bring your needle down in B, directly to the right. Then bring it back up in C, directly below point A. Continue in this manner, making horizontal parallel stitches all the way down.

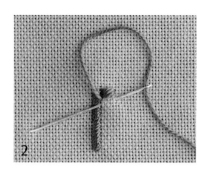

STEP 2

Begin the work at the top again. The large stripe is made over five threads of the weave. Proceed as before, from top to bottom, with horizontal parallel stitches. Continue the work by alternating a thin stripe with a thicker one.

THE DIAMOND DAMASK STITCH IN 3 STEPS

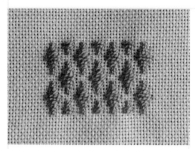

Level of Difficulty: Easy, accessible to beginners.

Threads and Fabrics: This stitch can be made on fabrics with a simple weave or on muslins, with cotton, linen, silk, or wool thread of Pearl, Cutwork and Embroidery, or stranded cotton floss varieties.

Direction: This stitch is worked horizontally, diamond by diamond and row by row, from top to bottom.

The diamond damask stitch almost entirely covers the surface of the fabric. Only two threads of the weave are left empty between the motifs to highlight the diamonds. The surface of the finished stitch, with its honeycomb pattern, looks like cotton pique fabric.

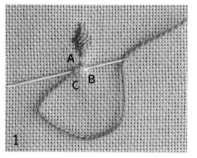
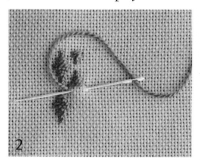

STEP 1

Each diamond is made up of ten horizontal straight stitches made over even numbers of threads of the weave. The stitches are situated on the straight of the goods with respect to the weave. Bring the needle up in A, at the top of the motif. Move your needle two threads of the weave to the right and bring it down in B. Bring it back up in C, directly below A, and make another horizontal straight stitch the same size as the first.

STEP 2

Shift one thread of the weave to the left and right of the first two stitches, and make two horizontal straight stitches of the same length over four threads of the weave. Continue in this manner, enlarging the straight stitches, then reducing them. Make ten straight stitches to form the diamond. Skip two threads of the weave to begin the next diamond, situated below the first.

TIP

The opposite side of the work is almost identical to the front. If you use a floss thread, be careful to allow the twist to return regularly so that the diamonds keep a smooth surface.

STEP 3

The next row is located to the right of the first, and the diamonds in this row are staggered between those in the first. Make the diamonds in the same way as before, skipping two threads of the weave between the two motifs. Make a half diamond on the top and bottom edges and a quarter diamond at the corners to make straight borders.

THE STAGGERED DAMASK STITCH IN 2 STEPS

Level of Difficulty: Easy, accessible to beginners.
Threads and Fabrics: This stitch can be made on fabrics with a simple weave or on muslins, with cotton, linen, silk, or wool thread of Pearl, Cutwork and Embroidery, or stranded cotton floss varieties.
Direction: This stitch is worked vertically in horizontal rows.

The beautiful geometry of the staggered damask stitch and its easiness to make mean that it is an ideal stitch for beginners. It would have the best effect worked tone on tone, in other words, the color of the thread should be the same as that of the fabric.

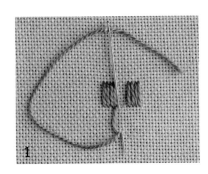

STEP 1

Begin at the top left with a group of four vertical straight stitches made over eight threads of the weave of fabric. Skip five threads to the right and repeat a new group of four vertical straight stitches. Form a second row of groups of four vertical stitches staggered with respect to the first.

STEP 2

Embroider three horizontal straight stitches in the spaces left open, skipping one thread of the weave after each stitch. In this manner, embroider all the empty spaces.

THE TRIANGLE DAMASK STITCH IN 2 STEPS

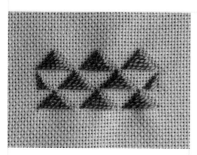

Level of Difficulty: Easy, accessible to beginners.

Threads and Fabrics: This stitch can be made on fabrics with a simple weave or on muslins, with cotton, linen, silk, or wool thread of Pearl, Cutwork and Embroidery, or stranded cotton floss varieties.

Direction: This stitch is worked horizontally, triangle by triangle and row by row.

TIP

Be sure to adapt the length of the stitches which form the triangle damask stitch based on the weave of the fabric and the thickness of the material. Avoid embroidering straight stitches that are so long they risk floating on the surface of the fabric.

In textiles, damask is a jacquard fabric with both matte and shiny surfaces. In embroidery, the triangle damask stitch, which imitates the perfection of damask fabrics, presents the appearance of raised and hollow areas which perfectly characterizes this family of stitches.

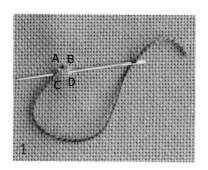 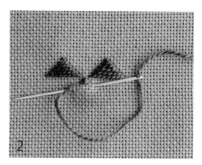

STEP 1

Each triangle is made up of horizontal, parallel straight stitches. The straight stitches are made over an even number of threads of the weave of fabric, and are situated on the straight of the goods with respect to the weave. Bring the needle up in A, at the top of the motif. Move the needle two threads of the weave to the right and bring it down in B. Bring it back up in C, one thread to the left of point A, and bring it down in D, moving one thread to the right of point B. Continue in this manner, enlarging the straight stitches. Each triangle is made up of six stitches.

STEP 2

Skip the equivalent of an upside-down triangle in the fabric between two embroidered triangles. To begin the next row, make a half triangle to align the borders of the stitches. The triangles in the second row are staggered with respect to those in the first row.

Repeat these two steps to work an embroidered background.

THE CHECKERBOARD DAMASK STITCH IN 2 STEPS

Level of Difficulty: Medium, for people who already have some experience.

Threads and Fabrics: This stitch can be made on fabrics with a simple weave or on muslins, with cotton, linen, silk, or wool thread of Pearl, Cutwork and Embroidery, or stranded cotton floss varieties.

Direction: This stitch is worked horizontally, in slanted rows.

TIP

When filling the squares, proceed from bottom to top and slanted to the left. This way, you will avoid threads hanging loose on the back of the embroidery. Straight stitches worked diagonally cover the fabric in a very dense fashion.

The checkerboard damask stitch is worked in two steps. The first step consists of creating a network of broken lines in the form of a stairway. Then, the spaces left open are filled with large straight stitches made on the opposite slant.

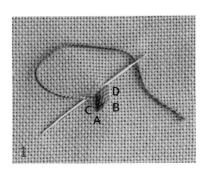
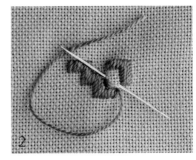

STEP 1

Form a stairway row with diagonal stitches over four threads of the weave of fabric. Each step of the stairs is made up of five slanted stitches. Bring the needle up in A, at the bottom, make the stitch slanting to the right, and bring the needle down in B. Bring the needle back up in C, above A, and back down in D. In this manner, make five points upwards, then, still following the same slant, make five stitches to the left. Continue to form the first stairway. Skip seven threads of the weave and form the second stairway, to the right of the first.

STEP 2

Re-stitching in the holes of the stitches which form the stairs, fill the spaces left empty. Make the slants in the opposite direction from the slants of the stairs.

The Lingerie Pouch

The refined nature of the fine linen fabric blends perfectly with the diamond motif for making little pouches and slipcovers for the home which are as functional as they are elegant. Easy to make, this pouch makes a beautiful holder for your most delicate lingerie.

OVERVIEW

Level of Difficulty:
Easy

Stitch Used:
Diamond damask stitch (see p. 150)

Finished Dimensions:
The finished pouch measures 12 x 9 inches.
The embroidered motif measures 8 x 2 inches.

MATERIALS

26 x 14 inches pale pink DMC fabric, size 7 mesh
1 skein of DMC Pearl cotton, art. 115, in each of the following colors: ecru (739) and yellow (744)
1 blunt-tipped tapestry needle
Embroidery hoop
Pins
Sewing thread to match the fabric
1 ecru frog closure

PREPARATION

By hand or with a sewing machine, whip stitch the edges of the fabric so that it does not unravel as you work.

With pins, mark the center of the motif, situated 4 inches from the edges of the rectangle.

EMBROIDERY

Stretch the material in the embroidery hoop.

Begin the work with the center square in yellow.

Make the framing diamonds in ecru.

Continue the embroidery with the squares situated on both sides of the central square motif.

Finish with the yellow squares along the ecru border and with the small yellow squares on the two ends.

Move the embroidery hoop as you finish each section and begin the next.

FINISHING TOUCHES

With an iron, make a first fold of ½ inch and then a second of ¾ inch on the long edges of the linen rectangle.

Baste and sew the hems.

On the short ends of the rectangle, make a first fold of ¾ inch and a second of 1 inch with an iron.

Baste and sew the hems.

ADVICE

Be careful with your finishing touches. Do not move from one motif to the next with the same thread, because the hanging end might be seen through the fine linen fabric. When you have finished embroidering a motif, fasten off the thread and cut it as close as possible to the surface of the fabric. Work the next motif with a new thread.

Fold the rectangle in three to make a 7½-inch flap at the top and an 8-inch base.

Pin the sides, then sew them together over the side stitch.

In the center of the flap, sew the top half of the frog closure, and on the bottom pocket, sew the bottom half.

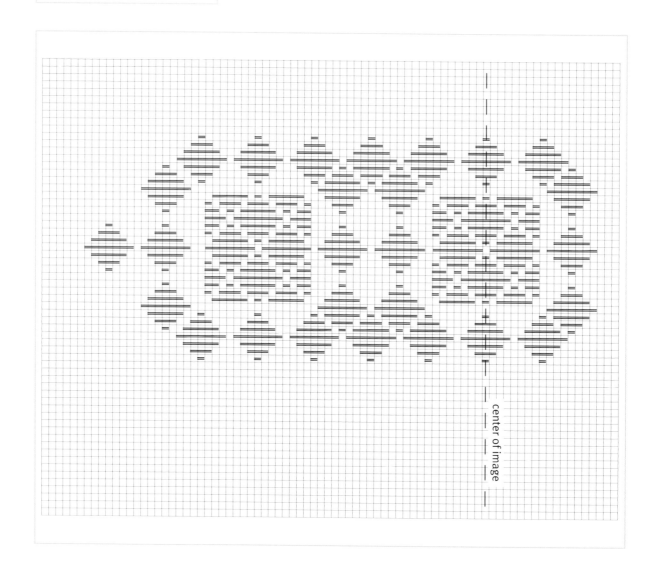

center of image

The Slavic Stitch Family

The filling stitches detailed in this chapter are most often of Eastern European origin. They can take on many fancy looks, but are often made as counted stitches on fabrics with an obvious weave. On these types of fabrics, the stitches offer a very uniform appearance.

THE KNOTTED SLAVIC STITCH IN 4 STEPS

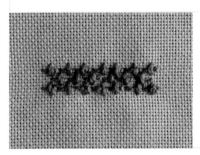

Level of Difficulty: Difficult, reserved for people who are experienced.

Threads and Fabrics: This stitch can be made on fabrics with a simple weave or on muslins, with cotton, wool, silk, or linen thread with twisted strands, such as Pearl.

Direction: This stitch is worked horizontally, from the right to the left.

Often used for embroidering clothing and household linens in western Slavic countries, the knotted Slavic stitch is a neat, raised stitch, ideal for highlighting the details in motifs.

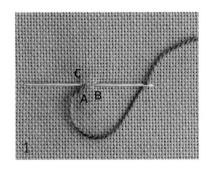

STEP 1

Bring your needle up in A and down in B, three threads of the weave to the right. Bring the needle back up in C, two threads to the left of A. Pull the thread and form the stitch.

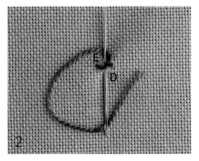

STEP 2

Slide the needle upwards under the first stitch, then bring it down in D, directly below the stitch, and bring the tip up vertically in E, directly above the stitch. Slide the thread behind the needle. Pull the thread to form a loop on the horizontal stitch.

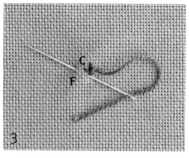

STEP 3

Bring the needle down in F, three threads of the weave to the left of point C, and begin again at step 1 to form the second stitch.

STEP 4

In this manner, work the entire row. To finish it, after having made the knot in step 2, bring the needle down into the fabric as close as possible to the knot.

TIP

This knot stitch worked on a straight cross will stand out even more if you embroider with a thick, twisted thread. Align the rows in a staggered fashion in order to cover the entire surface of the fabric.

THE BOSNIA STITCH IN 2 STEPS

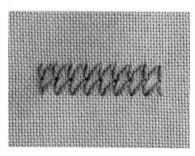

Level of Difficulty: Easy, accessible to beginners.
Threads and Fabrics: This stitch can be made on fabrics with a simple weave or on muslins, with cotton, wool, silk or linen thread with twisted strands, such as Pearl.
Direction: This stitch is worked horizontally in back and forth rows.

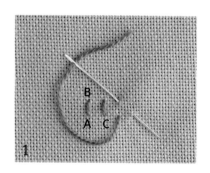

The Bosnia stitch is often used in the polychromatic embroideries of Bosnia, Dalmatia and Turkey, where it blends the cross-stitch with the line stitch to decorate the shawls and scarves of traditional women's clothing.

STEP 1

This stitch is made within a square of threads of the weave. The first row is made from left to right. Bring the needle up in A and down in B, five threads of the weave above A. Bring it back out in C, five threads of the weave to the right of A. Continue in this manner to form a line of vertical stitches.

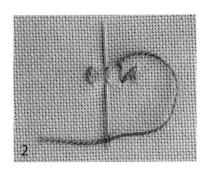

STEP 2

Return from right to left by stitching in the holes of the preceding row. Make slanted stitches working from top to bottom.

Start again at step 1 for the remaining rows. The rows should touch, and the vertical stitches are aligned on top of each other.

THE OKA STITCH IN 4 STEPS

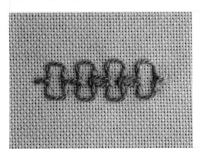

Level of Difficulty: Easy, accessible to beginners.
Threads and Fabrics: This stitch can be made on fabrics with a simple weave or on muslins, with cotton, wool, silk, or linen thread with twisted strands, such as Pearl.
Direction: This stitch is worked horizontally in back and forth rows.

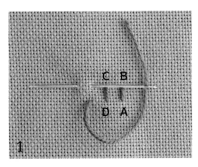

In many Slavic regions, the oka stitch is used in rustic embroidery to cover backgrounds. It takes its name from the Romanian word *oka*, which means "eye." Because it is easy to make, beginners love this stitch.

STEP 1

The first part of the first row is made from right to left. Bring the needle up in A and down in B, five threads of the weave above A. Bring the needle back up in C, five threads of the weave to the left of B. Bring the needle down in D, five threads of the weave below C. In this manner, make the entire row.

STEP 2

The second part of the row is made from left to right. Bring the needle up five threads to the left of the last stitch, on a line with the bottom of that stitch. Slide the needle under each of the vertical stitches in turn that form the first part of the row. Slide the needle upwards under one stitch and then downwards under the next stitch to obtain a line of crenels. End with a stitch to the right, in line with the bottom of the vertical stitches.

STEP 3

The second row is made below the first row of embroidery, stitching in the same holes. Place the vertical stitches of the second row directly below those in the first.

STEP 4

Begin the second step for the second row by bringing up the needle at the start of the side stitch made in step 2. Then work by sliding the needle downwards under the last vertical stitch. Continue the work by following step 2.

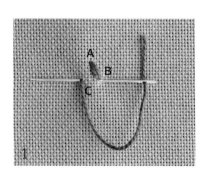

> **TIP**
>
> With its honeycomb look, the oka stitch is best suited to filling geometric shapes and for making borders. Used in cutwork embroidery, it brings much charm to a finished product.

THE TRIANGULAR TURKISH STITCH IN 4 STEPS

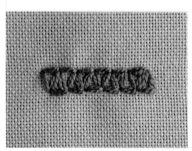

Level of Difficulty: Medium, for people who already have some experience.
Threads and Fabrics: This stitch can be made on fabrics with a simple weave or on muslins, with cotton, wool, silk, or linen thread with twisted strands, such as Pearl.
Direction: This stitch is worked horizontally or vertically.

Formed by triangles placed head to foot, the triangular Turkish stitch offers undeniable decorative qualities. It can be used to cover a foundation or to emphasize motifs, in which case it is used as a simple border.

STEP 1

Bring the needle up in A and down in B, diagonally to the right. Pull gently on the thread to form the stitch. Make the exact same stitch again. Then, bring the needle up in C, to the left of B, and bring it back down in B. Pull gently on the thread to form the stitch. Make the stitch again.

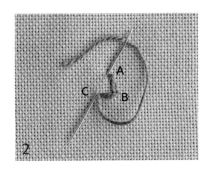

STEP 2

Bring the needle up in C and down in A to form the complete triangle. Make this stitch again. You have your first triangle made in double thickness.

STEP 3

Bring the needle up in D, to the left of point A. Bring the needle down in A and pull the thread to form the stitch. Make the stitch again.

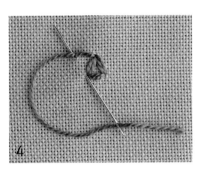

STEP 4

Bring the needle up in C and down in D to make the second triangle, then make the stitch again.

Start over at step 1 to continue working.

TIP

To make sure that the work is progressing well, verify that the back is the same as the front of the embroidery. Use a tightly twisted thread to make the triangular Turkish stitch stand out as much as possible.

You must stretch the fabric on a frame because the triangular Turkish stitch exerts a great deal of tension on the material, which therefore risks bunching up as you work the pattern.

The Tea Towel

More than a good opportunity to practice your counted stitch embroidery, this pattern made with the knotted Slavic stitch brings texture and originality to a simple linen tea towel. Its natural colors allow the work to find a home in all kitchens.

OVERVIEW

Level of Difficulty:
Medium

Stitch Used:
Knotted Slavic stitch (see p. 157)

Finished Dimensions:
The embroidered motif measures
3 x 2 inches.

MATERIALS

1 linen tea towel with obvious weave
1 skein of ecru (739) DMC Pearl cotton, art. 115
1 blunt-tipped tapestry needle
Embroidery hoop
Pins

PREPARATION

With pins, mark the center of the motif, situated in the center of the tea towel, 4 inches from the edge.

With long basting stitches, mark the edges of the pattern.

EMBROIDERY

Stretch the fabric in the embroidery hoop.

The diagram of counted stitches will guide you in making the pattern. Make one knot for each square indicated on the diagram.

Begin the work with the central stitch situated on the stem of the group of stylized flowers. Then make all the flowers and finish your work with the detail on the stems.

Move the embroidery hoop as you finish each section and begin the next.

When the embroidery is finished, remove the basting threads.

FINISHING TOUCHES

Press the work on the opposite side. If needed, starch it with spray starch.

ADVICE

The interesting thing about this stitch is its texture. It is important to use a round and twisted embroidery thread, such as size 5 Pearl cotton. Use this pattern on other items such as an apron, a linen tablecloth or place mats made of Aida muslin, which is the perfect fabric for working counted stitches.

The Looped Stitch Family

Created to imitate knotted tapestry stitches in embroidery techniques, looped stitches have a spectacular effect. They are used in making large works such as pillows, footstools or boxes, where the softness of the stitches is particularly highlighted. The motifs are generally very simple, and are worked in rows, squares, or patterns.

THE UNCUT TURKEY WORK STITCH IN 3 STEPS

Level of Difficulty: Difficult, for people who are experienced.
Threads and Fabrics: This stitch can be made on fabrics with a simple weave or on muslins, with cotton, wool, silk, or linen floss type thread.
Direction: This stitch is worked horizontally from left to right.

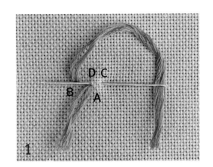

Although the uncut Turkey work stitch is made in the same way as the Malta stitch (see p. 166), it presents a different finish because its loops are not cut. Worked over a template such as a knitting needle or pencil, the loops will be all the same size.

STEP 1

Use doubled floss thread so that you have twelve strands. Bring your needle down in A, leaving ³⁄₄–1¹⁄₄ inches of thread hanging on the front of the work. Bring the needle up in B, a few threads of the weave to the left of A. Bring the needle down in C, a few threads to the right of A, and bring the tip of the needle back up in D, right next to A. As you pull gently on the thread to make the horizontal stitch, make sure that the working end of the thread is above the needle.

165

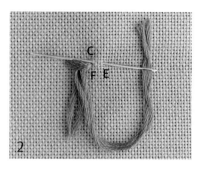

STEP 2

Bring the needle down in E, a few threads of the weave to the right, and back up in F, next to C. The working end of the thread should be below the needle. Pull the loop and, if necessary, slip it around a knitting needle to give it a standard length.

STEP 3

Make the remaining stitches by beginning again at step 1. Finish the row and leave the end of the thread hanging on the front of the work.

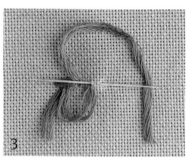

Cut the ends of the two hanging threads so that they are level with the loops.

If you run out of thread in the course of a row, fasten off the hanging end under the last loop. Begin a new thread and hide the hanging end under the next loop.

THE MALTA STITCH IN 2 STEPS

Level of Difficulty: Difficult, reserved for people who are experienced.

Threads and Fabrics: This stitch can be made on fabrics with a simple weave or on muslins, with cotton, wool, silk, or linen floss type thread.

Direction: This stitch is worked horizontally from left to right.

Originating in Asian countries, the Malta stitch is found on works from this region. It is made up of a knotted strand of thread that forms the tuft. Motifs embroidered with this stitch resemble knotted stitch tapestries.

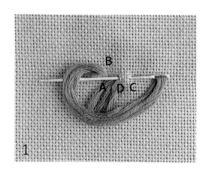

STEP 1

Use four cotton floss threads so that you have 24 strands. Bring your needle down in A, leaving ¾–1¼ inches of thread hanging on the front of the work. Bring the needle up in B, a few threads of the weave to the left of A. Bring the needle back down in C, to the left of A, and bring the tip up in D, right next to A. Place the

TIP

Malta stitch embroidery is always made from bottom to top so that the tufts of the working row are slightly staggered in relation to the tufts of the preceding row.

working end of the thread over the tip of the needle and pull gently on the thread to form a horizontal stitch.

STEP 2

Cut the threads to form the tuft.

A bit further away, make another Malta stitch.

THE POMPON STITCH IN 2 STEPS

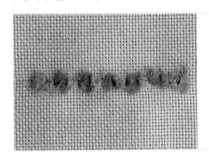

Level of Difficulty: Easy, accessible to beginners.

Threads and Fabrics: This stitch can be made on fabrics with a simple weave or on muslins, with cotton, wool, silk, or linen floss type thread.

Direction: This stitch is worked horizontally from right to left.

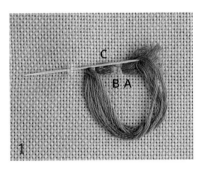

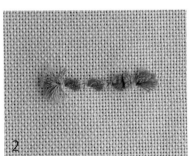

Very easy to make, this stitch is, however, not very stable. It is often used for little finishing touches in Maltese embroidery, where it highlights details, and it sometimes serves to underline a border of embroidered Malta stitches.

STEP 1

Use four cotton floss threads so that you have a total of twenty-four strands. Begin at the right of the line to be worked. Bring the needle down in A, leaving a small amount of thread hanging on the front of the work. Bring your needle up in B, to the left and not far from A, and then back down in C, 1 or 2 threads of the weave to the left of point B. Pull gently on the thread.

Proceed in this manner for the entire row.

STEP 2

With a pair of fine-tipped scissors, cut the center of the stitches in order to form little pompons.

THE ASTRAKAN STITCH IN 4 STEPS

Level of Difficulty: Difficult, reserved for people who are experienced.

Threads and Fabrics: This stitch can be made on fabrics with a simple weave or on muslins, with Pearl, stranded cotton floss, or cotton matte thread.

Direction: This stitch is worked horizontally, from left to right, beginning with the lowest row.

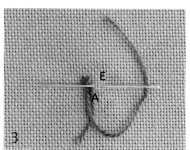

In the Astrakan stitch, also known as the "velvet stitch," the structure of the loop is supported on a cross stitch, which gives stability to the work. Depending on the desired results, the loops of this stitch can vary in length.

STEP 1

Bring your needle down in A, leaving the hanging end of the thread on the front of the fabric. Bring the needle up in B, to the left of point A. Then bring the needle back down in C, above point A, and up in D, above B.

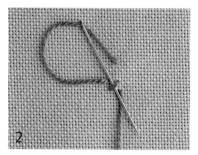

STEP 2

Slide the needle downwards and to the right under the half cross-stitch you just made.

STEP 3

Bring your needle down in E, a few threads of the weave to the right of point A. Bring the tip of the needle up in point A and pull gently to form the loop.

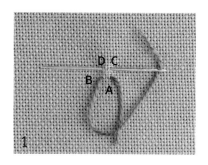

STEP 4

Bring your needle down in F, a few threads of the weave to the right of C, and bring the needle back up in C. Pull gently to form a half cross-stitch.

Begin the work again at step 2 and finish the row. The next row is situated above the first.

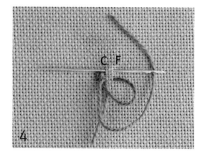

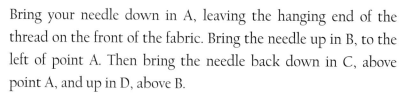

TIP

To obtain same-sized loops, use a template such as a knitting needle or a pencil in step 3.

THE RYA STITCH IN 4 STEPS

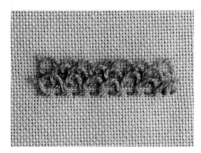

Level of Difficulty: Difficult, for people who are experienced.

Threads and Fabrics: This stitch can be made on fabrics with a simple weave or on muslins, with Pearl, stranded cotton floss, or cotton matte thread.

Direction: This stitch is worked horizontally, from left to right and beginning with the top row.

Imitating knotted tapestry, the Rya stitch presents a collection of small loops, all directed upwards.

STEP 1

Bring your needle down in A, leaving the hanging end of the thread on the front of the work. Bring the needle up in B, to the left of point A, and then bring it down in C, on the other side of A. Bring the needle back up in A. Pull thread through to make a horizontal stitch.

STEP 2

Bring the needle down in D, four threads of the weave to the right of C. Form a loop above the needle and bring the needle back up in C.

STEP 3

Continue the work by repeating steps 1 and 2. The backstitches which form the base of the loops must be the same length and worked over the same number of threads of the weave.

STEP 4

Make the next row beginning again on the left and working towards the right, staggering the loops between the loops of the first row.

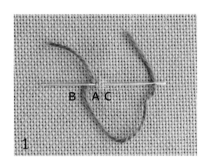
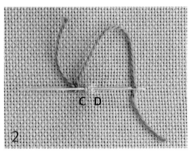
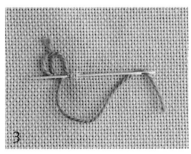

TIP

Keep your loops small so that you do not need a template to make them. Use the threads of the weave as a guide for the first row, and for the remaining rows, adopt the principle of covering half of the preceding row.

The Box Top

This box top in spring colors is a very original application of the loop stitch, which is voluminous and refined worked with cotton floss. It makes a stunning cover for a jewelry box or sewing case.

OVERVIEW

Level of Difficulty:
Easy

Stitch Used:
Uncut Turkey Work Stitch
(see p. 165)

Finished Dimensions:
The box measures 7 x 5 x 3 inches.
The embroidered motif measures
3½ x 2 inches.

MATERIALS

16 x 16 inches pale turquoise DMC
fabric, size 7 mesh
1 skein of DMC cotton floss,
art. 117, in each of the following
colors: light blue (3841), lavender
blue (340) and pale green (369)
1 7 x 5 x 3 inch cardboard box
1 blunt-tipped tapestry needle
1 #8 or #10 knitting needle
Embroidery hoop
16 inches lavender blue ½-inch
wide grosgrain ribbon
Pins
Fabric glue or spray adhesive

PREPARATION

Cut a rectangle of fabric measuring 8 x 6 inches.

By hand or with a sewing machine, whip stitch the edges of the fabric so that it does not unravel as you work. With pins, mark the center of the fabric and the area of the surface to be covered with the uncut Turkey work stitch, a 3½ x 2 inch rectangle.

EMBROIDERY

Stretch the material in the embroidery hoop.

Work with 12 strands of floss, in other words, double the thread.

Begin the work with the bottom row stitched in light blue, embroidering from left to right. Make the loop stitches around the knitting needle. You will make about twelve stitches to cover 3½ inches of fabric. When finished, make the next row in pale green. Then add the next row in lavender blue, then a pale green and then finish with light blue.

FINISHING TOUCHES

Press the work on the wrong side. Cover the top of the box with the embroidered fabric. Place the glue on the edges of the fabric on the inside of the box and hold them in place with pins as the glue dries. Cover the bottom of the box with fabric and glue the grosgrain ribbon around the edge of the lid.

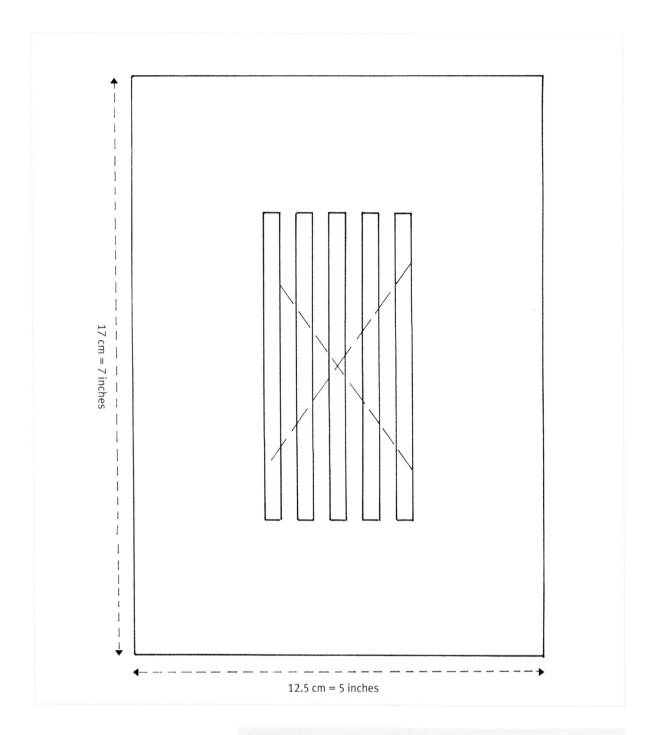

17 cm = 7 inches

12.5 cm = 5 inches

ADVICE

The uncut Turkey work stitches are very solid. To obtain a beautiful effect, use a thick embroidery thread and double or triple it. It is also important to stretch the fabric in a frame that is large enough so that you do not need to move it as you work. The thickness of the stitch will prevent you from stretching the fabric if it has to be moved as you work.

The name "cutwork embroidery" encompasses a great many stitches which are essentially drawn-thread work. Embroidery of this type presents a subtle and refined finish made of solid and empty spaces, gaps and voluminous fillings.

Each family—Madeira embroidery, cutwork embroidery, Hardanger or openwork embroidery, or drawn-thread work—has developed from different techniques to produce an array of stitches with complex designs which, made with finesse, combine lace stitches with needlework.

To obtain interesting contrasts, this embroidery is worked with rounded threads, which naturally give volume to motifs. A padding made up of floss thread is sometimes added for even more volume. Many stitches require preparatory work consisting of removing threads of the weave from certain areas of the surface of the fabric, or even cutting out motifs after filling them with embroidery stitches. The beautiful finish of our grandmothers' works requires only a bit of patience.

5

DRAWN-THREAD WORK STITCHES

The Madeira Embroidery Family

Madeira embroidery is a very old technique of embroidery on a fine white cloth. During the Renaissance, embroiderers combined it with needlework lace or embroidered netting motifs. It allows you to become familiar with the basic stitches of cutwork embroidery.

THE STEM STITCH OVER A BACKSTITCH IN 2 STEPS

Level of Difficulty: Easy, accessible to beginners.

Threads and Fabrics: This stitch can be made on cotton or linen fabrics (broadcloth, batiste, organdy), with round threads such as Cutwork and Embroidery thread, to which are added floss threads to give volume to the shapes.

Direction: The first step is worked in horizontal rows, from the right to the left, and the second in horizontal rows from the left to the right.

Offering more depth than the traditional stem stitch, the stem stitch over a backstitch is often used in cutwork embroidery to highlight fine details or to bring out certain motifs.

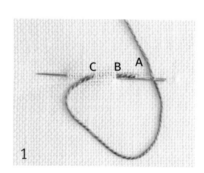

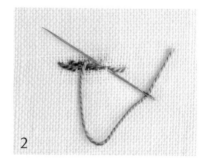

STEP 1

Bring your needle up in A, to the right of the tracing, and bring it back down in B, on the tracing, a few threads of the weave to the left, making a long horizontal stitch. Bring the tip of the needle up in C, a few threads of the weave away from B, and bring it back down in B. Continue the row in this manner, making large backstitches (see p. 25).

STEP 2

Bring the needle up on the left above the row of backstitches.

TIP

As you are working the stem stitch, the thread, which is very twisted, has a tendency to lose its twist. Therefore, in the course of your embroidery, make sure to let the needle hang so the thread recovers its twist on its own. Like a lead weight, the needle will cause the thread to return to its original twist.

Stitch a few threads of the weave to the right and bring the tip of the needle down below the row of backstitches in the middle of the first stitch. Direct the working end of the thread downwards. Make a second stitch to the right by re-stitching in the hole of the backstitch.

Continue in this manner for the remaining stitches. The backstitch from the first step is entirely covered.

THE STRAIGHT OVERCAST STITCH IN 2 STEPS

Level of Difficulty: Easy, accessible to beginners.

Threads and Fabrics: This stitch can be made on cotton or linen fabrics (broadcloth, batiste, organdy), with round threads such as Cutwork and Embroidery thread, to which are added floss threads to give volume to the shapes.

Direction: The first step is worked in horizontal rows, from the right to the left, and the second in horizontal rows from the left to the right.

The staff stitch and the straight overcast are one and the same. Depending upon who writes the directions in a cutwork embroidery pattern, this stitch can appear under either of its names.

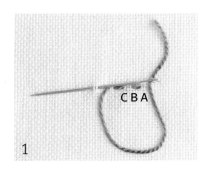 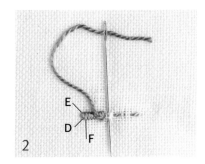

STEP 1

Make a row of running stitches (see p. 130). Bring the needle up in A, on the right, and down in B, a few threads of the weave to the left. Bring the tip of the needle up in C, making sure that the distance between B and C is the same as the distance between A and B.

STEP 2

Embroider a row of satin stitches (see p. 98) over the running stitches. Bring the needle up in D, on the left below the row of running stitches. Bring the needle down in E, vertical with D and over the row of running stitches. Bring the tip of the needle back up in F, level with and right next to D. As you work this row, the working end of the thread is always on the left.

THE SELF-PADDED SATIN STITCH IN 4 STEPS

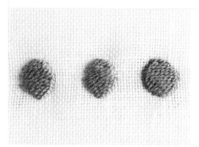

Level of Difficulty: Medium, for people who already have some experience.
Threads and Fabrics: This stitch can be made on cotton or linen fabrics (broadcloth, batiste, organdy), with round threads such as Cutwork and Embroidery thread or cotton Pearl, to which are added floss threads to give volume to the shapes.
Direction: This stitch is worked in all directions, as determined by the motif.

The self-padded satin stitch is used for working monograms or initials on household linens. It is made over a preparatory work called a "self padding." The denser the padding, the more voluminous your motif will be.

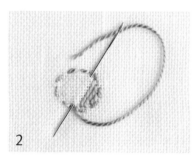

STEP 1

Make a row of running stitches (see p. 130) over the tracing of the shape.

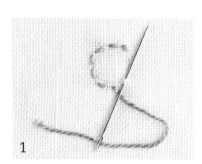

STEP 2

Inside the shape framed with running stitches, fill the surface with large slanted straight stitches (see p. 97). The stitches may be slightly spaced apart.

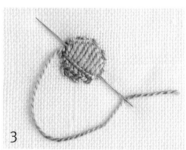

STEP 3

Make a second layer of straight stitches slanting in the opposite direction, still inside the shaped framed by the running stitches. Continue to embroider the layers of slanted stitches until you have the desired amount of padding, making sure your stitches always cross perpendicularly.

STEP 4

Take a new needle and proceed in covering the "self padding" of the shape. With large satin stitches (see p. 98) stitched very closely against each other, horizontally or vertically, embroider over the shape surrounded by running stitches.

THE OVERCAST EYELET STITCH IN 3 STEPS

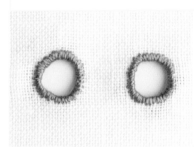

Level of Difficulty: Difficult, reserved for those who are experienced.

Threads and Fabrics: This stitch can be made on cotton or linen fabrics (broadcloth, batiste, organdy), with round threads such as Cutwork and Embroidery thread or cotton Pearl, to which are added floss threads to give volume to the shapes.

Direction: This stitch is worked based on the motif, in all directions.

One of the main principles of Madeira embroidery consists of making uniform hollowed-out motifs. We use the eyelet stitch to embroider cutouts whose edges are folded to the back of the fabric as you make the motif.

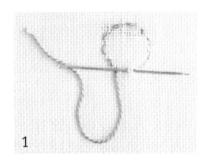

STEP 1

Make a row of running stitches (see p. 130) on the tracing of the shape.

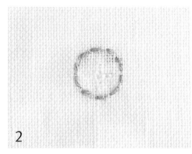

STEP 2

Cut the fabric on the inside of the shape framed by running stitches. Use fine, pointed embroidery scissors to make notches from the center of the motif towards the frame of running stitches.

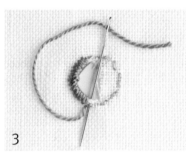

STEP 3

On the tracing of running stitches, make a row of straight overcast stitches (see p. 175), proceeding from left to right. As you continue the embroidery, fold the cut fabric to the back of the work. The cut material will be held in place on the back of the work by the overcast stitches.

TIP

The eyelet can take many different forms. This is often the case when making floral motifs. The center of the flower is open, and the shape comes from the petals. In this case, make the shape of the center of the flower with running stitches and then proceed with the petals using the self-padded stitch (see p. 176), finally covering them with satin stitches (see p. 98).

The Handkerchief

Fine batiste and small self-padded satin stitches pair their refinement to decorate the corner of this gorgeous handkerchief. The chosen floral motif, a delicate example of Madeira embroidery, also works well for a place mat or light sheer curtains.

OVERVIEW

Level of Difficulty:
Medium

Stitches Used:
Stem stitch over a backstitch
(see p. 174)
Self-padded satin stitch
(see p. 176)
Overcast eyelet stitch (see p. 177)
Knot stitch (see p. 74)
Blanket stitch (optional)
(see p. 181)

Finished Dimensions:
The finished handkerchief measures 9½ x 9½ inches. The embroidered corner motif measures 2 x 2 inches.

MATERIALS

11 x 11 inches white batiste fabric
1 skein of white #25 DMC Cutwork and Embroidery cotton, art. 107
1 skein of white DMC cotton floss, art. 17
1 fine-tipped embroidery needle
4-inch diameter embroidery hoop
Black hard lead pencil
Pins

PATTERN

Place the motif to trace under the batiste. Allow 1 ¼ inches of fabric around the corner to be worked, and then pin the fabric and the paper.

Using a sharp black pencil, trace the motif.

EMBROIDERY

Stretch the fabric in the embroidery hoop.

Thread one strand of floss and begin the preparatory work for the self-padded satin stitch on the leaves, as well as the preparatory work for the stem stitch over a backstitch and the eyelet stitch for the flowers.

Use the Cutwork and Embroidery thread to work the satin stitch of the leaves, the stem stitch, and the eyelet stitches for the flowers.

Finish the work with the knot stitches.

FINISHING TOUCHES

Embroidered finish: 1 ¼ inches from the edge of the fabric, trace the border design and embroider it with the blanket stitch. Once the shape is complete, trim the fabric as close to the blanket stitch as possible.

Quick finish: make a thin rolled hem. For this, cut the fabric so that you have a 9-inch square. Make a small roll between your thumb and index finger and sew it with small slip stitches.

ADVICE

The centers of the flowers, made of a fancy-shaped eyelet stitch, may be hollowed out as we described in the eyelet stitch earlier in the chapter. However, with a light batiste and a very fine motif, we do not recommend cutting the centers of the flowers. If the stitches on the petals are done well, the effect of depth on its own will give the impression of a cutout.

The Cutwork Embroidery Family

More complex than Madeira embroidery, cutwork embroidery also presents open areas of fabric bordered by embroidered stitches. With this family of stitches, it is possible to obtain large, irregularly shaped gaps because the borders of the fabric are kept in place by the bars. These little "bridges" of embroidered threads prevent the cut material from gaping, while bringing a supplementary element of decoration.

THE SIMPLE BLANKET STITCH IN 2 STEPS

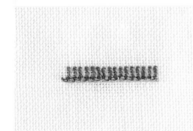

Level of Difficulty: Easy, accessible to beginners.

Threads and Fabrics: This stitch can be made on cotton or linen fabrics (broadcloth, batiste, organdy), with round threads such as Cutwork and Embroidery thread, to which are added floss threads to give volume to the shapes.

Direction: This stitch is worked in horizontal rows, from left to right.

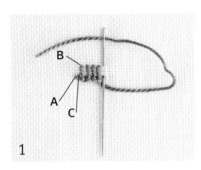

1

The blanket stitch is particularly well suited to working borders. Made of open parallel loops, it effectively maintains the threads of fabric borders and prevents fraying.

STEP 1

Bring the needle up in A, to the left of the tracing, and down in B, a few threads of the weave above A. Bring the tip of the needle up in C, next to A. Slide the thread under the needle and pull gently to form the first stitch. Continue in this manner for the entire row.

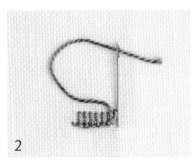

2

STEP 2

Finish the row by making a small stitch at the base of the blanket stitch in order to keep the thread against the fabric.

THE BUTTONHOLE STITCH IN 2 STEPS

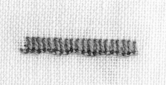

Level of Difficulty: Easy, accessible to beginners.

Threads and Fabrics: This stitch can be made on cotton or linen fabrics (broadcloth, percale, gabardine, batiste, organdy or lawn), with round threads such as Cutwork and Embroidery thread or cotton Pearl, to which are added floss threads to give volume to the shapes.

Direction: The first step is worked in horizontal rows, from the right to the left, and the second also in horizontal rows, but from the left to the right.

The buttonhole stitch has the same uses as the blanket stitch. It offers, however, a more voluminous appearance, which makes it perfect for working the edges of cutwork embroidery having large pointed or rounded corners.

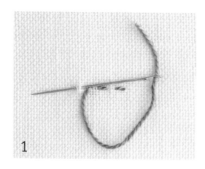
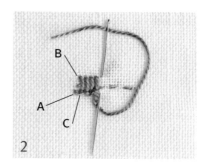

STEP 1

Make a horizontal row of running stitches (see p. 130), proceeding from right to left.

STEP 2

Bring the needle up in A, on the left of the tracing and below the row of running stitches, and bring it down in B, a few threads of the weave above A. Bring the tip of the needle up in C, next to A. Slide the thread under the needle and pull gently to form the first stitch. Continue the row in this manner, entirely covering the row of running stitches.

> **TIP**
>
> The buttonhole stitch that borders the edges of motifs in cutwork embroidery must be thin and uniform. They should measure between $1/8$ and $1/4$ inches in height, a dimension that has evolved based on the size of the thread used and the thickness of the fabric. Pull gently on the thread when you form the buttonhole stitch—if the thread is too tense, it will fold the fabric, and if it is too loose, the stitch looks very irregular.

THE OVERCAST BAR STITCH IN 4 STEPS

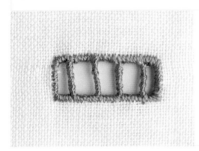

Level of Difficulty: Difficult, reserved for those who are experienced.

Threads and Fabrics: This stitch can be made on cotton or linen fabrics (broadcloth, percale, or gabardine), with round threads such as Cutwork and Embroidery thread, to which are added floss threads to give volume to the shapes.

Direction: This stitch is worked according to the shape of the motif.

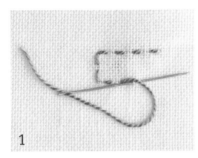

The overcast bar stitch is also found under the name "drawn-thread ladder stitch." A great classic of drawn-thread embroidery, the overcast bar stitch often borders the edge of linen or linen blend bed sheets. It is used in working geometric shapes, and allows you to join the edges of a motif with cut out shapes in a uniform way.

STEP 1

Surround the motif to be worked with running stitches (see p. 130). Proceed from the right to the left.

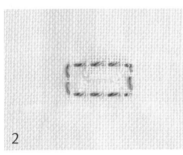

STEP 2

Using thin, sharp embroidery scissors, cut the fabric horizontally, then diagonally to the corners, inside the shape of the motif to be worked.

STEP 3

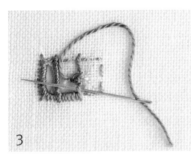

On the running stitch tracing, make a row of straight overcast stitches (see p. 175), proceeding from left to right. As you work, fold the cut fabric to the back and hold it in place with the overcast stitches. Make a bar to the opposite side by stitching the needle in the fabric, and then cover this bar by wrapping thread around it.

STEP 4

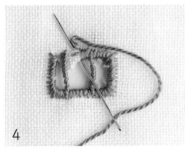

Finish the work with overcast stitches on the third and fourth sides of the motif to be embroidered.

THE BLANKET BAR STITCH IN 4 STEPS

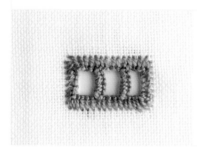

Level of Difficulty: Difficult, reserved for those who are experienced.
Threads and Fabrics: This stitch can be made on cotton or linen fabrics (broadcloth, batiste, organdy), with round threads such as Cutwork and Embroidery thread or cotton Pearl, to which are added floss threads to give volume to the shapes.
Direction: The first step is worked in horizontal rows, from the right to the left, and the second in horizontal rows from the left to the right.

The blanket bar stitch is very popular in cutwork embroidery techniques because the blanket stitch makes the shapes homogenous. The blanket stitches which decorate the bars of a work must be made in the same direction.

STEP 1

Surround the motif with running stitches (see p. 130). Proceed from right to left.

STEP 2

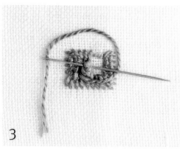

Frame the three sides of the motif with the blanket stitch (see p. 181), directing the loops of the stitches to the inside of the motif. In the middle of the fourth side, make a bar to the opposite side by bringing your needle down into the stitches without catching the fabric. Return to the base of the bar, which is made up of one thread.

STEP 3

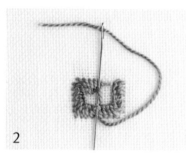

Cover the bar, without catching the fabric, with the blanket stitch. Attach the final blanket stitch to the base of the row with a small straight stitch, then finish the fourth side with the blanket stitch.

STEP 4

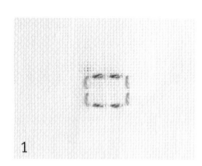

Using fine, sharp embroidery scissors, cut the fabric inside the motif. Be careful to pass the blade of the scissors under the bar so not to cut it.

THE PICOT BAR STITCH IN 5 STEPS

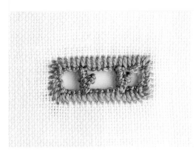

Level of Difficulty: Difficult, reserved for those who are experienced.
Threads and Fabrics: This stitch can be made on cotton or linen fabrics (broadcloth, percale, or gabardine), with round threads such as Cutwork and Embroidery thread or cotton Pearl, to which are added floss threads to give volume to the shapes.
Direction: This stitch is worked following the shape of the motif.

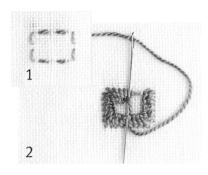

The small knots, called "picots," dot the bars of this openwork pattern. These decorations are also found in other types of bar embroidery, such as Venetian embroidery or Danish Hedebo embroidery.

STEP 1

Surround the motif with running stitches (see p. 130). Proceed from right to left.

STEP 2

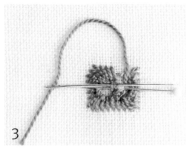

Surround three sides of the motif with the blanket stitch (see p. 181), directing the loops of the stitches to the inside of the motif. In the middle of the fourth side, make a bar to the opposite side by bringing your needle down into the stitches without catching the fabric. Return to the base of the bar, which is made up of one thread.

STEP 3

Cover the bar, without catching the fabric, with the blanket stitch. Stick a pin perpendicularly in the center of the bar. Slide the needle upward under the pin, then re-stitch across the bar.

STEP 4

Slide the needle once more under the pin and continue the work with the blanket stitch to the other end of the bar.

STEP 5

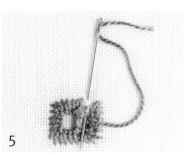

Finish the fourth side with the blanket stitch before cutting the fabric on the inside of the embroidered shape.

The Table Runner

The theme of ivy leaves gracefully renews the technique of cutwork embroidery. The elongated form of the table runner is perfectly suited to this refined work. The delicacy of this embroidery resides especially in using a fine embroidery thread and working tone-on-tone.

OVERVIEW

Level of Difficulty:
Difficult and time-consuming to make.

Stitches Used:
Blanket bar stitch (see p. 184)
Simple blanket stitch (see p. 181)
Stem stitch (see p. 22)
Self-padded satin stitch
(see p. 176)

Finished Dimensions:
The finished table runner measures 55 x 22 inches. The embroidered motif measures 20 x 8 inches.

MATERIALS

60 x 22 inches fine white linen fabric
3 skeins of white #25 DMC Cutwork and Embroidery cotton, art. 107
1 fine-tipped embroidery needle
4-inch diameter embroidery hoop
Black hard lead pencil
Pins

PATTERN

Using pins, mark the center of the rectangle of fabric. Place the motif to trace under the fabric. Match the center of the fabric with the center of the motif, and then pin the fabric and the paper.

Using a sharp black pencil, trace the motif.

EMBROIDERY

Stretch the material in the embroidery hoop.

Begin the work with the simple blanket stitch to embroider the ivy leaves. After making the border, embroider the blanket bar stitches in the places indicated on the diagram. Once the work is finished, carefully cut out the shapes.

With the same strand of Cutwork and Embroidery thread, prepare a padding for the motifs made with the self-padded satin stitch, namely the branches and the ivy berries. Embroider the satin stitch following the directions indicated on the diagram.

Finish the work with the veins in the leaves using the stem stitch.

FINISHING TOUCHES

With an iron, make a ¾-inch fold on the edges of the fabric. Pin, then make a 1-inch fold. Topstitch the hems ¾ inch from the edge. Steam press the work.

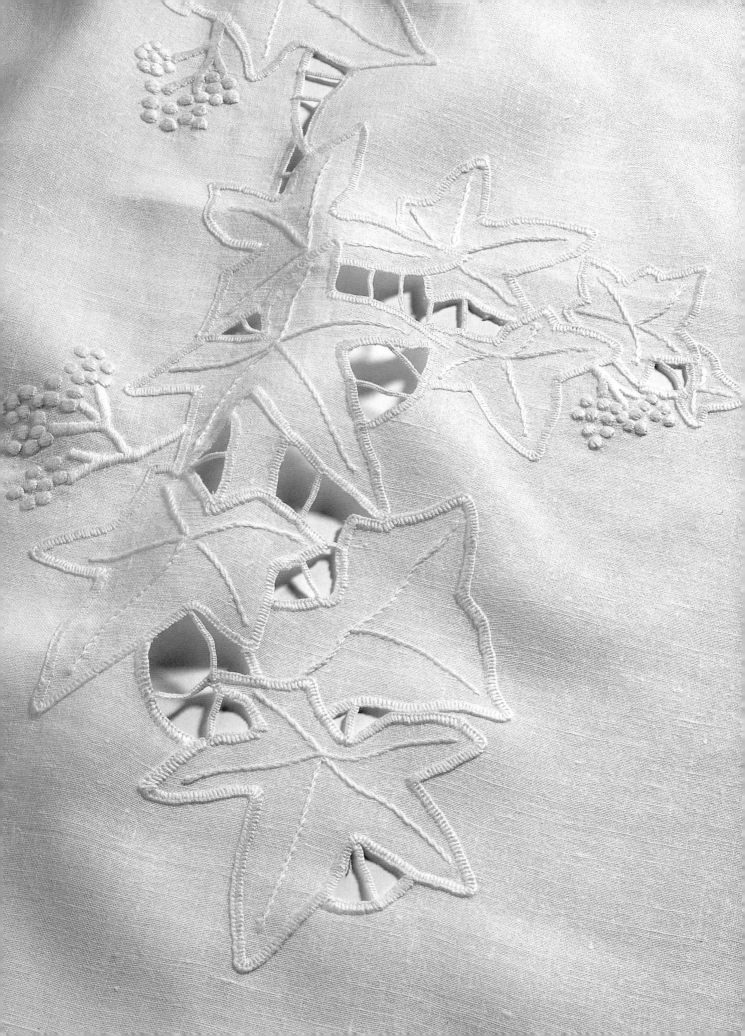

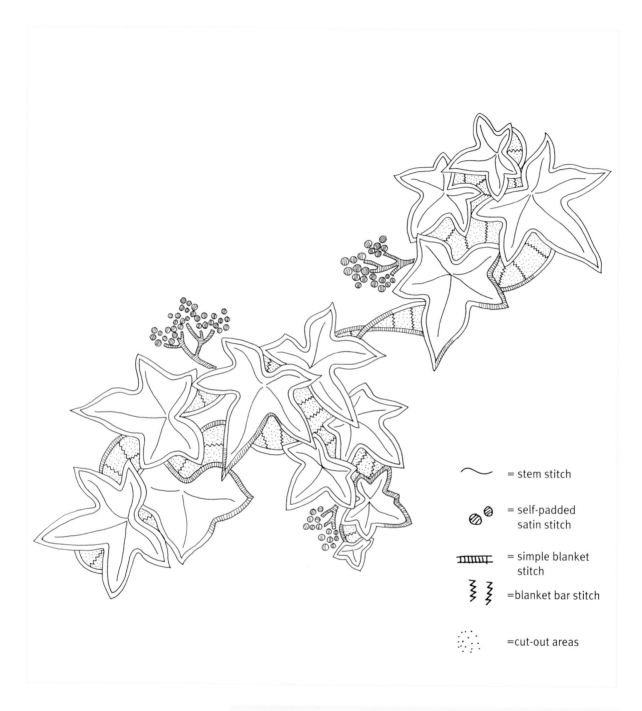

~ = stem stitch

⊘⊘ = self-padded satin stitch

▥▥▥▥ = simple blanket stitch

ʒ ʒ = blanket bar stitch

⋰⋱ = cut-out areas

ADVICE

Iron the work before you begin the cut-outs. The simple blanket stitches, which are still loose, will better adhere to the fabric. Cutting out the motifs should be done on the right side of the work with fine, sharp embroidery scissors. Use an embroidery hoop so that you do not cut the embroidery threads. If some loose threads of the fabric remain in the blanket stitches, turn the work over and cut these strands.

The Hardanger Embroidery Family

Hardanger embroidery comes from the region of Norway by the same name. This embroidery technique consists of bordering motifs with counted satin stitches using a thick cotton thread. The threads of the weave are trimmed as you finish the work. The cut threads are then drawn out to leave an open grid look, which is embroidered, bar by bar, with a thinner thread. These steps are the basis of many different embroidery stitches.

THE KLOSTER BLOCK BORDER STITCH IN 2 STEPS

Level of Difficulty: Easy, accessible to beginners.
Threads and Fabrics: This stitch can be made on cotton or linen fabrics with a simple and obvious weave, with round threads such as size 12 Cutwork and Embroidery thread or size 5 cotton Pearl.
Direction: This stitch is worked following the shape of the motif.

TIP

The principle of Hardanger embroidery consists of making a border with groups of uneven numbers of stitches (3, 5, or 7). On the other hand, the stitches are always made over an even number of threads of the weave (4, 6, or 8).

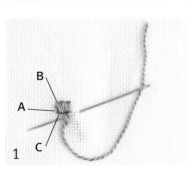

The Kloster block border stitch is the basic step of Hardanger embroidery. Worked in counted stitches, it is perfect for entirely surrounding a motif. It allows you to avoid unsightly unraveling when you cut the threads of the weave, and it maintains the edges of the fabric.

STEP 1

The Hardanger Kloster block border is made with the satin stitch (see p. 98), making a filling in a clockwise direction, starting at the top. Bring the needle up in A, skip four threads of the weave, and bring it down in B, above A. Bring the tip of the needle up in C, next to A, leaving only one thread of the weave between A and C. Make a group of five vertical satin stitches.

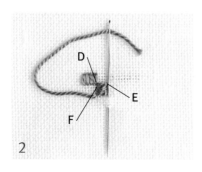

STEP 2

In the next group, the stitches are horizontal. Bring the needle up in D, in the same hole as the last stitch in the preceding group of vertical stitches, skip four threads of the weave, and bring it down in E. Bring the needle up in F, below D, leaving only one thread of the weave between F and D. Make a group of five horizontal satin stitches.

Continue the border by alternating groups of vertical stitches and groups of horizontal stitches.

THE CHEVRON BORDER STITCH IN 2 STEPS

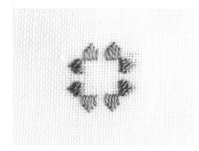

Level of Difficulty: Easy, accessible to beginners.

Threads and Fabrics: This stitch can be made on cotton or linen fabrics with a simple and obvious weave, with round threads such as size 12 Cutwork and Embroidery thread or size 5 cotton Pearl.

Direction: This stitch is worked following the shape of the motif.

TIP

On the back of the work you should see groups of five slightly slanted stitches. There should not be threads floating from one group of stitches to the next because they may be visible once you open up the work.

Like the Kloster block border stitch, the chevron border stitch must integrally surround the motif. The satin stitch is also used. The fact that the stitches are of different lengths makes this Hardanger stitch a bit fancier.

STEP 1

The border is made up of satin stitches (see p. 98), making the filling in a clockwise direction, starting at the upper right. Bring the needle up in A, skip four threads of the weave and bring it down in B, above A. Bring the tip of the needle up in C, one thread of the weave to the right of A. The first satin stitch was made over four threads of the weave, the second is made over five, the third is made over six, the fourth is made over five, and the final stitch is made over four. Make a group of vertical satin stitches.

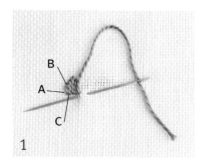

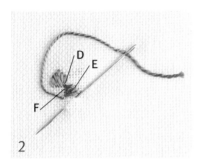

STEP 2

In the next group, the stitches are horizontal. Bring the needle up in D, in the same hole as the last stitch in the preceding group of vertical stitches, skip four threads of the weave, and bring it down in E. Bring the needle up in F, below D, leaving just one thread of the weave between F and D. Make a group of five horizontal satin stitches, regularly alternating the length of the stitches.

Continue the border by working groups of horizontal stitches at the sides of the motif and groups of vertical ones at top and bottom.

OPENING THE WORK IN 2 STEPS

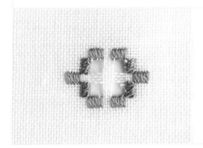

Level of Difficulty: Medium, requires precision, for people who have some experience.

Tools: Fine, sharp embroidery scissors, a pin for pulling the cut threads.

Direction: This stitch is worked following the shape of the motif.

TIP

To see your work better as you cut the threads of the weave, proceed in this fashion: for right-handed people, the group of five stitches should be situated to the right of the tip of the scissors, and for left-handed people, it should be to the left of the scissors. Working in this way, your field of vision is not hidden by your hand.

Opening the work is done when the motif is entirely surrounded by groups of satin stitches.

This step consists of cutting the threads marked out on the inside of the motif and held in place by the five satin stitches. Remove them in order to form a grid, which is then embroidered in the third step.

STEP 1

The work must always be stretched in a hoop. Hold the fabric face up and work vertically. The tip of the scissors works from behind the fabric upwards. Stick the lower blade of the scissors up in A, at the base of the first group of five stitches. Cut the four threads of the weave to point B, then turn the work one quarter turn and cut the threads of the weave to open up the corner formed by the groups of stitches.

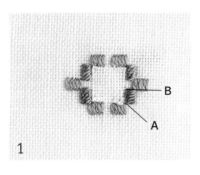

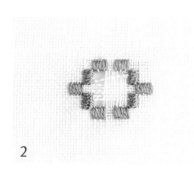

2

STEP 2

Cut the threads of the weave inscribed within the border of satin stitches. With the tip of a needle, raise the center of the threads whose ends have been cut. Pull the threads horizontally one by one, and then vertically one by one, until you see a grid of intact threads of the weave. Each branch of the grid is made up of four threads of the weave.

THE SIMPLE OVERCAST BAR STITCH IN 2 STEPS

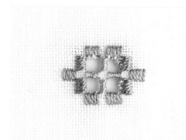

Level of Difficulty: Medium, for people who already have some experience.

Threads and Fabrics: This stitch can be made on cotton or linen fabrics with a simple and obvious weave, with round threads such as size 20 or 25 Cutwork and Embroidery thread or size 12 cotton Pearl.

Direction: This stitch is worked diagonally, from bottom to top and from right to left.

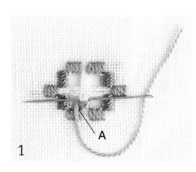

1

With the simple overcast bar stitch, begin with the third step of the Hardanger stitch, which consists of covering the branches of the grid formed by the remaining threads of the weave with an embroidery stitch. The overcast bar stitch is the most simple covering stitch.

STEP 1

Prepare a needle with a thread a bit thinner than the one you used to embroider the border. On the back, catch the thread under a group of five stitches. Bring the needle up in A, at the bottom of the motif and to the left of the first bar, and wrap it around the bar in a clockwise direction. Move to the next bar, situated diagonally above and to the left.

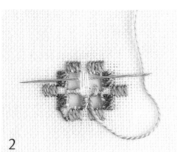

2

STEP 2

Once these two bars are entirely embroidered, fasten off the thread at the back of the work under the nearest group of five straight flat stitches. Cut the thread, take a new needle and begin the work at the remaining pair of bars to the right and top.

THE WOVEN OVERCAST BAR STITCH IN 2 STEPS

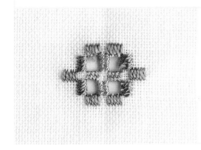

Level of Difficulty: Medium, for people who already have some experience.
Threads and Fabrics: This stitch can be made on cotton or linen fabrics with a simple and obvious weave, with round threads such as size 20 or 25 Cutwork and Embroidery thread or size 12 cotton Pearl.
Direction: This stitch is worked diagonally, from bottom to top and from right to left.

This is an exercise identical to the simple overcast bar stitch, but the bar of the grid here is separated in two in order to be covered in a more decorative manner.

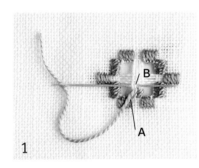

STEP 1

Prepare a needle with a thread a bit thinner than the one you used to embroider the border. On the back, catch the thread under a group of five stitches. Bring the needle up in A, at the bottom of the motif and to the left of the first bar. Bring the needle down in B, in the center of the group of four threads, and bring it back up to the right of the bar. Stitch back down in the center of the bar and bring your needle back up to the left of the bar. Proceed in this way, systematically moving the needle through the center of the four threads of the weave.

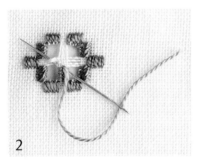

STEP 2

Move to the next bar, situated diagonally to the upper left. Place the needle under the horizontal bar and bring it down in the center, dividing the group of four threads. Continue the woven work as in the preceding step.

> **TIP**
> The woven stitch made on the bars of the grid justifies counting the threads of the weave in the first step. The groups of straight flat stitches on the border must always be worked over even numbers of threads of the weave. Then, when you are doing the woven bar work, the needle passes through the middle of the group of threads of the weave, leaving the same number of strands on each side.

193

THE PICOT WOVEN OVERCAST BAR STITCH IN 2 STEPS

Level of Difficulty: Difficult, reserved for those who are experienced.

Threads and Fabrics: This stitch can be made on cotton or linen fabrics with a simple and obvious weave, with round threads such as size 20 or 25 Cutwork and Embroidery thread or size 12 cotton Pearl.

Direction: This stitch is worked diagonally, from bottom to top and from right to left.

The picot woven overcast bar stitch, or picot bar, is made on a base of woven stitches. A small picot is embroidered in the center of each bar. This pretty detail brings much charm to Hardanger embroidery.

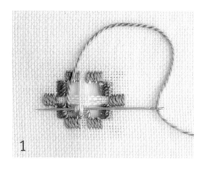

STEP 1

Prepare a needle with a thread a bit thinner than the one you used to embroider the border. On the back, catch the thread under a group of five stitches. Work the bar with the darning stitch (see p. 110). In the middle of the bar, keep the needle underneath and behind the threads of the weave. Wind the thread around the needle and pull gently to form a small knot, or picot.

STEP 2

Pass the needle under and behind the threads of the bar, and wrap the thread around the middle to make a picot on the other side of the bar. Pull gently on the thread.

Begin the work again on the bar with the woven stitch, then move to the next bar.

TIP

The picot woven overcast bars, in order to stand out as much as possible, must be worked with a thin thread such as size 25 Cutwork and Embroidery cotton or size 12 Pearl cotton. With a thicker thread, the volume of the picot would completely fill the open part of the grid. As a result, you would not be able to distinguish the branches of the grid, and the work would then lose its finesse.

THE WOVEN OVERCAST BAR WITH SPIDER STITCH IN 2 STEPS

Level of Difficulty: Difficult, reserved for those who are experienced.

Threads and Fabrics: This stitch can be made on cotton or linen fabrics with a simple and obvious weave, with round threads such as size 20 or 25 Cutwork and Embroidery thread or size 12 cotton Pearl.

Direction: This stitch is worked diagonally, from bottom to top and from right to left.

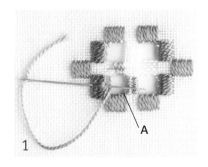

TIP

The spider stitch can also be made in different way. Once the four bars are embroidered, stitch in the next corner, slide the thread under the needle, pull gently, and move to the next corner, turning counter-clockwise. You will obtain a spider stitch that is diagonal in relation to the squares of the grid. When done in this way, it is called a "spider web stitch."

The spider stitch, filling the open center of the grid with great flair, brings a touch of fancy contrast to the tempered geometry of Hardanger embroidery.

STEP 1

Prepare a needle with a thread a bit thinner than the one you used to embroider the border. On the back, catch the thread under a group of five stitches. Bring the needle up in A, at the bottom of the motif and to the left of the first bar. Bring the needle down in the center of the group of four threads, and bring it back up on the right of the bar. Stitch back down in the center of the bar and bring your needle back up on the left of the bar. Proceed in this way, systematically moving the point of the needle through the center of the four threads of the weave.

Move to the next bar, situated diagonally to the upper left. This bar completes the frame for the lower left opening. Weave to the center of this bar, then slide the needle left to right in the satin stitch block to the left of the opening. Slide the thread under the needle and pull gently on the thread.

STEP 2

Stitch in the center of the next side, proceeding in counter-clockwise direction. Return to the center of the bar and finish the work using the woven stitch. Continue around motif.

The Napkin Corner

Hardanger embroidery is perfectly suited to working with colors. Decorate the corner of napkins with the pretty open work of geometric shapes. Its rose shades will spruce up even the simplest of napkins.

OVERVIEW

Level of Difficulty:
Medium

Stitches Used:
Kloster block border stitch
(see p. 189)
Woven overcast bar stitch
(see p. 193)
Woven overcast bar with spider
stitch (see p. 195)
Cross-stitch (see p. 138)

Finished Dimensions:
The finished napkin measures 18 x
18 inches. The embroidered corner
measures 3¼ inches on each side.

MATERIALS

20 x 20 inches mauve linen DMC
fabric, size 7 mesh
1 skein of pale pink (761) DMC
size 5 Pearl cotton, art. 15
1 skein of bright pink (893) DMC
size 20 Cutwork and Embroidery
cotton, art. 107
1 round-tipped embroidery needle
4-Inch diameter embroidery hoop
Mauve sewing thread
Sewing needle or sewing machine

PATTERN

The motif does not need to be traced since it is made in counted stitches following the grid. It is placed 100 threads of the weave from the cut edges of the fabric.

EMBROIDERY

Stretch the fabric in the embroidery hoop. Thread a needle with the pale pink Pearl cotton. Begin the border work with the satin stitches. Each group of stitches is made up of seven satin stitches worked over six threads of the weave of fabric. Once the shape is completely finished, cut the fabric along the groups of satin stitches. Do not cut the parts of the fabric left unworked between the groups.

Thread a needle with bright pink Cutwork and Embroidery cotton and work the bars. Proceed diagonally with the woven stitch. The spider stitch is worked in staggered rows.

Finish the work with the small cross-stitch motif made using the bright pink Cutwork and Embroidery cotton. Each cross is made over two threads of the weave.

FINISHING TOUCHES

With an iron, make a first fold of ¾ inch toward the wrong side of the napkin. Pin, and then make a second fold of 1 inch, mitering the corners. Baste before sewing the hem either by hand or with a sewing machine.

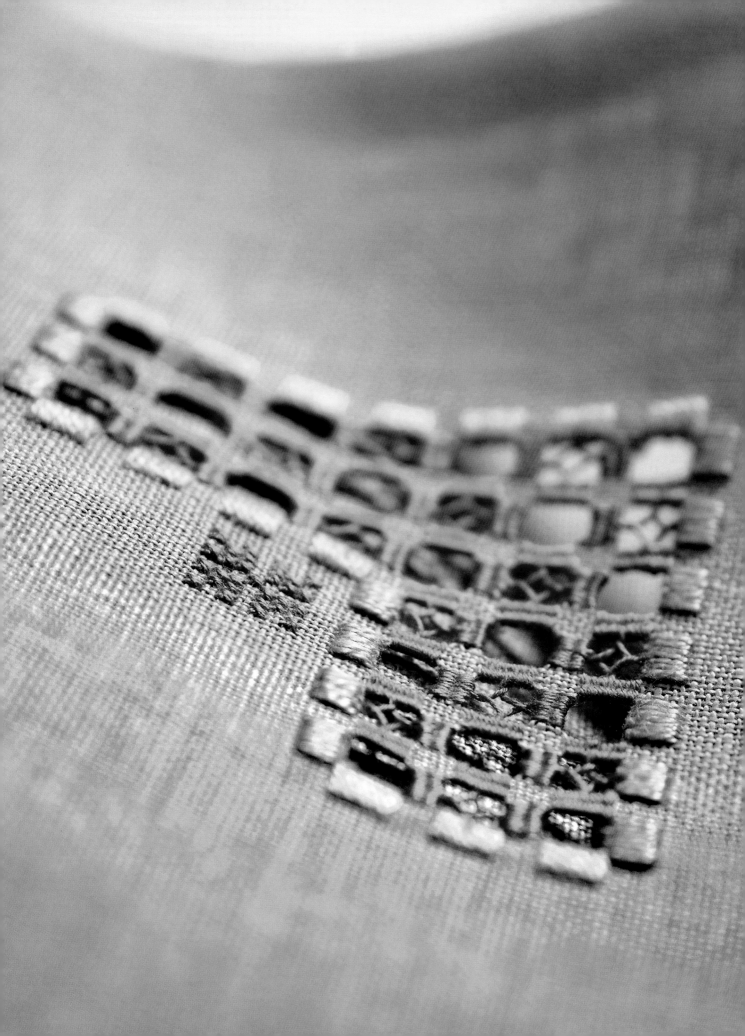

Model reduced to 45%

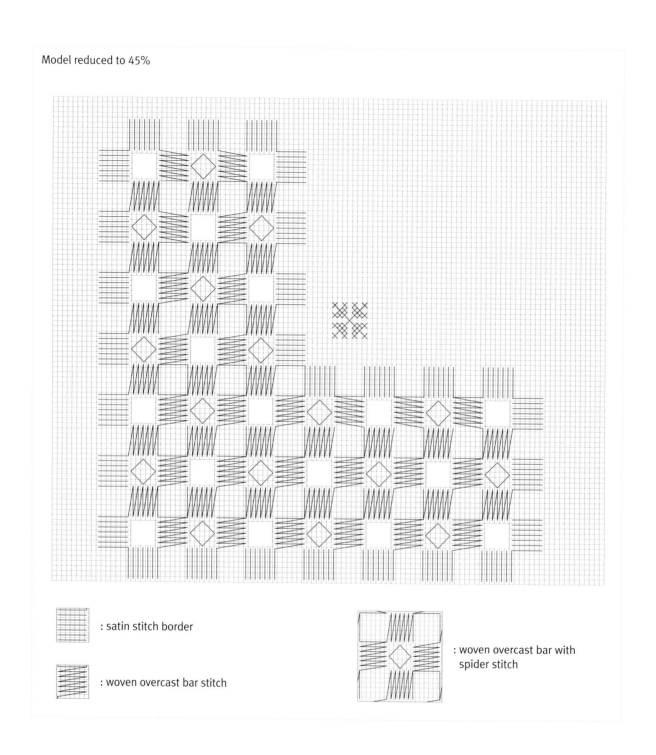

: satin stitch border

: woven overcast bar stitch

: woven overcast bar with spider stitch

ADVICE

Only geometric motifs can be used in Hardanger embroidery. If you are look-ing for original motifs, use the grids of other counted stitch works, such as those for cross-stitch, and adapt the pattern. Create your own grid on graph-ing paper before beginning your final project.

The Drawn-Thread Embroidery Family

The technique for drawn-thread embroidery differs a bit from the other cutwork embroidery techniques. Here, the fabric must be prepared. Certain parts of the fabric will be fashioned based on the motif desired. The threads of the weave or of the warp are delicately removed so as to leave only a row of parallel threads which serve as a support for embroidery stitches. Drawn-thread work is often joined with other stitches, such as self-padded satin stitches.

PREPARATION OF THE DRAWN-THREAD WORK IN 2 STEPS

Level of Difficulty: Easy, accessible to beginners.
Tools: Embroidery scissors, basting thread, sewing needle, pin. The finer the fabric, the more difficult it is to draw out the threads. Beginners should practice with fabrics that have an obvious weave.
Direction: The first step is worked as determined by the border.

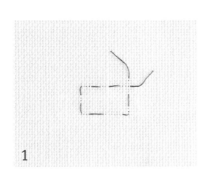

Preparing for drawn-thread work consists of removing the threads of the weave or the warp of the fabric to leave only parallel threads. This primary step is necessary for making all the drawn-thread stitches to follow.

STEP 1

With large running stitches (see p. 130), sew a basting thread around the border. Cut the cross threads of the weave at each side edge of this delineated border.

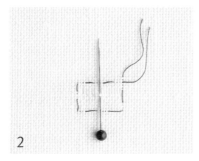

STEP 2

Using the tip of a pin, raise ¾–1¼ inches of a cross thread situated at the center of the interior and pull it out completely. Continue to remove all the parallel threads inside the basted border.

THE LADDER HEMSTITCH IN 3 STEPS

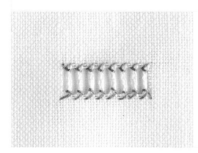

Level of Difficulty: Medium, for people who already have some experience.

Threads and Fabrics: This stitch can be made on cotton or linen fabrics (toile, broadcloth, or percale), with thin round threads such as size 20 or 25 Cutwork and Embroidery thread or size 12 cotton Pearl.

Direction: This stitch is worked horizontally, from left to right.

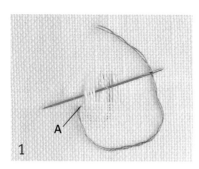

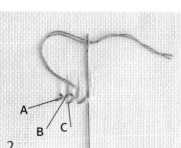

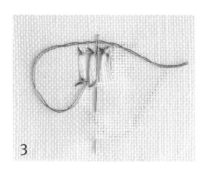

To offer a ladder appearance, the ladder hemstitch, also called the "open ladder," is worked on the upper and lower edge of a border. It constitutes the base for all other drawn-thread work.

STEP 1

Prepare the fabric for the drawn-thread embroidery (see p. 199). Work the lower edge of the border first. Bring the needle up in A, to the left below the border. Slide the needle from the right to the left under four threads of the weave, then pull gently to tighten the base of the threads of the weave.

STEP 2

Bring the needle down in B, to the right of the first bundle of threads of the weave, and bring the tip of the needle back up in C, below point B. Continue with these two steps to form the remaining stitches.

STEP 3

Once the lower border is entirely embroidered, turn the work so that you can work the upper border as you just did the first. Proceed from left to right, taking the same groups of threads of the weave.

> **TIP**
>
> With drawn-thread work, the threads of the weave grouped together in bundles are called "rivers." The technique used here differs from "bars" of cutwork and Hardanger embroidery.

THE TRELLIS HEMSTITCH IN 3 STEPS

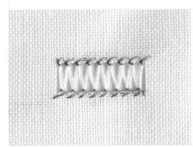

Level of Difficulty: Medium, for people who already have some experience.

Threads and Fabrics: This stitch can be made on cotton or linen fabrics (toile, broadcloth, or percale), with thin round threads such as size 20 or 25 Cutwork and Embroidery thread or size 12 cotton Pearl.

Direction: This stitch is worked horizontally, from left to right.

The trellis hemstitch, also known as the serpentine hemstitch, is a variation of the ladder hemstitch, in which the bundles of threads are inset into each other as you work the embroidery on the upper and lower borders.

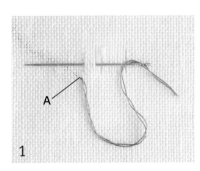

STEP 1

Prepare the fabric for the drawn-thread embroidery (see p. 199). Work the lower edge of the border first. Bring the needle up in A, to the left below the border. Slide the needle from the right to the left under four threads of the weave, then pull gently to tighten the base of the threads of the weave.

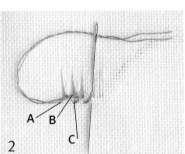

STEP 2

Bring the needle down in B, to the right of the first bundle of threads of the weave, and bring the tip of the needle back up in C, below point B. Continue with these two steps to form the remaining stitches.

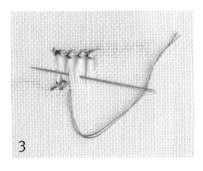

STEP 3

Once the lower border is entirely embroidered, turn the work so that you can work the upper border as you just did the first. Proceed from left to right, taking two threads of the weave from the first bundle and two threads from the second. Continue to group threads in this manner to form a line of chevrons.

> **TIP**
>
> The bundles of threads absolutely must be made up of even numbers of threads. Therefore, as you are working the upper edge, you can separate the groups into two to obtain the uniform zigzag effect.

THE WOVEN DRAWN-THREAD BAR STITCH IN 3 STEPS

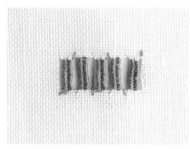

Level of Difficulty: Difficult, reserved for those who are experienced.

Threads and Fabrics: This stitch can be made on cotton or linen fabrics (toile, broadcloth, or percale), with thin round threads such as size 20 or 25 Cutwork and Embroidery thread or size 12 cotton Pearl.

Direction: The two steps are worked horizontally, the first from left to right and the second from right to left.

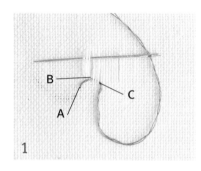

The woven drawn-thread bar stitch joins the bar stitch with the woven stitch already learned in Hardanger embroidery. The preparatory technique of this stitch is completely different, though. This stitch makes a solid river with old-fashioned charm.

STEP 1

Prepare the fabric for the drawn-thread embroidery (see p. 199). Bring the needle up in A, at the bottom left of the border. Bring the needle down in B, in the middle of the group of six threads of the weave, and bring it back up in C, to the right of the bundle. Proceed in this manner systematically passing the tip of the needle through the center of six threads of the weave.

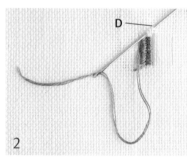

STEP 2

With the bundle entirely covered, bring your needle up in D, on the upper edge of the weave, to form a small straight stitch to attach the thread.

STEP 3

Move to the next bar, situated to the right. Slide your needle in E, in the center of six threads of the next bar, and work the woven stitch, this time moving down the bar. Make a small straight stitch at the bottom to attach the thread before moving to the next bundle.

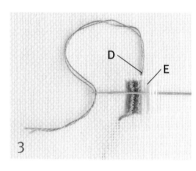

THE INTERLACED DRAWN-THREAD STITCH IN 2 STEPS

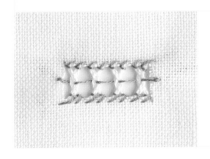

Level of Difficulty: Difficult, reserved for those who are experienced.

Threads and Fabrics: This stitch can be made on cotton or linen fabrics (toile, broadcloth, or percale), with thin round threads such as size 20 or 25 Cutwork and Embroidery thread or size 12 cotton Pearl.

Direction: The two steps are worked horizontally, the first from left to right and the second from right to left.

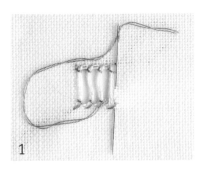

The interlaced drawn-thread stitch, or knotted drawn-thread stitch, is a much more elaborate river than the previous ones and offers a very decorative look to the fabrics on which it is embroidered. It requires a fairly large space—at least ½ inch in height—to showcase all its beauty.

STEP 1

Prepare the fabric for the drawn-thread embroidery (see p. 199). Work the border using the ladder hemstitch (see p. 200).

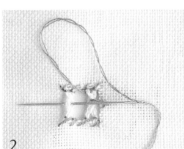

STEP 2

Thread a new needle and attach it on the right side of the border. From the back of the work, slide the needle under the second bundle, then over the first, with the tip of the needle pointing to the right. Pivot the needle to orient the point to the left. Pull gently on the thread, and the bundles will cross over each other. Repeat this step for the entire border.

> **TIP**
>
> In the second step, it is important for the thread of the needle to be a bit longer than the length of the border. This work will not permit stops, which would look terrible and would risk giving a twisted appearance to the interlacing. To obtain a straight border, make sure that your thread is all one piece.

The Curtain

Light as air, this little white linen curtain allows just enough sunshine to pass through to give your rooms comfortable and harmonious light. The interlaced drawn-work borders give it all the charm of household linen of days gone by.

OVERVIEW

Level of Difficulty:
Difficult

Stitches Used:
Preparation of drawn-thread work (see p. 199)
Ladder hemstitch (see p. 200)
Interlaced drawn-thread stitch (see p. 203)

Finished Dimensions:
The finished curtain measures 60 x 30 inches. The embroidered borders measure ¾ x 30 inches.

MATERIALS

67 x 32 inches white linen fabric
1 skein of white DMC size 20 Cutwork and Embroidery cotton, art. 107
1 fine-tipped embroidery needle
6-inch diameter embroidery hoop
Pins
White sewing thread
Sewing needle or sewing machine

PATTERN

Place the first drawn-thread border 12 inches from the bottom edge, and the second at 16 inches. Place pins in the fabric to mark these places. Stitch a basting thread at the edges of the borders to be worked, then draw the threads out in preparation for the embroidery, using the tip of a needle.

EMBROIDERY

Stretch the material in the embroidery hoop. Begin with the drawn-thread borders. Make the ladder hemstitch by taking eight threads of the weave to form the bundles. Cut a piece of cotton thread a few inches longer than the border. Attach it to one end of the border and pass the needle through the weave, interlacing the bundles. At the other end of the border, attach another thread to the edge of the fabric. Proceed in the same way, sliding a second thread to form opposite interlaced bundles.

Make a second drawn-thread border in the same way as the first.

FINISHING TOUCHES

With an iron, on the sides of the curtain, make a first fold of ¼ inch. Pin, and then make a second fold of ½ inch. Stitch the hems at ¼ inch from the edge. At the bottom of the curtain, make a first fold of 1¾ inches, pin, and make a second fold of 2¼ inches. Stitch ½ inch from the top of the second fold. Make the top of the curtain based on the type of curtain rod you have. Steam press the entire work.

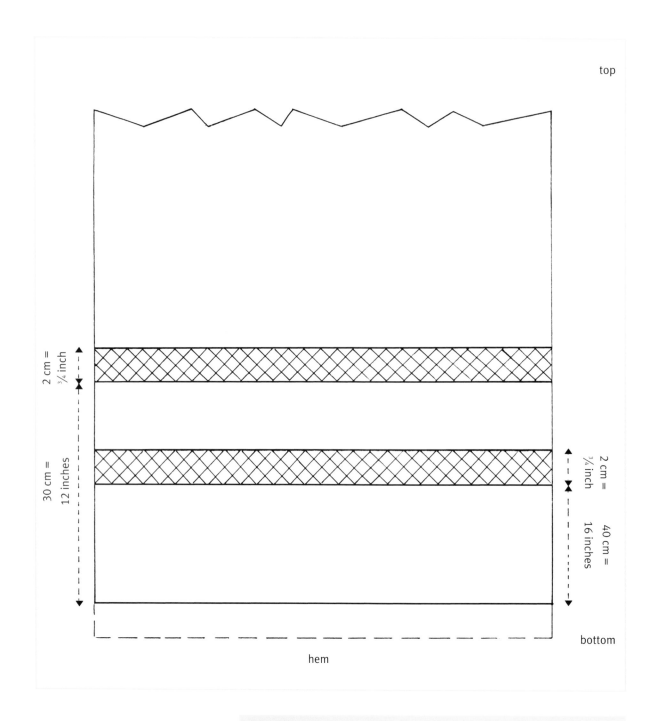

top

2 cm =
¾ inch

30 cm =
12 inches

2 cm =
¾ inch

40 cm =
16 inches

hem

bottom

ADVICE

It is often difficult to pull the threads over a large length of fabric when preparing for drawn-thread work. First, lightly dampen the linen fabric so the fibers become less brittle. Then, pull the first thread from the center of the piece of fabric. With the help of a needle, raise ¾–1¼ inches of thread, then pull while gathering the fabric. This method allows you to loosen the tension on the pulled thread and prevents it from breaking.

Coming from the Orient where it decorated the sumptuous clothing of the elite, golden embroidery arrived in the West in the 17th century. Made of copper, silver, vermeil, or gold, the traditional furnishings—thin strips of metal, braids, and twisted threads—lacked flexibility and could not always pass through the foundation material. These metallic threads were generally placed, "couched," on the surface of the fabric to be embroidered. And so this method is known as "couching."

Today, metallic threads look nothing like the old materials. Made of synthetic fibers, they are available in many varieties, but are still not used in the same way as natural fibers. They are less flexible and wear out much more rapidly. Therefore, we must embroider them just as our ancestors did, in other words, by using these time-tested stitches.

Golden embroidery, which is no longer reserved for the elite, guarantees brilliant results for beginning embroiderers.

6

COUCHING STITCHES

The Oriental Stitch Family

The people of Asia have excelled in the art of golden embroidery, which we find in the Near East as well as the Far East. Most frequently worked using metallic threads, the stitches which hold it together are also embroidered with beautiful threads such as silk or wool. The following stitches serve to fill large surfaces or to make fancy borders. The metallic threads are worked in large flat satin stitches to cover the surface, which are then are held in place in the second step by small stitches made in cotton or silk thread.

THE BOULOGNE STITCH IN 3 STEPS

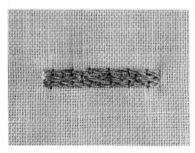

Level of Difficulty: Easy, accessible to beginners.

Threads and Fabrics: This stitch can be made on fabrics with a tight weave, such as taffeta, velour or brocade, with metallic stranded embroidery thread or metallic Pearl, to which is added stranded embroidery cotton.

Direction: The first step is worked in large horizontal stitches, and the second in small vertical stitches.

The famous Bayeux Tapestry, which is actually embroidery, offers us a perfect example of how to use the Boulogne stitch. Made during the Middle Ages mostly with woolen thread, this stitch was used to cover surfaces which featured people, boats and horses. With metallic thread, this is one of the most basic stitches used in the "couching" technique.

STEP 1

Thread a needle with metallic thread and bring the needle up in A, on the upper left of the surface to cover. Bring it down in B, horizontal with A, to form the first large couching stitch. Bring the needle back up in C, below point B, and bring it down in D, below point A. The second stitch is parallel to the first. Continue in this way to cover the entire surface.

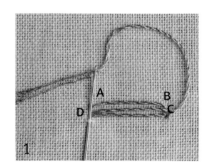

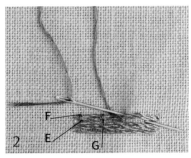

STEP 2

Thread two strands of embroidery cotton and bring the needle up in E, on the left, under the first two horizontal stitches. Bring it down in F to form the first small vertical stitch over the first two couching stitches. Bring your needle back up in G, a bit to the right, and make another small vertical stitch to hold the metallic thread against the surface of the fabric.

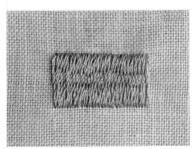

STEP 3

For the second row of small vertical stitches, work from right to left and stagger the stitches in relation to the ones in the first row. Continue to attach the couching stitches to the fabric in this manner.

THE BOKHARA COUCHING STITCH IN 3 STEPS

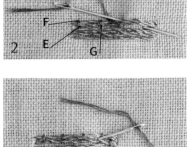

Level of Difficulty: Medium, for people who already have some experience.
Threads and Fabrics: This stitch can be made on fabrics with a tight weave, such as taffeta, velour or brocade, with metallic stranded embroidery thread or metallic Pearl.
Direction: The first step is worked vertically, from top to bottom.

The Bokhara couching threads, worked in large satin stitches, cross and offer a fleecy look, as if the surface has been padded.

This embroidery stitch is mostly used as a filling for large surfaces of fabric. The back of the work is also completely covered.

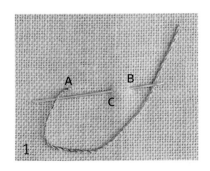

STEP 1

Bring your needle up in A. Bring it down in B, horizontal to A and about ½ inch to the right to form a long stitch. Bring the needle back up in C, one-third of the way between A and B on the right, just slightly below the horizontal of those two points.

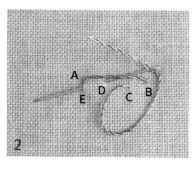

STEP 2

Slide your needle from top to bottom under the horizontal thread and bring it down in D, halfway between A and C, just slightly above the horizontal stitch. Bring the needle up in E, below point A.

STEP 3

Bring your needle down in F, below point B, to form the second horizontal stitch, parallel to the first. Bring the needle up in G, below point C. Continue the work, beginning again at step 2.

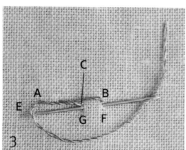

TIP

This stitch uses a great deal of thread. Because metallic thread is not very flexible, you must pull a bit harder to keep it flat against the surface of the fabric. Therefore, it is useful to make this stitch on fabric that is stretched tightly in an embroidery hoop.

THE TURKISH ZIGZAG COUCHING STITCH IN 2 STEPS

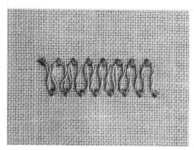

Level of Difficulty: Easy, accessible to beginners.

Threads and Fabrics: This stitch can be made on fabrics with a tight weave (taffeta, velour, or brocade), or on thin fabrics (organza or cotton voile), with metallic stranded embroidery thread or metallic Pearl, to which is added stranded embroidery cotton.

Direction: This stitch is worked horizontally.

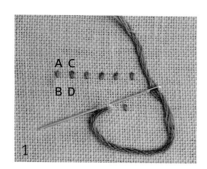

Very delicate, the Turkish zigzag couching stitch was used by the Ottomans to cover small geometric surfaces or to make flower and foliage motifs.

STEP 1

Thread a needle with six strands of embroidery cotton and bring your needle up in A, on the upper left of the shape to embroider. Bring your needle down in B, below A, to make the first small vertical stitch. Bring the needle up in C, to the right of A, and bring it down in D to create the second small vertical stitch, parallel with the first. Complete the row. On the second row, work from right to left, staggering the vertical stitches between those of the first row.

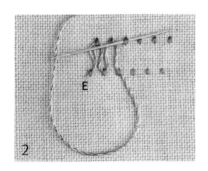

STEP 2

Thread a metallic thread and bring it up in E, on the bottom left of the shape. Slide the needle from left to right under the first stitch on the bottom row. Then slide it from left to right under the first stitch of the top row. Continue in this manner, going from top to bottom, to form the zigzag.

TIP

To cover the surface to be embroidered, the stitches on the horizontal rows should be very close to each other, and the distance between the rows (in other words, the height of the zigzag), must be uniform. Made in this way, the Turkish zigzag couching stitch will hide the fabric completely.

THE TURKISH DIAMOND COUCHING STITCH IN 3 STEPS

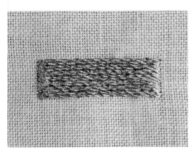

Level of Difficulty: Difficult, reserved for those who are experienced.

Threads and Fabrics: This stitch can be made on fabrics with a tight weave, such as taffeta, velour or brocade, with metallic stranded embroidery thread or metallic Pearl, to which is added stranded embroidery cotton.

Direction: The first step is worked in large horizontal stitches, and the second in small vertical stitches.

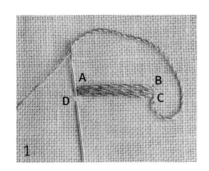

Like the Boulogne stitch, the Turkish diamond couching stitch is made on a foundation of threads lying on the fabric. Its damask effect is the result of working the small stitches that hold the metallic threads in place. It is particularly striking when it is used to work large foundations.

STEP 1

Thread a metallic thread and bring your needle up in A, on the upper left of the surface to cover. Bring it down in B, horizontal with A, to form the first large couching stitch. Bring the needle up in C, below point B, and bring it down in D, below point A. Continue in this manner until you have covered the entire surface.

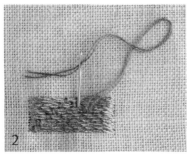

STEP 2

Beginning at the bottom left of the surface covered with couching stitches, make small vertical stitches with two strands of cotton embroidery floss. Each stitch holds two couching stitches. Work up and to the right to create the first slant, then work down and to the right to form the next slant. Chevrons will be formed.

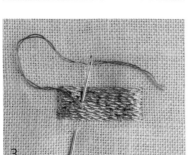

STEP 3

Proceed in the opposite direction beginning the work of small stitches from the upper left of the surface covered with couching stitches. Work down and to the right to create the first slant, then up and to the right to create the second. In this manner, complete the diamonds.

THE IRANIAN COUCHING STITCH IN 3 STEPS

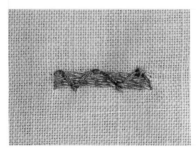

Level of Difficulty: Medium, for people who already have some experience.
Threads and Fabrics: This stitch can be made on fabrics with a tight weave, such as taffeta, velour, or brocade, with metallic stranded embroidery thread or metallic Pearl, to which is added stranded embroidery cotton.
Direction: The first step is worked in large horizontal stitches, and the second in small vertical stitches.

TIP

This fancy couching stitch is very quick to make. It would be even more spectacular if you use metallic threads in two different colors. Be careful to pull the second couching stitch tightly enough to make neat zigzags.

The part of western Asia corresponding to ancient Persia presents a spectrum of very rich embroidery stitches. Used on borders, the Iranian couching stitch, also called the "Persian filling stitch," decorates the garments of men and women as well as wall-hangings, pillows, or even Koran covers with its delicate scrolls.

STEP 1

Thread a metallic thread and bring your needle up in A, on the upper left of the surface to cover. Bring it down in B, horizontal with A, to form the first large couching stitch. Bring the needle up in C, below point B, and bring it down in D, below point A.

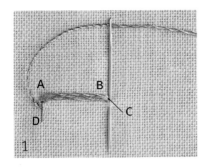

The second stitch is parallel to the first. Continue in this manner until you have covered the entire surface.

STEP 2

The second step consists of making a zigzag couching with metallic thread held in place with small vertical stitches.

Bring the second metallic thread up in E, on the bottom right of the couching stitch border. Move your needle up and to the left. Thread six strands of embroidery cotton on another needle and bring it up in F, just above the couching stitch border and over the new metallic thread. Bring it back down in G, vertical with F, to hold the thread and form the first branch of the zigzag.

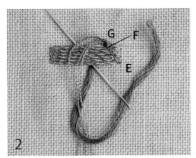

STEP 3

Direct the zigzag metallic thread down and to the left, and make a small vertical stitch over it to maintain the second branch of the zigzag.

Continue working the zigzag in this manner over the entire surface of the border. When this is complete, bring the second metallic thread being used for the zigzag down through the fabric at the base of the border and fasten it off.

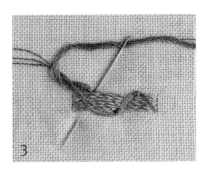

THE SPIRAL COUCHING STITCH IN 3 STEPS

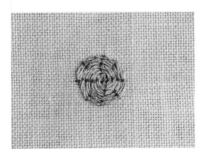

Level of Difficulty: Medium, for people who already have some experience.
Threads and Fabrics: This stitch can be made on fabrics with a tight weave (taffeta, velour, or brocade), or on thin fabrics (organza or cotton voile), with metallic stranded embroidery thread or metallic Pearl, to which is added stranded embroidery cotton.
Direction: This stitch is worked in a circle, in a clockwise direction.

The spiral couching stitch is a decorative element used on its own. Very simple to make, it is used in heavy-fill and loose-fill patterns on the chosen fabric. Depending on the effect sought, add fewer or more turns to the spiral to obtain different sized dots.

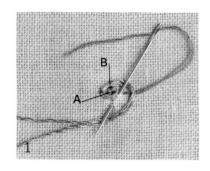

STEP 1

Thread two metallic threads and bring your needle up in A, in the center of the circle to be worked. Thread two strands of embroidery cotton and also bring the needle up in A, then wind the metallic threads in a circle around the central point. With the cotton thread, make a small stitch in point B over the metallic thread to maintain the curve. Make four small stitches in the shape of a cross to hold the turns of each spiraling couching thread.

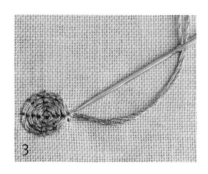

STEP 2

On the third turn of the metallic thread, add small slanted stitches midway between the cross stitches to form the diagonals of the circle. Proceed in this manner to fill the pattern completely.

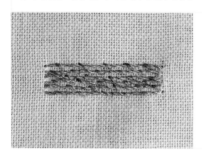

STEP 3

When the motif is completed, thread the two metallic threads onto a large needle and bring it down into the fabric on the edge of the embroidered circle. Fasten the threads on the back of the work. Fasten the embroidery cotton in the same manner.

THE ROMANIAN COUCHING STITCH IN 2 STEPS

Level of Difficulty: Easy, accessible to beginners.

Threads and Fabrics: This stitch can be made on fabrics with a tight weave, such as taffeta, velour or brocade, with metallic stranded embroidery thread or metallic Pearl, to which is added stranded embroidery cotton.

Direction: The first step is worked in large horizontal stitches, and the second with small slanted stitches.

Also known as "Uzbekistan embroidery," the Romanian couching stitch is inspired by the golden embroidery of the Turks. In Romania, this stitch is used to embroider golden thread motifs on velour to make men's caps.

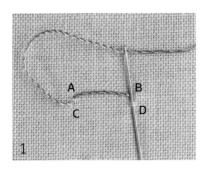

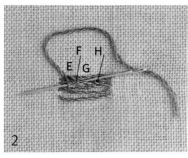

TIP

So that your metallic thread does not wear out quickly, use a large-eyed embroidery needle in the first step. The large eye will not ruin the surface of the couching stitch and it will space the threads of the weave of fabric more widely, allowing the thread to pass through with plenty of room.

STEP 1

Thread a metallic thread and bring your needle up in A, on the upper left of the surface to cover. Bring it down in B, horizontal with A, to form the first large couching stitch. Bring the needle up in C, a few threads of the weave below point A, and bring it down in D, below point B. The second stitch is parallel to the first. Continue in this manner until you have covered the entire surface.

STEP 2

This step is worked using two strands of embroidery cotton over one strand of metallic thread. Bring the needle up in E, on the upper left, above the first couching stitch. Bring it down in F, to the right, over the metallic thread. The first slanted stitch is formed. Bring the needle back up in G, a bit to the right and above the first couching stitch, and bring it down in H, to the right and over the metallic thread to form the second slanted stitch.

Work the second row of slanted stitches from right to left, but keep the direction of the slant the same as the preceding row. Stagger the slanted stitches.

Jeweled Buttons

A perfect idea for the busiest of embroiderers: by practicing the assortment of Oriental stitches described in this chapter, you can make a series of jeweled buttons with very few materials and just a little bit of time. They will be the perfect accessories to set off your dresses, shirts, or coats, giving them some "haute couture" flair.

OVERVIEW

Level of Difficulty:
Easy and quick

Stitches Used:
Boulogne stitch (see p. 208)
Turkish zigzag couching stitch
(see p. 210)
Satin stitch (see p. 98)
Straight stitch (see p. 97)
Knot stitch (see p. 74)

Finished Dimensions:
The finished buttons measure
1¼ inches in diameter.

MATERIALS

An assortment of orange silk
taffetas in madras plaids
1 skein of DMC metallic embroidery thread, art. 317, in each of
the following colors: gold (5282),
copper (5279), red (5270)
Buttons to cover, 1-inch diameter
Embroidery needle and hoop
Compass, basting thread
Sewing needle

PATTERN

On the silk, trace 1¼-inch circles with a compass with a graphite point (or black pencil).

Place the circles at the intersection of the plaid squares so that you have two to four different colors upon which to embroider. Space the circles about 2 inches apart in every direction.

EMBROIDERY

Use two strands of metallic embroidery thread for all stitches except the knots, which are made using three strands.

Stretch the material in the embroidery hoop.

Following the directions on the patterns, embroider the motifs, respecting the direction as well as the colors of the stitches.

Make sure you do not make knots to fasten the threads on the back of the embroidered pieces.

Move the embroidery hoop as you finish each section and begin the next.

FINISHING TOUCHES

Cut each of the circles, leaving about 1 inch of fabric around the embroidered motifs. Make a gathering stitch ½ inch from the edge of the embroidery.

ADVICE

These precious buttons are very fragile. Before washing the garment on which they have been sewn, remove the buttons and wash them separately, by hand.

Place the top of the button-to-cover behind the embroidered work and tighten the gathering thread. Knot the ends. The silk fabric will perfectly mold itself over the shape of the button.

Finish mounting the buttons according to the manufacturer's directions.

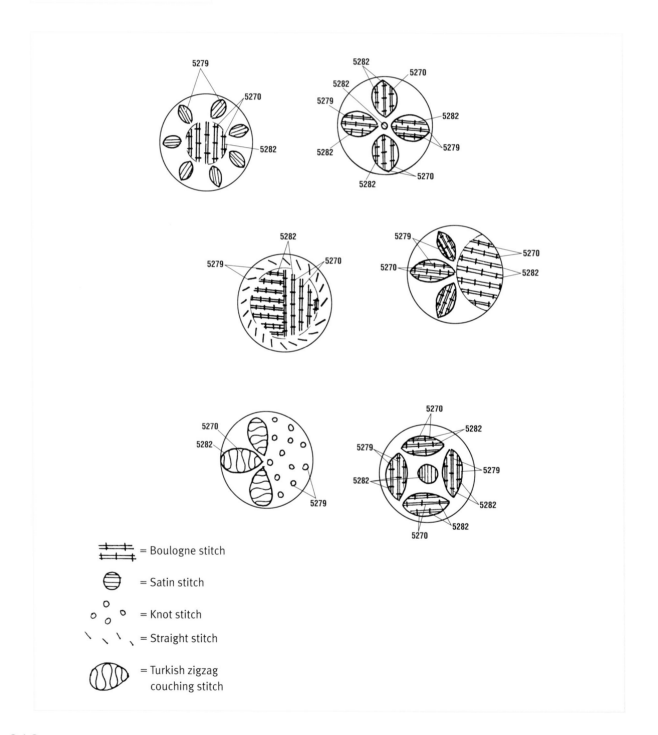

≈ = Boulogne stitch

⊖ = Satin stitch

∘ = Knot stitch

＼ ＼ ＼ ＼ = Straight stitch

⬯ = Turkish zigzag couching stitch

The Soutache Family

The application of a ribbon trim to decorate or to frame a motif that has already been embroidered with a basic filling stitch is called "soutache." This technique is found today in golden embroidery because the laces, large ribbons, and even thick metallic threads cannot easily pass through fabric to make stitches. The trims are placed on the fabric and attached using small stitches.

THE FLAT LACE SOUTACHE IN 1 STEP

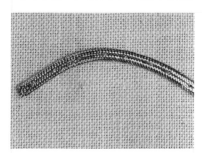

Level of Difficulty: Easy, accessible to beginners.

Threads and Fabrics: This stitch can be made on fabrics with a tight weave (taffeta, velour, or brocade), or on thin fabrics (organza or cotton voile), with flat, thin braids, to which is added stranded embroidery cotton.

Direction: This stitch is worked following the shape of the motif, from right to left.

The flat lace soutache can be used to make up a motif on its own, following a continuous tracing, or to set off an already-made embroidery. This technique is a perfect exercise for beginners.

STEP 1

Place the flat lace on the tracing and keep it securely in place with a row of running stitches (see p. 130) made in the center of the trim.

Thread a needle with two strands of embroidery cotton. Bring the needle up in A, on the right, and bring it down in B, directly to the left. Bring the tip of the needle back up in C. Keep a uniform distance between the stitches throughout your work.

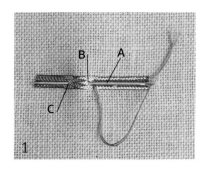

TIP

Use pins to make holding the trim against the fabric easier. Place them perpendicular to the trim and remove them as your work progresses. As a finishing touch, fold the ends of the trim under to prevent them from unraveling.

219

THE CORDED SOUTACHE IN 2 STEPS

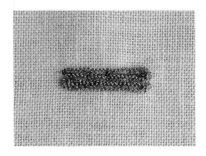

Level of Difficulty: Easy, accessible to beginners.

Threads and Fabrics: This stitch can be made on fabrics with a tight weave (taffeta, velour, or brocade), or on thin fabrics (organza or cotton voile), with thin rounded braids to which is added sewing thread.

Direction: This stitch is worked following the shape of the motif.

TIP

The work of placing the braid must be nearly invisible. For this, use a sewing thread in the same color as the braid. For gold braids, it is best to use golden yellow or bronze green colored thread.

The corded soutache is made using rounded braids with a small diameter. It is very flexible, and adapts perfectly to working shapes as well as fillings.

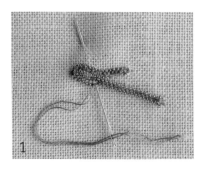 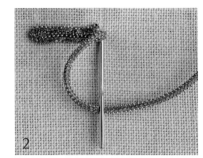

STEP 1

Place the braid on the tracing and hold it in place with a row of running stitches (see p. 130) made in the center of the braid with a needle threaded with sewing thread. Proceed in the same way as you did for the flat lace soutache. Here, the stitches must be very short, and they should become invisible because they enter into the thickness of the trim.

STEP 2

Using a tapestry needle, bring the ends of the trim down through the work and hold them against the surface of the fabric with a few backstitches.

THE LARGE RIBBON SOUTACHE IN 2 STEPS

Level of Difficulty: Difficult, reserved for those who are experienced.

Threads and Fabrics: This stitch can be made on fabrics with a tight weave (taffeta, velour, or brocade), or on thin fabrics (organza or cotton voile), with thick, flat braids, to which is added stranded embroidery cotton.

Direction: This stitch is worked following the shape of the motif, from right to left.

TIP

Instead of attaching the ribbon to the fabric with pins, which can prove to be annoying as you work the backstitches, glue the ribbon. Use textile or ribbon glue, apply a thin layer on the back of the ribbon, place it on the fabric, and wait until it is completely dry before beginning the backstitches.

Because of its spectacular effect, working the large ribbon soutache is reserved for works that require a very strong, pronounced border. In this example, we show you the technique that allows you to form the corners of a motif.

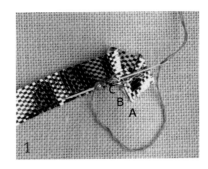
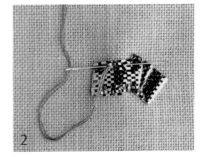

STEP 1

Place the ribbon on the tracing and pleat it when you reach the corners. Hold it in place with pins. Thread a needle with two strands of embroidery cotton and work the backstitch (see p. 25) on the lower edge of the ribbon. Bring the needle up in A, on the right of the ribbon, and bring it back down in B, directly to the left, to make a horizontal stitch. Bring the tip of the needle back up in C, just to the left of point B, and make a backstitch into B. Continue in this manner along the entire edge of the ribbon.

STEP 2

Make a backstitch on the upper edge of the ribbon to completely attach it to the surface of the fabric. Fold both ends of the ribbon under about ¼ inch to prevent them from unraveling, and stitch them to the fabric.

THE INTERLACED TRIM STITCH IN 3 STEPS

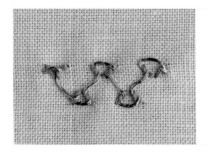

Level of Difficulty: Difficult, reserved for those who are experienced.

Threads and Fabrics: This stitch can be made on fabrics with a tight weave (taffeta, velour, or brocade), with thick metallic threads or thin braids of Lurex thread, to which is added stranded embroidery cotton.

Direction: This stitch is worked in horizontal rows.

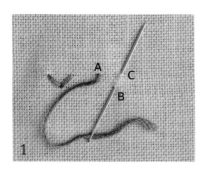

Originating in the Greek Isles where it is known as the "Astipalaia stitch," the interlaced trim stitch is embroidered with a thin braid, or, as seen here, a thick metallic thread.

STEP 1

Use six strands of embroidery cotton and form rows of chevron stitches. Bring the needle up in A and down in B, slanted down and to the right. Bring the needle up in C, to the right of and level with point A. Bring it back down in B to form the first chevron. Make other chevrons to the right, spacing them about ¼–½ inch apart. Embroider a second row of chevrons in the opposite direction of the first row and stagger them in between the chevrons of the first row.

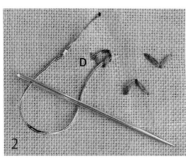

STEP 2

Thread a thick strand of metallic thread on a tapestry needle and bring the needle up in D, on the left-hand side of the first chevron. Slide the needle down and from right to left under the second branch of the chevron and pull gently.

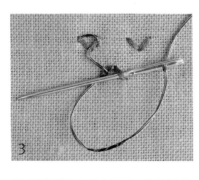

STEP 3

Slide the needle from right to left, over and then under the first branch of the lower chevron. Slide the needle under the second branch of the lower chevron, guiding the needle from right to left. Pull gently on the needle to form the interlacing. Continue embroidering through each branch of each chevron in this way, alternating the work on the chevrons from top to those on the bottom.

TIP

Thick metallic thread has a tendency to lose its twist. To bring the twist back, turn the needle in a clockwise direction.

The Evening Bag

Arabesques intermingle to make this little evening bag a ravishing accessory. The soutache in this pattern offers a remarkable looks of depth, which highlights the pastel colors of the silk taffeta on which the trim is embroidered.

OVERVIEW

Level of Difficulty:
Medium

Stitches Used:
Corded soutache (see p. 220)
Satin stitch (see p. 98)

Finished Dimensions:
The finished bag measures
7 x 9 inches.

MATERIALS

10 x 10 inches turquoise silk taffeta
10 x 10 inches lavender silk taffeta
20 x 20 inches turquoise synthetic lining
1 skein of DMC metallic embroidery thread, art. 317, silver (5283)
6 ½ yards light blue thin round ribbon trim
3 ¼ yards porcelain blue thin round ribbon trim
Embroidery needle
Embroidery hoop
Carbon paper for light fabrics
Light blue sewing thread
Sewing needle

PATTERN

Cut the squares of taffeta in half. With right sides together, alternately sew a turquoise rectangle to a lavender one, joining long edges. In this manner, form a band of four rectangles. Using the carbon paper, trace the arabesque design on the taffeta band. Place the seam that joins the two fabrics in the center of the arabesque motif leaving about 1½ inches of fabric above the top of the design. Transfer the design over the seams.

EMBROIDERY

Stretch the material in the embroidery hoop. Thread a needle with the light blue thread. Fold the end of the light blue ribbon under and attach it to the fabric with two backstitches.

Begin attaching the ribbon at the top left of the motif. Attach the ribbon along the tracing as you advance in your work. When you have finished attaching the ribbon, fold the end under and attach it to the work with two backstitches.

Thread two strands of metallic thread and work satin stitches perpendicularly over the ribbon. Make a stitch every ¼ inch following the curves of the arabesques. Move the embroidery hoop as you finish each section and begin the next.

FINISHING TOUCHES

Cut the lining to the exact dimensions of the embroidered band formed by the sewn rectangles of taffeta.

ADVICE

The ribbon used for this work is made of synthetic fibers, which offers much flexibility, a very useful quality for attaching it to the arabesque design.

If you wish to use another trim, try silk or cotton cord. Metallic trims risk being too stiff for this type of motif, and will result in very marked curves.

Fold the taffeta with right sides together to form the side and the bottom; stitch the side seam. Refold bag so the untrimmed seam (just sewn) is at the center back of the bag. Stitch across the bottom, making the bottom seam about ½ inch below the bottom of the design.

Press the top of the taffeta, folded under about ¼ inch from the soutache trim. Turn the bag and the lining with right sides together. Sew the top at the fold. Turn right side out. Slipstitch the opening in the lining by hand and slide the lining into the bag.

Fold the porcelain blue ribbon in two and twist it until it folds in half on its own, forming the shoulder strap. Sew the ends of the shoulder strap inside the bag.

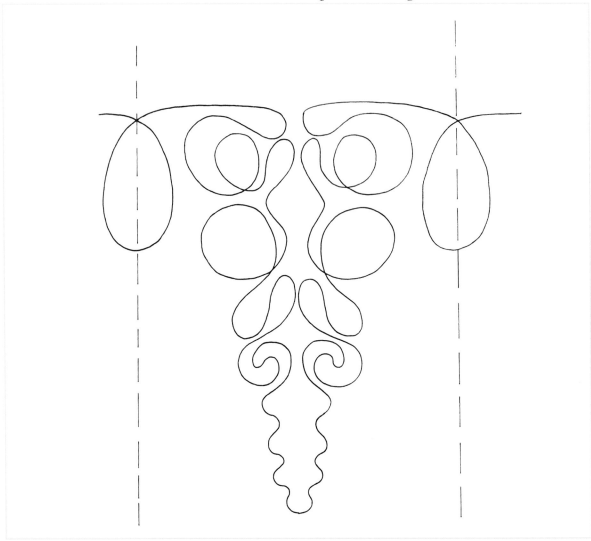

The Trellis Stitch Family

All made up of long crossed couching stitches, the stitches in this chapter form a network of threads which look like a trellis. They are used to fill many different surfaces or for making decorative borders. It is interesting to embroider them on fabrics with an obvious weave to bring out all the uniformity that these stitches offer.

THE STRAIGHT TRELLIS STITCH IN 2 STEPS

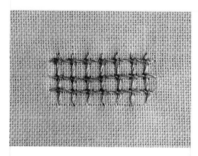

Level of Difficulty: Easy, accessible to beginners.

Threads and Fabrics: This stitch can be made on fabrics with an obvious weave (muslins) or on fabrics with a tight weave (taffeta, velour, or brocade), with metallic embroidery floss or metallic Pearl, to which is added stranded embroidery cotton.

Direction: The first step is worked in long vertical and horizontal stitches to form the trellis. The second step is worked in horizontal rows.

The straight trellis stitch is a very old stitch which was traditionally worked with wool. Very decorative, it allows you quickly to fill large surfaces. For the best effect, embroider this stitch with threads of two different colors.

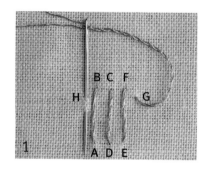 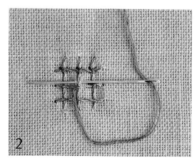

STEP 1

Make long vertical stitches with the metallic thread. Bring the needle up in A, on the lower left, and bring it down in B, about an inch above A. Bring the needle back up in C, six threads to the right of B, and bring it down in D to form the second vertical stitch. Bring the needle up in E, and bring it down in F. Bring the needle up in G, diagonally below and to the right of F, to begin the first horizontal stitch. Bring the needle down in H, to the left of the first vertical stitch. In this manner, complete the remaining branches of the trellis.

TIP

If you use a fabric with a tight weave, it would be helpful to trace the trellis first with tailor's chalk to obtain a uniform shape.

STEP 2

Embroider a cross-stitch with two strands of embroidery cotton over each intersection of the branches of the trellis. Proceed row by row, forming a complete cross-stitch at each crossing. Begin the work at the upper left of the trellis.

THE SLANTED TRELLIS STITCH IN 2 STEPS

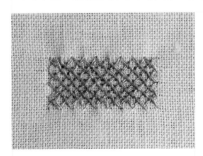

Level of Difficulty: Medium, for people who already have some experience.

Threads and Fabrics: This stitch can be made on fabrics with an obvious weave (muslins) or on fabrics with a tight weave (taffeta, velour, or brocade), with metallic embroidery floss or metallic Pearl, to which is added stranded embroidery cotton.

Direction: The first step is worked in long slanted stitches to form the trellis. The second step is worked in horizontal rows.

The slanted trellis stitch is a more elaborate variation of the preceding stitch. The trellis here is composed of large slanted stitches, held in place at each cross by a small vertical stitch.

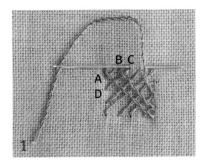
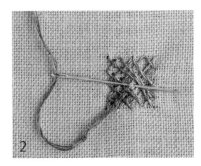

STEP 1

Make long slanted stitches with the metallic thread. Bring the needle up in A, on the upper left, and bring it down in B, diagonally up and to the right. Bring the needle back up in C, six threads to the right of B. Bring it back down in D, six threads of the weave below point A. In this manner, form the first set of large slanted stitches. To make the second set of stitches slanted in the opposite direction, stitch again in the holes you made for the first set, but this time direct the stitches to the left.

TIP

When the trellis is large and airy, it is possible to embroider cross stitches over each intersection. When it is tight, make small straight stitches in the second step instead.

STEP 2

Thread two strands of embroidery cotton and embroider a small straight stitch (see p. 97) vertically over each intersection of branches of the trellis. Proceed in vertical rows, forming a small straight stitch over two threads of the weave on each crossing. Begin the work at the upper left of the trellis.

THE SHEAF STITCH IN 2 STEPS

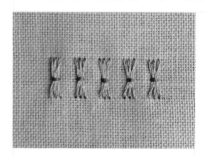

Level of Difficulty: Medium, for people who already have some experience.

Threads and Fabrics: This stitch can be made on fabrics with an obvious weave (muslins) or on fabrics with a tight weave (taffeta, velour or brocade), with metallic embroidery floss or metallic Pearl, to which is added stranded embroidery cotton.

Direction: The first step is worked in long straight vertical stitches, and the second in horizontal rows.

TIP

To obtain a beautiful result, work the sheaf stitch in horizontal rows. Make sure that the groups of three are placed in staggered rows in relation to the groups in the preceding row.

Also called the "cluster stitch," the sheaf stitch is mostly used for the creation of borders. It is also worked in uniform patterns to highlight a surface that is only lightly filled. It has a particularly decorative effect.

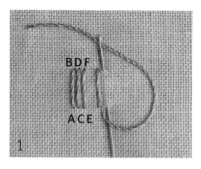 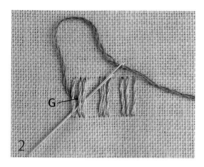

STEP 1

Form three long vertical satin stitches (see p. 98) with the metallic thread. Bring the needle up in A, on the lower left, and bring it down in B, about ¼ inch above A. Bring your needle back up in C, two threads of the weave to the right of A, and bring it back down in D, two threads of the weave to the right of B. Bring the needle up in E and back down in F. The first group of three stitches is formed. Embroider another group of three vertical stitches seven threads of the weave to the right of the first group of stitches. In this manner, continue the entire row.

STEP 2

Thread two strands of embroidery cotton and bring the needle up in G, under the strands of the first group of three stitches, at the center, then sliding the needle out of the left of the group. Slide the needle from left to right over and then from right to left under the stitches in the first group and tighten the stitch. Bring your needle back down in G. Two horizontal stitches will form around the first group of three vertical stitches. Bring your needle up under the next group of three stitches and begin again at step 2.

THE KNOTTED SHEAF STITCH IN 2 STEPS

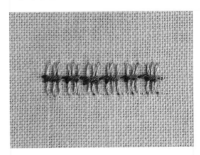

Level of Difficulty: Difficult, reserved for those who are experienced.

Threads and Fabrics: This stitch can be made on fabrics with an obvious weave (muslins) or on fabrics with a tight weave (taffeta, velour, or brocade), with metallic embroidery floss or metallic Pearl, to which is added stranded embroidery cotton.

Direction: The first step is worked in long horizontal stitches, and the second vertically from top to bottom.

TIP

You can make this stitch look a bit more padded by working in groups of four or five parallel straight stitches. As the number of branches increases, leave a larger space between the groups of stitches so that they stand out from each other.

Derived from the preceding stitch, the knotted sheaf stitch is solely adapted for making borders. The groups of stitches are linked together with a twisted chain stitch which forms the central line.

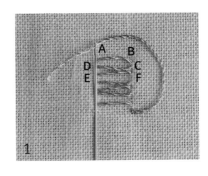

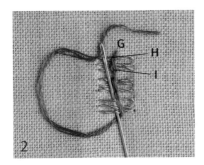

The finished stitch forms a horizontal border, but if it is easier, it can be worked vertically.

STEP 1

Form three long horizontal satin stitches (see p. 98) with the metallic thread. Bring the needle up in A, on the upper left, and bring it down in B, about ½ inch to the right of A. Bring it back up in C, below B, and bring it down in D, below A. Bring the needle up in E and down in F. The first group of three stitches is formed. Embroider a new group of three horizontal stitches four threads of the weave below the first group of stitches. In this manner, continue the row.

STEP 2

Embroider a row of twisted chain stitches (see p. 33) with two strands of embroidery cotton. Bring the needle up in G, under the center of the first horizontal stitch, and bring it back down in H, below and a bit to the left of G. Bring the tip of the needle up in I, vertical with G, and then slide the thread under the tip of the needle and pull gently to form a loop which passes over the first group of three straight stitches. Work the row of twisted chain stitches by repeating the maneuvers indicated above.

THE TRELLIS STITCH ON COUCHING STITCH IN 3 STEPS

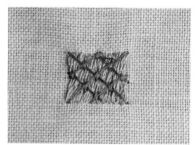

Level of Difficulty: Difficult, reserved for those who are experienced.

Threads and Fabrics: This stitch can be made on fabrics with an obvious weave (muslins) or on fabrics with a tight weave (taffeta, velour, or brocade), with metallic embroidery floss or metallic Pearl, to which is added stranded embroidery cotton.

Direction: The first step is worked in long vertical stitches. The second step is worked in long slanted stitches to form the trellis. The third step is worked in small vertical stitches in horizontal rows.

TIP

To obtain perfect work with a very beautiful effect of depth, it is important that the couching threads in the first step completely cover the background fabric. Use three or four strands of metallic thread for this step.

The trellis stitch on a couching stitch gets its richness from working three threads, which give it extraordinary depth. This is one of the most beautiful couching stitches, and it is reserved for precious works whose scope is sufficient for the development of its design.

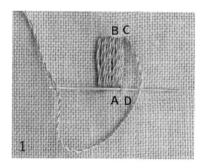
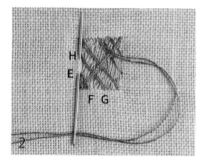

STEP 1

Make long vertical stitches with the metallic thread. Bring the needle up in A, on the lower left of the surface to be covered, and bring it down in B, vertical with A, to form the first long couching stitch. Bring the needle back up in C, directly to the right of B and bring it down in D, right next to point A. The second stitch is parallel to the first. Continue in this manner to cover the entire surface with large vertical stitches.

STEP 2

Make long slanted stitches with two strands of metallic thread. Bring the needle up in E, on the lower left, and bring it down in F, diagonally down and to the right. Bring the needle back up in G, six threads of the weave to the right of point F. Bring it down in H, six threads of the weave below point E. In this manner, form the first set of large slanted stitches.

To make the second step, which is composed of stitches slanted in the opposite direction, stitch again in the holes you made for the first set, but this time slant the stitches to the left.

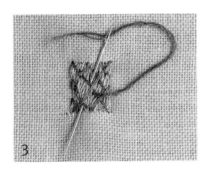

STEP 3

Thread two strands of embroidery cotton and embroider a small straight stitch (see p. 97) vertically over each intersection of the trellis. Proceed row by row, vertically, beginning with the top left of the trellis.

The Eyeglass Case

The sheen of gold and the richness of the trellis stitches come together to decorate the most original eyeglass case. To be successful with this stylish pattern, all you need to do is count the threads of the weave of fabric.

OVERVIEW

Level of Difficulty: Easy

Stitches Used:
Straight trellis stitch (see p. 226)
Slanted trellis stitch (see p. 227)

Finished Dimensions:
The finished glasses case measures 7 x 3½ inches; only the front of the case is embroidered.

MATERIALS

8 x 8 inches blue cotton 25 count Lugana DMC fabric
1 skein of DMC metallic embroidery thread, art. 317, in the following colors: gold (5282), copper (5279)
Embroidery needle
Embroidery hoop
Blue sewing thread

PATTERN

Whip stitch the fabric.

Fold the fabric in two to make two rectangles; only one of the rectangles is embroidered.

Sew a basting stitch to establish the edges of the rectangle.

The trellis motifs are made as counted stitches. Use the diagram as a guide to make the designs.

EMBROIDERY

Use two strands of metallic embroidery thread.

Stretch the material in the embroidery hoop.

Begin the work with the four motifs in the straight trellis stitch, then continue the embroidery with the borders on the top and bottom of the case.

Move the embroidery hoop as you finish each section and begin the next.

When you have completed the work, remove the basting thread.

FINISHING TOUCHES

At the top of the fabric, make a hem in the following manner: make a first fold of ¼ inch with an iron. Baste, and then form a second fold of ½ inch. Sew by hand or with a sewing machine.

Fold the fabric in two with right sides together to form the case. Sew the open side and the bottom of the work at ½ inch from the edge.

Press the work and turn it inside out.

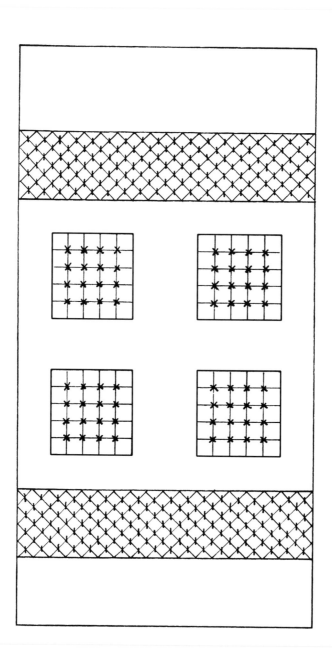

ADVICE

These couching stitches are very solid. However, to preserve the surface of the threads or to prevent them from getting snagged in the arms of the glasses, we recommend that you add a lining to the inside of the eyeglass case. A thin cotton toile or a synthetic lining will do the trick. Before beginning the assembly of the case, place the work on the lining (which you have cut to the exact dimensions of the embroidered work) with wrong sides together. Whip stitch the two pieces of fabric together, and then assemble the glasses case as indicated in the "Finishing Touches" step.

The Woven Stitch Family

The woven stitches hope to imitate rich woven fabrics—warp and weft—for the effects of jacquard and damask materials. Made in several steps, they offer such a pronounced depth, in some cases, to the point of giving the fabric a matelassé or quilted appearance. They are used for filling large surfaces to highlight the design of their weave.

THE MOSAIC STITCH IN 3 STEPS

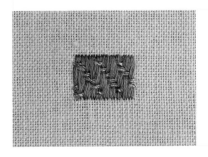

Level of Difficulty: Difficult, reserved for those who are experienced.

Threads and Fabrics: This stitch can be made on fabrics with a tight weave such as taffeta, velour, or brocade, with metallic embroidery floss or metallic Pearl, to which is added stranded embroidery cotton.

Direction: The first step is worked in long vertical stitches, and the second step is worked in small horizontal stitches.

TIP

So that the geometric designs remain uniform, consider preparing your weave work on graphing paper first. This way, you can determine the exact dimensions and spacing for the horizontal stitches.

Presenting a pretty raised effect, the mosaic stitch adapts to all sorts of geometric designs to form triangle, diamond, and chevron motifs, just to name a few. As with all woven stitches, there is a first preparatory step, which consists of making stitches to cover the background of the fabric. The geometric motif is then woven using metallic thread.

STEP 1

Thread six strands of embroidery cotton on a needle, and bring it up in point A, on the upper left of the surface to cover. Bring it down in B, vertical with A, to form the first long couching stitch. Bring the needle back up in C, next to A, and bring it back down in D, next to point B. The second stitch is parallel to the first. Continue in this manner to cover the entire surface.

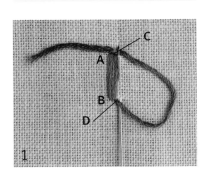

235

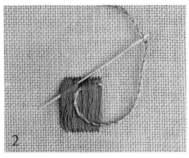

STEP 2

Beginning on the upper right of the surface covered with couching stitches, make small horizontal stitches using two strands of metallic embroidery thread. Each stitch is made over two couching stitches, and the needle is then slipped under the next four stitches. Proceed in this manner for the entire row.

STEP 3

For the remaining rows, proceed in the same way as in step 2, but shift the weave by two couching stitches in order to obtain slanted lines formed by rows of small horizontal stitches. At the end of each row, bring the needle down into the fabric before moving to the next row.

THE WOVEN STRIPED BORDER STITCH IN 3 STEPS

Level of Difficulty: Difficult, reserved for those who are experienced.
Threads and Fabrics: This stitch can be made on fabrics with an obvious weave (muslins) or on fabrics with a tight weave (taffeta, velour, or brocade), with metallic embroidery floss or metallic Pearl, to which is added stranded embroidery cotton.
Direction: The first step is worked in long horizontal stitches, and the second is a vertical weave.

TIP

For the woven work, use blunt-tipped tapestry needles so that you do not snag the ladder stitches.

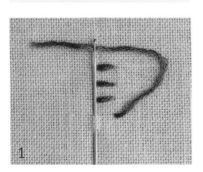

The woven striped border stitch is, as its name suggests, generally used for borders.

As with all the other woven stitches, it is made on a base of straight stitches which provide a structure for the woven stitches in the two subsequent steps.

STEP 1

Thread six strands of cotton thread and make a ladder of horizontal straight stitches (see p. 97).

Keep a uniform spacing between the stitches, as well as the same stitch length for each.

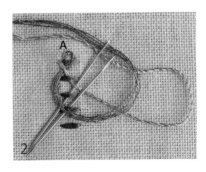

STEP 2

Thread one needle with gold metallic thread and another with copper metallic thread. Bring the needles up in A, just above the first ladder stitch. Slide the gold thread over the first ladder stitch, and then continue the row alternating your weave stitches over and under each ladder stitch. Slide the copper thread under the first ladder stitch and under the gold thread. Continue working the copper thread under and over the each ladder stitch. Continue the weave between the ladder stitches, each time crossing the two metallic threads.

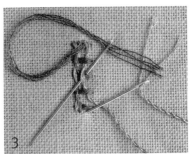

STEP 3

Begin the next row of weaves to the right of the first and start again at step 2. You must make three or four rows of two colors to complete the border.

THE INTERLACING UKRAINIAN STITCH IN 3 STEPS

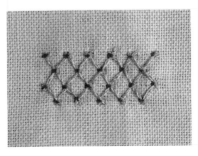

Level of Difficulty: Easy, accessible to beginners.

Threads and Fabrics: This stitch can be made on fabrics with a tight weave (taffeta, velour, or brocade), or in thinner cotton or linen fabrics, with metallic embroidery floss or metallic Pearl, to which is added stranded embroidery cotton.

Direction: The first step is worked in long horizontal stitches, and the second is a slanted weave.

TIP

This woven stitch can also be made using thin ribbon, which beautifully replaces the metallic thread.

A country of great and long-standing textile culture, the Ukraine has always produced embroiderers who are in a class all their own. The interlacing stitch is intended for household linens as well as for decorating traditional garments.

STEP 1

Thread six strands of embroidery cotton and make a line of horizontal running stitches (see p. 130). Keep a uniform spacing between the stitches, as well as the same length for each stitch. In the next row, stagger the stitches between those of the first row.

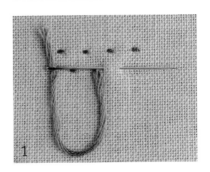

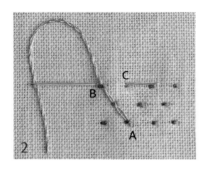

STEP 2

Thread a needle with metallic thread and bring it up in A, on the bottom of the surface to be worked. Slide the needle up and to the left under the running stitches to form a slant. At the top of the motif, bring your needle down in B to hold the thread and bring it back up in C, just above the next running stitch to the right. Slide the needle down and to the right under the running stitches to form the next slant. Cover the surface with parallel slants.

STEP 3

For this step, make slants in the opposite direction in order to complete the trellis. At the end of each row, bring the needle down into the fabric and back up just above the next running stitch.

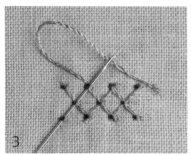

THE TURKISH BASKET STITCH IN 3 STEPS

Level of Difficulty: Difficult, reserved for those who are experienced.
Threads and Fabrics: This stitch can be made on fabrics with a tight weave with metallic embroidery floss or metallic Pearl, to which is added stranded embroidery cotton.
Direction: The first step is worked in long vertical stitches, the second step in long horizontal stitches, and the third in small vertical straight stitches worked in horizontal rows.

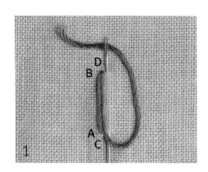

The Turkish basket stitch is embroidered over two sets of perpendicular couching stitches. This first step serves to pad the stitch and give it a very dense look. Because of its thickness, it is reserved for decorative objects and fashion accessories.

STEP 1

Thread a needle with six strands of embroidery cotton and form long vertical stitches. Bring the needle up in A, on the lower left of the surface to be covered, and bring it down in B, vertical with A, to form the first large couching stitch. Bring the needle back up in C, directly to the right of A, and bring it back down in D,

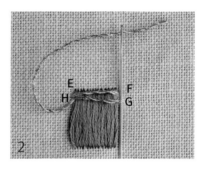

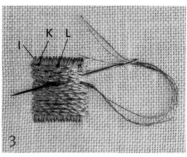

TIP

The first set of couching stitches must completely disappear, and so the color of the thread does not matter. Nonetheless, consider using embroidery cotton, through which you will be able to more easily pass the tip of your needle in the third step.

right next to point B. The second stitch is parallel to the first. Continue in this manner to cover the entire surface with large vertical stitches.

STEP 2

Thread two strands of gold metallic thread and form long horizontal stitches perpendicular to the first set to cover the surface once more. Bring the needle up in E, on the upper left of the surface, and back down in F on the right, to form the first horizontal stitch. Bring the needle back up in G, below F, and bring it down in H, below point E. Continue in this manner to make horizontal couching stitches over the first set of couching stitches. The first set should disappear entirely.

STEP 3

Embroider rows of small vertical straight stitches (see p. 97) with two strands of copper metallic thread. Bring your needle up in point I, on the left under the first two horizontal couching stitches, and bring it down in K to form the first vertical stitch. Bring your needle back up in L, directly to the right, and make another small vertical stitch to hold the metallic couching stitches to the fabric. In the second row, stagger the vertical stitches between the ones in the first row.

THE LINEN STITCH IN 2 STEPS

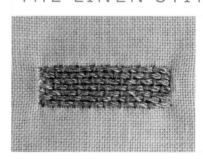

Level of Difficulty: Medium, for people who already have some experience.
Threads and Fabrics: This stitch can be made on fabrics with a tight weave such as taffeta, velour, or brocade, with metallic embroidery floss or metallic Pearl, to which is added stranded embroidery cotton.
Direction: The first step is worked in long horizontal stitches, and the second step small woven vertical stitches.

The linen stitch looks like the brother of the Boulogne stitch, but it is made in a completely different way and used for a different purpose. While the Boulogne stitch is embroidered to fill in small details of motifs, the linen stitch is only embroidered as a foundation.

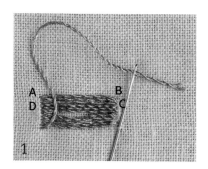

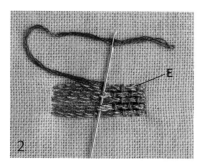

STEP 1

Thread two strands of metallic thread and bring the needle up in A, on the upper left of the surface to be covered, and bring it down in B, horizontal with A, to form the first long couching stitch. Bring the needle back up in C, directly below B, and bring it down in D, below point A. The second stitch is parallel to the first. Continue in this manner to cover the entire surface.

STEP 2

Proceed with the weaving, made in vertical rows with two strands of embroidery cotton. Bring the needle up in E, on the upper right of the area covered with couching stitches. Slide the needle downwards alternately under two couching stitches and over the next two couching stitches. At the end of the row, bring your needle down into the fabric. Bring it back up a few threads of the weave to the left and begin weaving upwards. Make a uniform weave over the whole surface of metallic threads.

The Pin Cushion

This pin cushion is a small refined object where the linen stitch in gold thread contrasts with the simplicity of the natural linen fabric. It will be the jewel in your sewing kit.

OVERVIEW

Level of Difficulty:
Medium

Stitches Used:
Linen stitch (see p. 239)

Finished Dimensions:
The finished pin cushion measures 5 x 5 inches.

MATERIALS

6 x 11 inches natural-colored linen fabric
1 skein of DMC metallic embroidery thread, art. 317, gold (5282)
1 skein DMC stranded embroidery cotton, art. 177, ecru (712)
20 inches of dark ochre yellow thin round ribbon
Embroidery needle
Embroidery hoop
Blue carbon paper
Natural-colored sewing thread
Sewing needle
Synthetic fiber filling

PATTERN

On the back of the linen, mark the shape of the pin cushion twice with pins.

Then, using carbon paper, mark the geometric pattern on the front of the fabric.

EMBROIDERY

Stretch the material in the embroidery hoop.

Begin the work with the central motif. The couching stitches are made with six strands of cotton embroidery thread. The woven work is done with two strands of metallic embroidery thread.

Embroider the four triangle motifs. The couching stitches are made with three strands of metallic embroidery thread, and the woven work is done with two strands of ecru embroidery cotton. Finish the work with the small squares on the corners, made in the same way as the central square.

FINISHING TOUCHES

Cut the two pieces of fabric which make up the pin cushion adding ¾ inch beyond the marked outline for a seam allowance. Whip stitch the edges.

Place the fabrics with right sides together and pin. Seam the pieces together, leaving one side open.

Those embroiderers who are comfortable with the linen stitch might like to enlarge the pattern and work the motif on the center of a pillow. To keep all its charm and refinement, the linen stitch must, however, remain the same size as that of the pin cushion.

Press the seams open. Turn the pin cushion right side out, stuff with the filling, and close the open side with slip stitches.

Sew the round ribbon around the edge of the pin cushion by hand with slip stitches.

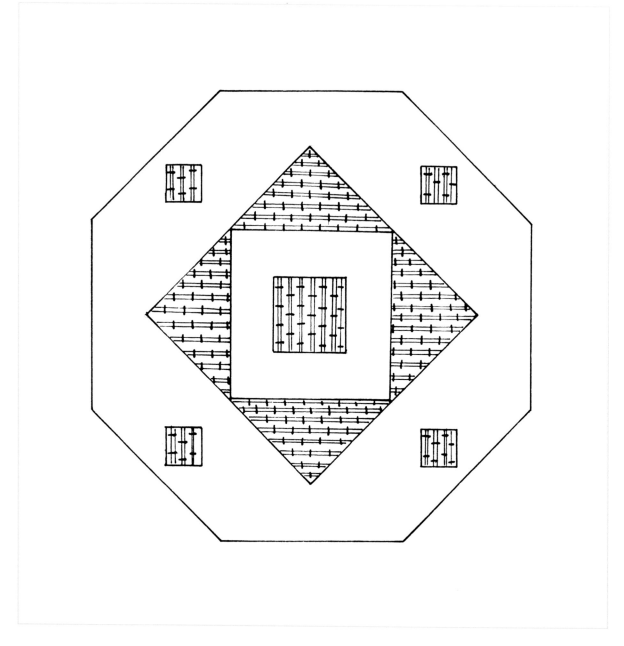

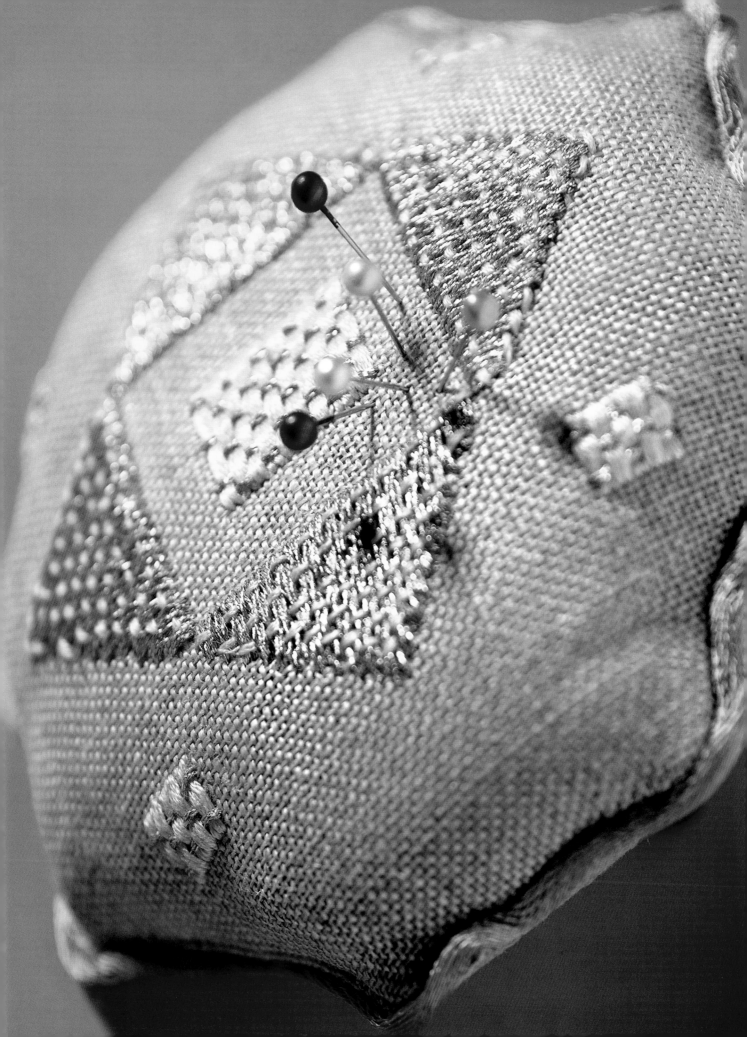

APPENDIX

Index of Stitches

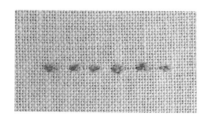

Opening the Work
p. 191

The Spider Web Stitch
p. 107

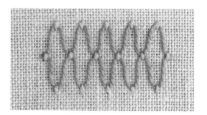

The Cloud Stitch
p. 113

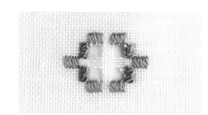

The Fishbone Outline Stitch
p. 45

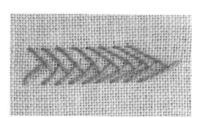

The Fishbone Filling Stitch
p. 93

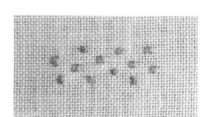

The Cable Stitch
p. 80

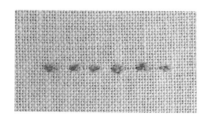

The Knotted Cable Stitch
p. 81

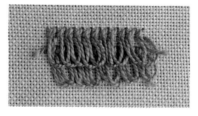

The Astrakan Stitch
p. 168

The Assisi Stitch
p. 140

The Split Running Stitch
p. 24

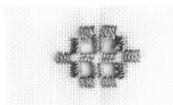

The Woven
Overcast Bar Stitch   p. 193

The Picot Woven
Overcast Bar Stitch   p. 194

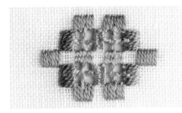

The Woven Overcast Bar
with Spider Stitch   p. 195

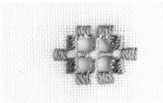

The Simple Overcast
Bar Stitch   p. 192

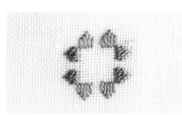

The Chevron Border Stitch
p. 190

The Kloster Block Border Stitch
p. 189

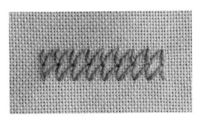

The Bosnia Stitch
p. 158

The Uncut Turkey
Work Stitch p. 165

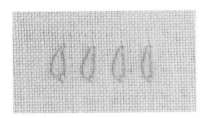

The Lazy Daisy Stitch
p. 37

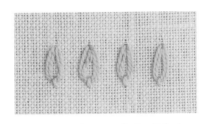

The Double Lazy Daisy Stitch
p. 38

The Boulogne Stitch
p. 208

The Overcast Bar Stitch
p. 183

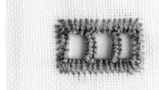

The Blanket Bar Stitch
p. 184

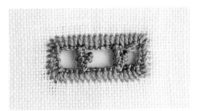

The Picot Bar Stitch
p. 185

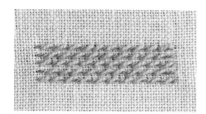

The Brocatello Stitch
p. 122

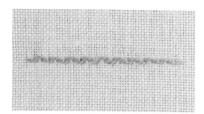

The Cable Stitch
p. 23

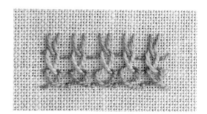

The Ceylon Stitch
p. 114

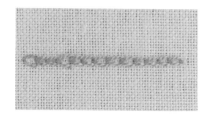

The Chain Stitch
p. 32

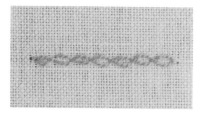

The Cable Chain Stitch
p. 34

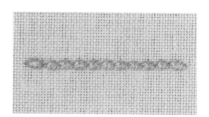

The Reversed Chain Stitch
p. 36

The Whipped Chain Stitch
p. 39

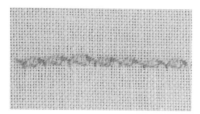

The Twisted Chain Stitch
p. 33

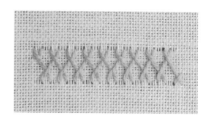

The Herringbone Stitch
p. 54

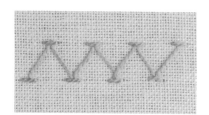

The Chevron Stitch
p. 56

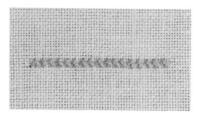

The Coral Stitch
p. 69

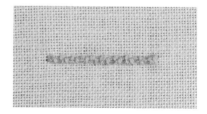

The Corded Double Knot Stitch
p. 66

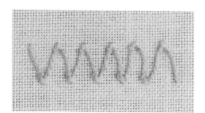

The Zigzag Corded Pearl Stitch
p. 67

The Straight Overcast Stitch
p. 175

The Bokhara Couching Stitch
p. 209

The Iranian Couching Stitch
p. 212

The Crossed Featherstitch
p. 48

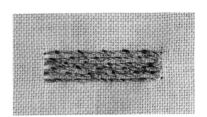

The Romanian Couching Stitch
p. 214

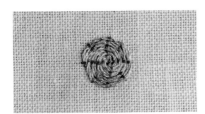

The Spiral Couching Stitch
p. 213

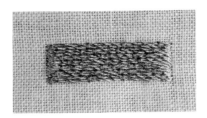

The Turkish Diamond
Couching Stitch   p. 211

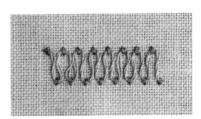

The Turkish Zigzag
Couching Stitch   p. 210

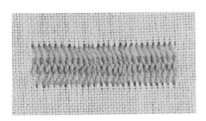

The Cretan Stitch
p. 50

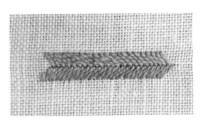

The Crossed Stitch
p. 92

The Cross-Stitch
p. 138

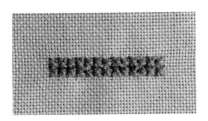

The Two-Sided Cross-Stitch
p. 144

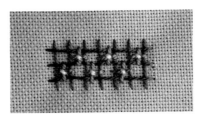

The Hungarian Cross-Stitch
p. 143

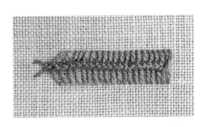

The Overlapping Cross-Stitch
p. 91

The Checkerboard Damask Stitch
p. 153

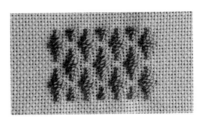

The Diamond Damask Stitch
p. 150

The Staggered Damask Stitch
p. 151

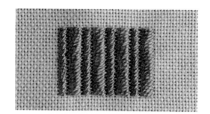

The Striped Damask Stitch
p. 149

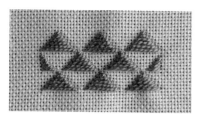

The Triangle Damask Stitch
p. 152

The Checkboard Stitch
p. 112

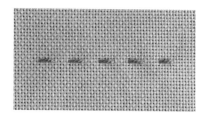

The Running Stitch
p. 130

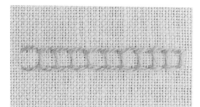

The Ladder Stitch
p. 35

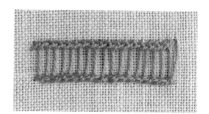

The Woven Ladder Stitch
p. 111

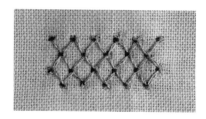

The Interlacing Ukrainian Stitch
p. 237

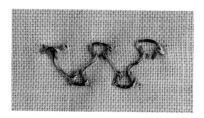

The Interlaced Trim Stitch
p. 222

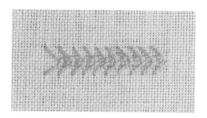

The Wheat Stitch
p. 46

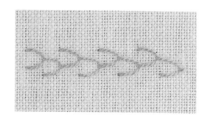

The Featherstitch
p. 43

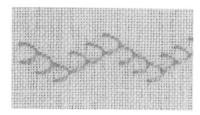

The Double Featherstitch
p. 44

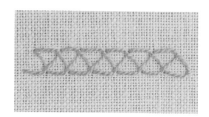

The Closed Featherstitch
p. 49

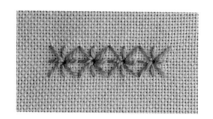

The Star Stitch
p. 141

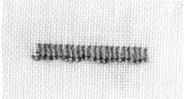

The Buttonhole Stitch
p. 182

The Simple Blanket Stitch
p. 181

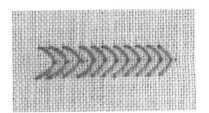

The Leaf Stitch
p. 86

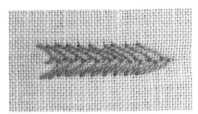

The Double Leaf Stitch
p. 87

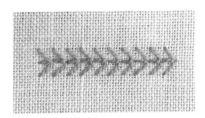

The Fern Stitch
p. 90

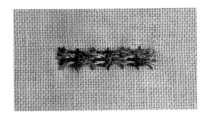

The Woven Striped Border Stitch
p. 236

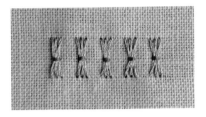

The Sheaf Stitch
p. 228

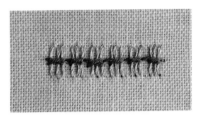

The Knotted Sheaf Stitch
p. 229

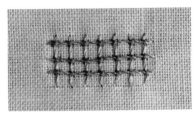

The Straight Trellis Stitch
p. 226

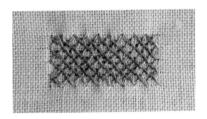

The Slanted Trellis Stitch
p. 227

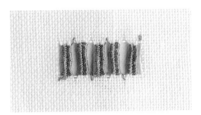

The Woven Drawn-Thread
Bar Stitch   p. 202

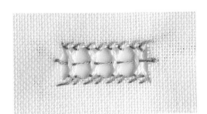

The Interlaced Drawn-Thread
Stitch   p. 203

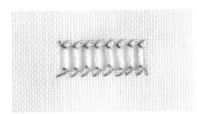

The Ladder Hemstitch
p. 200

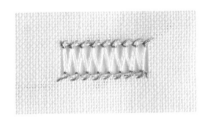

The Trellis Hemstitch
p. 201

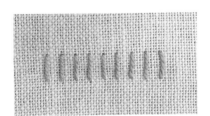

The Straight Stitch
p. 97

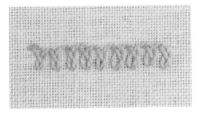

The Link Stitch
p. 65

The Malta Stitch
p. 166

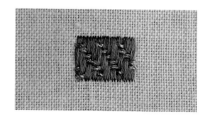

The Mosaic Stitch
p. 235

The Mosul Stitch
p. 123

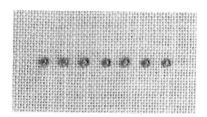

The Knot Stitch
p. 74

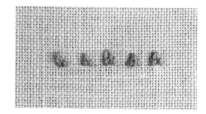

The German Knot Stitch
p. 77

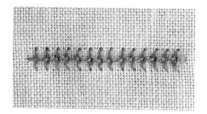

The Basque Knot Stitch
p. 82

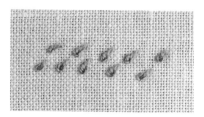

The Knotted Stem Stitch
p. 79

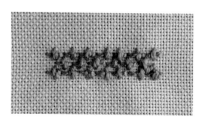

The Knotted Slavic Stitch
p. 157

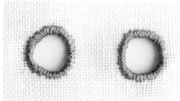

The Overcast Eyelet Stitch
p. 177

The Oka Stitch
p. 159

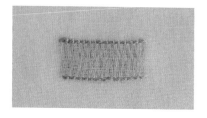

The Shadow Stitch
p. 119

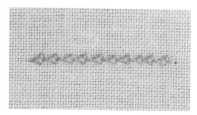

The Palestrina Stitch
p. 63

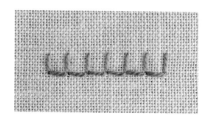

The Paris Stitch
p. 121

The Long and Short Stitch
p. 99

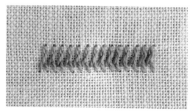

The New England Laid Stitch
p. 102

The Encroaching Satin Stitch
p. 101

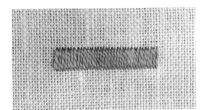

The Satin Stitch
p. 98

The Crossed Satin Stitch
p. 103

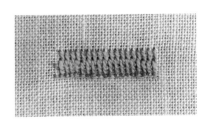

The Re-Stitched Satin Stitch
p. 100

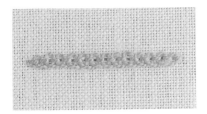

The Pekinese Stitch
p. 26

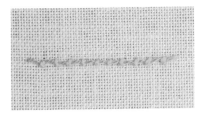

The Pearl Stitch
p. 64

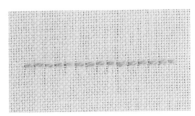

The Backstitch
p. 25

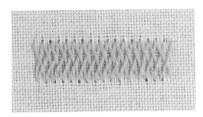

The Crossed Backstitch
p. 55

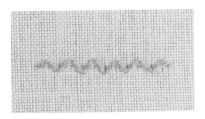

The Re-Embroidered Backstitch
p. 28

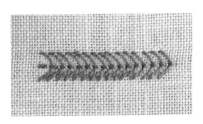

The Plume Stitch
p. 89

The Self-Padded Satin Stitch
p. 176

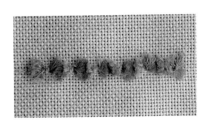

The Pompon Stitch
p. 167

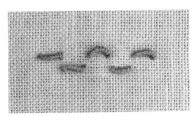

The Bullion Stitch
p. 75

Preparation of the
Drawn-Thread Work   p. 199

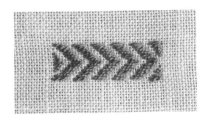

The Darning Stitch
p. 110

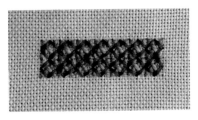

The Rice Stitch
p. 142

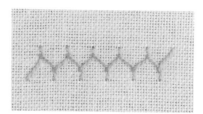

The Roman Stitch
p. 57

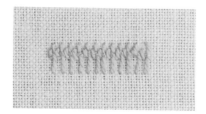

The Russian Stitch
p. 58

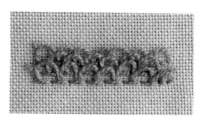

The Rya Stitch
p. 169

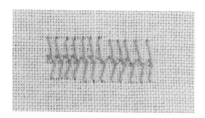

The Shisha Stitch
p. 124

The Sind Stitch
p. 68

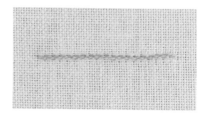

The Sorbello Stitch
p. 78

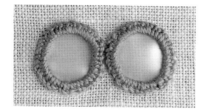

The Corded Soutache
p. 220

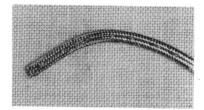

The Flat Lace Soutache
p. 219

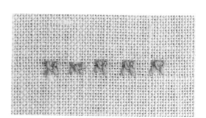

The Large Ribbon Soutache
p. 221

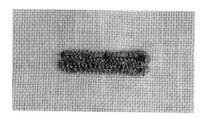

The Seed Stitch
p. 76

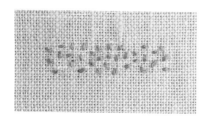

The Sylrnie Stitch
p. 134

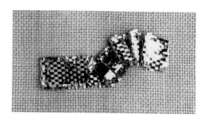

The Stem Stitch
p. 22

The Stem Stitch
over a Backstitch   p. 174

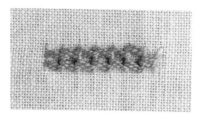

The Woven Portuguese Stitch
p. 108

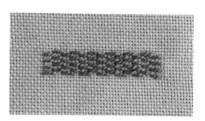

The Simple Woven Stitch
p. 133

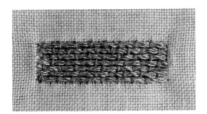

The Linen Stitch
p. 239

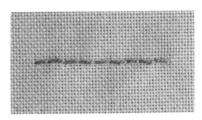

The Line Stitch
p. 131

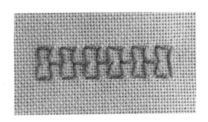

The Japanese Line Stitch
p. 132

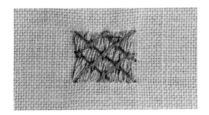

The Trellis Stitch on
Couching Stitch   p. 230

The Triangular Turkish Stitch
p. 160

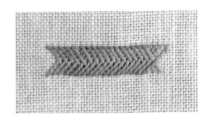

The Basket Stitch
p. 88

The Turkish Basket Stitch
p. 238

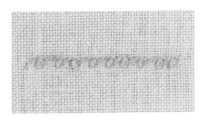

The Scroll Stitch
p. 27

List of Stitches

METRIC EQUIVALENTS CHART
Inches to Millimeters and Centimeters

MM=MILLIMETERS   CM=CENTIMETERS

INCHES	MM	CM	INCHES	CM	INCHES	CM
⅛	3	0.3	9	22.9	30	76.2
¼	6	0.6	10	25.4	31	78.7
⅜	10	1.0	11	27.9	32	81.3
½	13	1.3	12	30.5	33	83.8
⅝	16	1.6	13	33.0	34	86.4
¾	19	1.9	14	35.6	35	88.9
⅞	22	2.2	15	38.1	36	91.4
1	25	2.5	16	40.6	37	94.0
1¼	32	3.2	17	43.2	38	96.5
1½	38	3.8	18	45.7	39	99.1
1¾	44	4.4	19	48.3	48	101.6
2	51	5.1	20	50.8	41	104.1
2½	64	6.4	21	53.3	42	106.7
3	76	7.6	22	55.9	43	109.2
3½	89	8.9	23	58.4	44	111.8
4	102	10.2	24	61.0	45	114.3
4½	114	11.4	25	63.5	46	116.8
5	127	12.7	26	66.0	47	119.4
6	152	15.2	27	68.6	48	121.9